Trading For Dummies®

Cheat Sheet

W9-BKQ-624

Steps to Using Fundamental and Technical Analysis

1. Determine economic cycle position.
2. Determine position within sector rotation.
3. Decide which sectors are ascending.
4. Determine leading stocks in the ascending sector.
5. Evaluate the Fed position.
6. Confirm economic cycle with index charts.
7. Determine if leading sectors are range bound or trending.
8. Determine if leading stocks are range bound or trending.
9. Enter the trade only if the stop-loss point is nearby.
10. Trade within your preferred time frame.

Order Types

Buying a share of stock can be as easy as calling a broker and saying that you want to buy such and such a stock, but you can place an order in a number of other ways that gives you better protection. The way you trade and the types of orders you place are critical to your success as a trader. Here are the most common order types:

- **Market order** is an order to buy or sell stock at the current market price. This is the type of order your broker will place unless you give different instructions.
- **Limit order** is an order to buy or sell stock in which you specify the price at which you will buy or sell that stock. A buy limit order will be executed at the price indicated or lower. A sell limit order will be executed at the same price or higher.
- **Stop order** is an order that automatically becomes a market order when the stock reaches the price you specify. Buy stop orders are entered at a price higher than the current market price, while sell stop sell orders are entered at a price lower than the current market price.
- **Stop-limit order** is an order that incorporates features of both a stop and a limit order. When the stock reaches your specified price, the order becomes a limit order rather than a market order.
- **Day orders** are only good on the day you place the order. They do not carry over to the next trading day.
- **Good 'til canceled orders** are orders placed at a limit price and remain in force until actually executed or cancelled, which can be days or weeks.

For much more information on order types, see Chapter 2.

For Dummies: Bestselling Book Series for Beginners

Trading For Dummies®

Cheat Sheet

Signs You've Found a Good Trading Opportunity

You're looking at a fundamentally strong company . . .

- With earnings that are growing faster than average
- In a strong sector
- In a growing economy
- While the stock is approaching a technical buy signal on its bar chart
- And performing better than the average stock with high relative strength

Steps to Developing Your Own Trading System

1. **Select system development tools.**
2. **Gather historical data to test your system.**
3. **Develop and test your system design.**
4. **Identify system optimization pitfalls.**
5. **Test with blind simulation.**
6. **Account for slippage.**
7. **Keep a trading journal.**
8. **Frequently evaluate your trades.**

Top Ten Trading Web Sites

- Stock Charts (stockcharts.com)
- Investor's Business Daily (investors.com)
- Trade Station Securities (tradestation.com)
- Wall Street Journal (wsj.com)
- eSignal (esignal.com)
- Decision Point (decisionpoint.com)
- Morningstar (morningstar.com)
- Reuters (investor.reuters.com)
- Quote Tracker (quotetracker.com)
- SEC's Edgar (sec.gov/edgar.shtml)

Copyright © 2004 Wiley Publishing, Inc.
All rights reserved.

Item 5689-4.

For more information about Wiley Publishing,
call 1-800-762-2974.

Wiley, the Wiley Publishing logo, For Dummies, the Dummies Man logo, the For Dummies Bestselling Book Series logo and all related trade dress are trademarks or registered trademarks of John Wiley & Sons, Inc. and/or its affiliates. All other trademarks are property of their respective owners.

For Dummies: Bestselling Book Series for Beginners

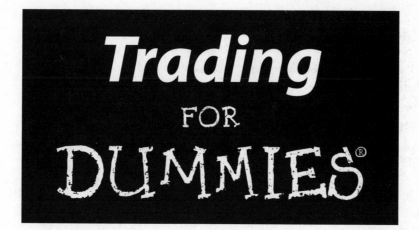

Trading
FOR
DUMMIES®

by Michael Griffis and Lita Epstein

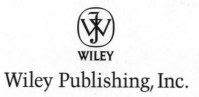

WILEY

Wiley Publishing, Inc.

Trading For Dummies®

Published by
Wiley Publishing, Inc.
111 River St.
Hoboken, NJ 07030-5774
www.wiley.com

Copyright © 2004 by Wiley Publishing, Inc., Indianapolis, Indiana

Published by Wiley Publishing, Inc., Indianapolis, Indiana

Published simultaneously in Canada

No part of this publication may be reproduced, stored in a retrieval system, or transmitted in any form or by any means, electronic, mechanical, photocopying, recording, scanning, or otherwise, except as permitted under Sections 107 or 108 of the 1976 United States Copyright Act, without either the prior written permission of the Publisher, or authorization through payment of the appropriate per-copy fee to the Copyright Clearance Center, 222 Rosewood Drive, Danvers, MA 01923, 978-750-8400, fax 978-646-8600. Requests to the Publisher for permission should be addressed to the Legal Department, Wiley Publishing, Inc., 10475 Crosspoint Blvd., Indianapolis, IN 46256, 317-572-3447, fax 317-572-4355, e-mail: brandreview@wiley.com.

Trademarks: Wiley, the Wiley Publishing logo, For Dummies, the Dummies Man logo, A Reference for the Rest of Us!, The Dummies Way, Dummies Daily, The Fun and Easy Way, Dummies.com and related trade dress are trademarks or registered trademarks of John Wiley & Sons, Inc. and/or its affiliates in the United States and other countries, and may not be used without written permission. All other trademarks are the property of their respective owners. Wiley Publishing, Inc., is not associated with any product or vendor mentioned in this book.

LIMIT OF LIABILITY/DISCLAIMER OF WARRANTY: THE PUBLISHER AND THE AUTHOR MAKE NO REPRESENTATIONS OR WARRANTIES WITH RESPECT TO THE ACCURACY OR COMPLETENESS OF THE CONTENTS OF THIS WORK AND SPECIFICALLY DISCLAIM ALL WARRANTIES, INCLUDING WITHOUT LIMITATION WARRANTIES OF FITNESS FOR A PARTICULAR PURPOSE. NO WARRANTY MAY BE CREATED OR EXTENDED BY SALES OR PROMOTIONAL MATERIALS. THE ADVICE AND STRATEGIES CONTAINED HEREIN MAY NOT BE SUITABLE FOR EVERY SITUATION. THIS WORK IS SOLD WITH THE UNDERSTANDING THAT THE PUBLISHER IS NOT ENGAGED IN RENDERING LEGAL, ACCOUNTING, OR OTHER PROFESSIONAL SERVICES. IF PROFESSIONAL ASSISTANCE IS REQUIRED, THE SERVICES OF A COMPETENT PROFESSIONAL PERSON SHOULD BE SOUGHT. NEITHER THE PUBLISHER NOR THE AUTHOR SHALL BE LIABLE FOR DAMAGES ARISING HEREFROM. THE FACT THAT AN ORGANIZATION OR WEBSITE IS REFERRED TO IN THIS WORK AS A CITATION AND/OR A POTENTIAL SOURCE OF FURTHER INFORMATION DOES NOT MEAN THAT THE AUTHOR OR THE PUBLISHER ENDORSES THE INFORMATION THE ORGANIZATION OR WEBSITE MAY PROVIDE OR RECOMMENDATIONS IT MAY MAKE. FURTHER, READERS SHOULD BE AWARE THAT INTERNET WEBSITES LISTED IN THIS WORK MAY HAVE CHANGED OR DISAPPEARED BETWEEN WHEN THIS WORK WAS WRITTEN AND WHEN IT IS READ.

For general information on our other products and services or to obtain technical support, please contact our Customer Care Department within the U.S. at 800-762-2974, outside the U.S. at 317-572-3993, or fax 317-572-4002.

Wiley also publishes its books in a variety of electronic formats. Some content that appears in print may not be available in electronic books.

Library of Congress Control Number: 2004110826

ISBN: 0-7645-5689-4

Manufactured in the United States of America

10 9 8 7 6 5 4 3 2

1O/QZ/QY/QU/IN

WILEY

About the Authors

Michael Griffis became an active trader in the mid 1980s. He first traded commodities and precious-metals after taking a commodities trading class as part of his MBA program at Rollins College. He turned his interest in trading into a profession and became a stock broker in 1992, where he helped businesses and individuals manage investments in stocks, bonds, mutual funds, retirement plans, 401(k) employee-savings plans, and asset management programs. Today, he mostly trades stocks and exchange-traded funds for his own account.

In addition, Michael is an author and a freelance writer. From 1997 through 2002, he wrote a weekly column about stock trading for online audiences. Today, he writes about investing and marketing for clients in the banking and brokerage industries. Outside of the business and investment world, he is active in his community and volunteers his time and talents as a fundraiser for civic and nonprofit organizations, and is a member of an investment advisory board for a local nonprofit.

Lita Epstein, who earned her MBA from Emory University's Goizueta Business School, enjoys helping people develop good financial, investing, and tax planning skills. She designs and teaches online courses on topics such as investing for retirement, getting ready for tax time, and finance and investing for women. She has written over ten books, including *Streetwise Retirement Planning* and soon to be released *Reading Financial Reports For Dummies*.

Lita was the content director for a financial services Web site, MostChoice. com and managed the Web site Investing for Women. As a Congressional press secretary, Lita gained first hand knowledge about how to work within and around the Federal bureaucracy, which gives her great insight into how government programs work. In the past Lita has been a daily newspaper reporter, magazine editor, and fundraiser for The Carter Presidential Center.

For fun, Lita enjoys scuba diving and is even certified as an underwater photographer. She hikes, canoes, and enjoys surfing the Web to find all its hidden treasures.

Authors' Acknowledgments

We would like to thank all of the people who have been instrumental in making this book a reality. In particular, we'd like to thank Jessica Faust at BookEnds for getting us connected with Wiley. We'd also like to thank all of the wonderful *For Dummies* folks at Wiley, especially Natasha Graf and Tim Gallan for shepherding this project to completion, and to Neil Johnson, our friendly neighborhood copy editor, for his advice and suggestions.

Also, we appreciate the extraordinary efforts of Darla D. Tuttle, the Manager of Strategic Relations for TradeStation Technologies, Inc., for her help providing software to generate the example charts.

Publisher's Acknowledgments

We're proud of this book; please send us your comments through our Dummies online registration form located at www.dummies.com/register/.

Some of the people who helped bring this book to market include the following:

Acquisitions, Editorial, and Media Development

Senior Project Editor: Tim Gallan

Acquisitions Editor: Natasha Graf

Copy Editor: E. Neil Johnson

Assistant Editor: Holly Gastineau-Grimes

Technical Editor: Dan Chesler

Editorial Manager: Christine Meloy Beck

Editorial Assistants: Melissa S. Bennett, Courtney Allen

Cover Photos: © Alan Schein Photography/ CORBIS

Cartoons: Rich Tennant, www.the5thwave.com

Composition

Project Coordinator: Maridee Ennis

Layout and Graphics: Jonelle Burns, Andrea Dahl, Denny Hager, Joyce Haughey, Michael Kruzil, Lynsey Osborn

Proofreaders: Laura Albert, TECHBOOKS Production Services

Indexer: TECHBOOKS Production Services

Publishing and Editorial for Consumer Dummies

Diane Graves Steele, Vice President and Publisher, Consumer Dummies

Joyce Pepple, Acquisitions Director, Consumer Dummies

Kristin A. Cocks, Product Development Director, Consumer Dummies

Michael Spring, Vice President and Publisher, Travel

Brice Gosnell, Associate Publisher, Travel

Kelly Regan, Editorial Director, Travel

Publishing for Technology Dummies

Andy Cummings, Vice President and Publisher, Dummies Technology/General User

Composition Services

Gerry Fahey, Vice President of Production Services

Debbie Stailey, Director of Composition Services

Contents at a Glance

Table of Contents

Introduction

● ●

*T*rading used to be the purview of institutional and corporate entities that had direct access to closed securities trading systems. Recent technical advances have leveled the playing field, making securities trading much more accessible to individuals. After the stock market crash of 2000, when many lost large sums of money because professional advisors or mutual fund managers didn't protect their portfolio principal, investors chose one of two options — getting out of the market altogether and seeking safety or finding out more about how to manage their own portfolios.

The concept of buying and holding forever died after that stock crash. People are now looking for new ways to invest and trade. While investors still practice careful portfolio balancing using a buy and hold strategy, they look much more critically at what they are holding and are more likely to change their holdings now than they were before the crash. Others have gotten out of the stock market completely.

Still others have moved on to the world of trading. Many kinds of traders ply their skills in the markets. The ones who like to take on the most risk and want to trade as a full-time business look to day trading. They never hold a position in a security overnight. Swing traders hold their positions a bit longer, sometimes for a few days or even a few weeks.

But we're not focusing on the riskier types of trading in this book; instead, we're focusing on position trading, which involves executing trades in and out of positions and holding positions for a few weeks or months and maybe even a year or more, depending on trends that are evident in the economy, the marketplace, and ultimately individual stocks.

About This Book

Many people have misconceptions about trading and its risks. Most people think of the riskiest type of trading — day trading — whenever they hear the word *trader*. We're definitely not trying to show you how to day trade. Instead, we want to introduce you to the world of position trading, which is much safer, less risky, and yet a great way to build a significant portfolio.

Don't get the wrong idea; trading in securities always carries risks. You should never trade with money that you can't risk losing. That means trading with your children's education savings isn't a good idea. If you want to trade, set aside a portion of your savings that isn't earmarked for any specific use and that you believe you can put at risk without ruining your lifestyle.

Obviously, we plan to show you ways to minimize risk, but we can't promise that you won't take a loss. Even the most experienced traders, the ones who put together the best trading systems, don't have a crystal ball and periodically get hit by a market shock and accompanying loss. By using the basics of fundamental and technical analyses, we show you how to minimize your risk, how to recognize when the market is ripe for a trade, when specific sectors in the market are the right places to be, how to figure out which phases economic and market cycles are in, and how to make the best use of all that knowledge.

Foolish Assumptions

We've made a number of assumptions about your basic knowledge and stock-trading abilities. We assume that you're not completely new to the world of investing in stocks and that you're familiar with the stock market and its basic language. Although we review many key terms and phrases as we explore the basics of trading, if everything you read sounds totally new to you, you probably need to read a basic book on investing in stocks before trying to move on to the more technical world of trading.

We also assume that you know how to operate a computer and use the Internet. If you don't have high-speed access to the Internet now, be sure you do have it before trying to trade. Many of the resources we recommend in this book are available online, but you'll need high-speed access to be able to work with many of these valuable tools.

How the Book Is Organized

We've broken this book down into six logical parts. Well, we tried anyway. The first focuses on tools, and then we explore the basics of fundamental analysis right before delving into technical analysis. After getting the basics out of the way, we discuss how you can use your newly discovered tools to develop and begin building your own strategies and trading system. Just in case you want to move on to riskier types of trading, we include some basic information about day trading, swing trading, and trading derivatives and foreign currency. That said, we highly recommend that you seek additional training before trying any of the riskier forms of trading.

Part I: So You Want to Be a Trader: Gathering Your Tools

Trading is a business, and just like any other business, you need to put together a good set of tools to be successful. In Part I, we talk about the basics of trading, introduce the markets and the exchanges, discuss various alternatives for finding a broker and setting up your brokerage account, and describe the minimum computer hardware and software necessities you need to succeed as a trader. We also discuss your Internet needs and point you to some good basic resources on the Internet that can help get you started.

Part II: Reading the Fundamentals: The Basics of Fundamental Analysis

Many traders don't use fundamental analysis. They believe technical analysis is the only thing you need to understand. We don't agree. You can gather plenty of valuable information about the economy, markets, sectors, and individual stocks that can help you excel as a trader. We start you out with the economy, the basics of the business cycle, sector rotation, and various economic indicators, because they can help you make your calls. Next we show you how to delve into financial statements to find the crucial information you need to pick the companies whose stocks you want to trade. Finally, we talk about analysts and what information you can get and use from them and what you shouldn't use. We also explain how you can listen in on analysts' calls to get the most current information about a company and how executives perceive their company numbers.

Part III: Reading the Charts: The Basics of Technical Analysis

You can't even begin thinking about trading if you don't understand technical analysis and how to build and read charts so you can pick entry and exit points when buying and selling stocks. We take you step by step through the process of building a chart, and we describe how to identify trends and distinguish between transitions from one trend to another. In this part, you find out how to recognize bull and bear patterns and how to differentiate between a stock that is range bound and one that is trending. We also introduce you to some of our favorite tools and give you several examples of how to use them.

Part IV: Developing Strategies for When to Buy and Sell Stocks

After finding out how to use the tools of fundamental and technical analyses, you're ready to develop strategies for your own trading. First you need to explore good money discipline to avoid taking major losses and be around to trade for another day. You also need to determine when to stay in a position and when to trade out of it. You certainly want to take your profits at the right time, but you also want to avoid standing idly by as a profit turns into a loss. Next we talk about how you can gather key information through fundamental analysis and then add the results of your technical analysis to build an optimum trading strategy. And we talk about the mechanics of trading before finally exploring how you can build your own trading system.

Part V: Risk-Taker's Paradise

You may want to try the riskier forms of trading, such as swing trading, day trading, or trading in derivatives and foreign currency. We definitely won't be sharing any strategies for actually participating in these types of trading, but we will introduce you to the basics and warn you about what you need to become familiar with before entering these wilder forms of trading. Be careful out there and don't get caught up in any of the many frauds and scams that are common with these types of trading.

Part VI: The Part of Tens

The final part of the book is a hallmark of the *For Dummies* series — the Part of Tens. In it, we highlight the top ten huge trading mistakes and ways you can avoid them, and we review the top ten basics you'll need to remember for surviving in the world of trading.

Icons Used in This Book

For Dummies books use little pictures, called icons, to flag certain chunks of text. Here's what they actually mean:

Watch for these little flags to get ideas on how to improve your trading skills or where you can find other useful resources.

If there is something that is particularly important for you to remember, we mark it with this icon.

The trading world is wrought with many dangers and perils. A minor mistake can cost you a bunch of money, so we use this icon to point out particularly perilous areas.

When you see this icon, we're discussing higher-end, more technical material for the experienced trader.

Where to Go from Here

You're ready to enter the exciting world of trading. You can start anywhere in the book. Each of the chapters is self-contained. But, if you're totally new to trading, starting with Chapter 1 of *Trading For Dummies* is the best way to understand the basics. If you already know the basics, understand everything about the various markets and exchanges that you care to know, and already have a broker picked out and have all the tools you'll need, you may want to start with fundamental analysis in Part II. Remember, though, to have fun and enjoy your trip through the exciting world of trading.

Part I

So You Want to Be a Trader: Gathering Your Tools

The 5th Wave   By Rich Tennant

Defining your investment risk with the:
TOAST RETRIEVING RISK TOLERANCE TEST

| LOW RISK | Waits for toast to pop up even though it's burning. |

| MODERATE RISK | Goes after toast with wooden toast prongs. |

| HIGH RISK | Goes after toast with all metal butter knife. |

| ULTRA HIGH RISK | Goes after toast with metal butter knife wearing a wet swim suit and a stainless steel colander on head. |

In this part . . .

Want to discover how you can be a successful trader and why you should want to get involved in trading? That's what you get in Part I. You'll explore the nuances of the various markets and trading exchanges on which you place your trades and find out about the brokers and the types of brokerage houses frequently used by traders. In addition, we describe what computer hardware and software and Internet access you'll need and provide you with several useful Internet resources to get you started.

Chapter 1

The Ins and Outs of Trading Stocks

Making lots of money is the obvious goal of most people who decide to enter the world of trading. How successful you become as a trader depends on how well you use the tools, gather the needed information, and interpret what you've got. You need to develop the discipline to apply all that you know about trading toward developing a winning trading strategy.

Discovering how to avoid getting caught up in the emotional aspects of trading — the highs of a win and the lows of a loss — is key to developing a profitable trading style. Trading is a business and needs to be approached with the same logic you'd apply in your approach to any other business decision. Setting goals, researching your options, planning and implementing your strategies, and assessing your success are just as important for trading as they are for any other business venture.

In this book, we help you traverse these hurdles, and at the same time, we introduce you to the world of trading. In this chapter, we give you an overview of trading and an introduction to the tools you need, the research skills you must use, and the basics of developing all this information into a successful trading strategy.

Trading versus Investing

First, we need to discuss how trading differs from investing. Investors buy stocks and hold them for a long time — many times too long, riding a stock all the way down and possibly even buying more along the way. Traders, on the other hand, hold stocks for as little as a few minutes or as long as several months, and sometimes possibly even a year or more. The specific amount of time depends on the type of trader you want to become.

Investors want to carefully balance an investment portfolio between growth stocks, value stocks, domestic stocks, and foreign stocks, along with long-, short-, and intermediate-term bonds. A well-balanced portfolio generally offers the investor a steady return of between 5 percent and 12 percent, depending on the type of investments and amount of risk he or she is willing to take.

For investors, an aggressive portfolio with a mix of 80 percent invested in stocks and 20 percent in bonds, if well balanced, can average about a 12 per-cent annual return during a 20 year period; however, in some years, the port-folio will be down, and in others, it will go through periods of high growth. The opposite, a conservative portfolio with 20 percent invested in stocks and 80 percent in bonds, is likely to provide a yield on the lower end of the spectrum, closer to 5 percent. The volatility and risk associated with the latter portfolio, however, would be considerably less. Investors who have 10 or more years before they need to use their investment money tend to put together more aggressive portfolios, but those who need to live off the money tend to put together less aggressive portfolios that give them regular cash flows, which is what you get from a portfolio invested mostly in bonds.

As a trader, you look for the best position for your money and then set a goal of exceeding what an investor can otherwise expect from an aggressive port-folio. During certain times within the market cycle, your best option may be to sit on the sidelines and not even be active in the market. In this book, we show you how to read the signals to decide when you need to be in the market, and how to find the best sectors in which to play the market and the best stocks within those sectors.

Why Trade?

Improving your potential profit from stock transactions is obviously the key reason most people decide to trade. People who want to grow their portfo-lios rather than merely maintain them, hope the way they invest in them does better than the market averages. Regardless of whether traders invest through mutual funds or stocks, they hope the portfolio of securities they select gives them superior returns — and they're willing to work at it.

People who decide to trade make a conscious decision to take a more active role in increasing their profit potential. Rather than just riding the market up and down, they search for opportunities to find the best times and places to be in the market based on economic conditions and market cycles.

Traders who successfully watched the technical signals before the stock crash of 2000 moved into cash positions before stocks tumbled and then carefully jumped back in as they saw opportunities for profits. Some position traders simply stayed on the sidelines, waiting for the right time to jump back in. Even though they were waiting, they also carefully researched their opportunities, selected stocks for their watch lists, and then let technical signals from the charts they kept tell them when to get in or out of a position.

Successful Trading Characteristics

To succeed at trading, you have to be hard on yourself and, more than likely, work against your natural tendencies, fighting the urge to prove yourself right and accepting the fact that you're going to make mistakes. As a trader, you must develop separate strategies for when you want to make a trade to enter a position and for when you want to make a trade and exit that position, all the while not allowing emotional considerations to affect the decisions you make on the basis of the successful trading strategy you've designed.

You want to manage your money, but in doing so, you don't have to prove whether your particular buying or selling decision was right or wrong. Setting up stop-loss points for every position you establish and adhering to them is the right course of action, even though you may later have to admit that you were wrong. Your portfolio will survive, and you can always reenter a position whenever trends indicate the time is right again.

You need to make stock trends your master, ignoring any emotional ties that you have to any stocks. Although you may, indeed, miss the lowest entry price or the highest exit price, you nevertheless will be able to sleep at night, knowing that your money is safe and your trading business is alive and well.

Traders find out how to ride a trend and when to get off the train before it jumps the tracks and heads toward monetary disaster. Enjoy the ride, but know which stop you're getting off at so you don't turn profits into losses.

Tools of the Trade

The first step you need to take in becoming a trader is gathering all the right tools so you can open and operate your business successfully. Your computer needs to meet the hardware requirements and other computer specifics we describe in Chapter 4, including processor speed, memory storage, and screen size. You may even want more than one screen, depending on your trading style. High-speed Internet access is a must; otherwise, you may as well never open up shop.

We also introduce you to the various types of software in Chapter 4, showing you what can help your trading business ride the wave to success. Traders' charting favorites such as Metastock, MyTrack, AmiBroker, and Trade Station are evaluated along with data-feed services. And we talk about the various trading platforms that are available and how to work with brokers.

After you have all the hardware and software in place, you need to hone your analytical skills. Many traders advocate using only technical analysis, but we show you how using technical and fundamental analyses can help you excel as a trader.

Taking Time to Trade More than Just Stocks

The ways traders trade are varied. Some are day traders, while others are swing traders and position traders. Although many of the tools they use are the same or similar, each variety of trader works within differing time frames to reach goals that are specific to the type of trades they're making.

Position trading

Position traders use technical analysis to find the most promising stock trends and enter and exit positions in the market based on those trends. They can hold positions for just a few days, a few months, or possibly as long as a year or more. Position trading is the type of trading that we discuss the most in this book. After introducing you to the stock markets, the types of brokers and market-makers with whom you'll be dealing, and the tools you need, we discuss the basics of fundamental analysis and technical analysis to help you become a better position trader.

Short-term swing trading

Swing traders work within much shorter time frames than position traders, rarely holding stocks for more than a few days and looking for sharp moves that technical analysis uncovers. Even though we won't show you the specifics of how to become a swing trader, we nevertheless discuss the basics of swing trading and its strategies in Chapter 16. You can also read about the basics of technical analysis and money management strategies, both of which are useful topics to check out if you plan to become a swing trader. However, you definitely need to seek additional training before deciding to pursue this style of trading.

Day trading

Day traders never leave their money in stocks overnight. They always cash out. They can trade into and out of a stock position in a matter of hours, minutes, or even seconds. Many outsiders watch day traders in action and describe it as more like playing a video game than trading stocks. We discuss this high-risk type of trading in Chapter 17, but we won't be showing you the specifics of how to do it. If day trading is your goal, this book will only take you part of the way there. You'll discover the basics of technical analysis, but you need to seek out additional training before engaging in this risky trading style.

Weathering a bear market

By the end of the 1990s, it was no secret that the bull market had gotten carried away. Stocks with no earnings and few prospects for any were trading for hundreds of dollars. Wall Street was pumping out initial public offerings (IPOs) for questionable companies at a remarkable and alarming rate. You didn't need a crystal ball to see that things were going to turn out badly for technology stocks, especially for high-flying Internet stocks on the NASDAQ.

When traders and investors become exuberant, they tend to party long past the time everyone knows that they need to go home. We can't claim any special foresight or knowledge of when a bull market will end, because we don't have a crystal ball. But we were able to get most of our money out of the markets before the bear market did the worst of its catastrophic damage.

By using strategies that we discuss throughout this book, we were able to exit our positions before giving back most of the profits that accumulated during the bull market — many others unfortunately had to do just that. Sensing the huge pullback was not like a switch was flipped on, we knew it was time to sell everything. Instead, we closed each individual position as technical conditions for each stock deteriorated. The tools we describe in this book enabled us to recognize that risk levels had changed, that few stocks were attractive, and that simply leaving most of our trading capital in cash was the best course of action.

We had no idea how long the bear market would last. In fact, we certainly wouldn't have guessed that it would last as long as it did or be as brutal as it was. Nevertheless, adhering to the techniques featured in this book kept us from committing the bulk of our trading capital until risk levels became more favorable, and we were able to weather the bear market with the majority of our trading capital intact and even make a little money during those trying times by shorting a few stocks. Thanks to the tools we show in this book, we were ready to trade aggressively when the technical condition of stocks began improving in late 2002.

Going Long or Short

Before you start trading, you absolutely have to know what stocks you want to buy and hold for a while, which is called *going long,* or holding a long stock position. You likewise have to know at what point holding that stock is no longer worthwhile. Similarly, you need to know at what price you want to *enter* or trade into a position and at what price you want to *exit* or trade out of a position. You may be surprised to find out that you can even profit by selling a stock without ever owning it, in a process called *shorting.* We discuss these vital trading strategies in Chapter 13.

You can even make money buying and selling options on stocks to simulate long or short stock positions. Buying an option known as a *call* enables you to simulate a long stock position, in much the same way that buying an option known as a *put* enables you to simulate a short stock position. You make money on calls when the option-related stock rises in price, and you make money on a put when the option-related stock falls in price.

When placing orders for puts and calls, you're never guaranteed to make money, even when you're right about the direction a stock will take. The values of options are affected by how volatile stock prices are in relationship to the overall direction (up or down) in which they are headed. We discuss options and how they work in greater detail in Chapter 18.

Managing Your Money

Managing your trades so that you don't lose a bunch of money is critical. Although we can't guarantee that you'll never lose money, we can provide you with useful strategies for minimizing your losses and getting out before your stock portfolio takes a huge hit. The key is knowing when to hold 'em and when to fold 'em, and we cover that in great detail in Chapter 12.

One thing that we can't emphasize enough is that you must think of your trading as a business and the stocks that you hold as its inventory. You can't allow yourself to fall in love with and thereby hang onto a stock out of loyalty. You'll find it especially hard to admit you've made a mistake; nevertheless, you have to bite the bullet and exit the position before you take a huge hit. You'll discover that housecleaning and developing successful strategies for keeping your inventory current are important parts of managing a trading portfolio.

Setting a target price for exiting a position before ever trading into it is the best way to protect your business from major losses. Stick with those predetermined price stops and you'll avoid a major pitfall that many traders face — holding a position too long and losing everything. You obviously don't want to turn a profit into a loss, so as your position in a stock produces a profit, you can periodically raise your target exit price while continuing to hold the position to ensure that you keep most of that profit.

Understanding your risks — market risks, investment risks, and trading risks — helps you to make better trading decisions. We review the different kinds of risks as they relate to specific situations at several points throughout the book.

Understanding Fundamental Analysis

You've probably heard the phrase, "It's the economy, stupid." Well that's true, and we show you how understanding the basics of the business cycle can help you improve your trading successes. In Chapter 5, you find out how to identify periods of economic growth and recession and how these differing periods impact bull and bear stock markets. You can also explore sector rotation and how to use it to pick the right sectors for your trading activities.

You can also discover plenty of information about how money supply, inflation rates, deflation, joblessness, and consumer confidence impact the mood of the market and stock prices and how the economy can be driven by how confidently (or not) political and monetary leaders speak out about it. We discuss the role of the Federal Reserve (Fed) and how when Fed Chairman Alan Greenspan speaks, the markets listen.

Understanding how the economy works isn't the only fundamental analysis tool that's important to you. You also need to read financial statements to understand the financial status of the companies you want to buy. We'll delve into financial statements in Chapter 6.

A company's income statements, on the other hand, give you a look at the results of the most recent period and provide a basis for comparison with prior years and periods. You can use these statements to look at whether revenues are growing, and if they are, by what percentage. You also can see how much profit the company is keeping from the revenue it generates. The cash flow statement shows you how efficiently a company is using its cash and whether it's having problems meeting its current obligations. The balance sheet gives you a snapshot of a company's assets and liabilities and stockholder's equity.

You can use this information to develop your own estimate of a company's growth and profit potential. In Chapter 6, we show you how to do a few basic ratio calculations that you can use to compare similar stocks and then choose the one with the best potential.

Analysts use this information to project a company's financial growth and profits. You never should depend entirely on what analysts say, but you always should do your own research and collect the opinions of numerous analysts. One of the best ways to find out what analysts are saying and what aspects of the financial statements may raise a red flag is the analyst call. In Chapter 7, we explain how you can listen in on these calls and understand the unique language used in them to make better choices when selecting stocks. We also discuss the pros and cons of using analyst reports.

Getting a Grip on Technical Analysis

You use fundamental analysis to determine what part of the business cycle the economy is in and what industries offer the best growth potential. Then you use that information to select the best target companies and identify prices at which you'd want to buy their stocks.

After choosing your targets, you then use technical analysis to follow trends in the prices of the target stocks, so you can find the right time to get in and ultimately to get out of a stock position. These targets become part of your stock-watch list. After you've established that list, you then use the tools of technical analysis to make your trades.

In Chapter 8, we introduce you to the basics of technical analysis, how it works, and how it needs to be used. Although some people think of technical analysis as no more than fortune-telling, others believe it yields significant information that can help you make successful trades. We obviously believe that technical analysis provides you with extensive tools for your trading success, and we show you how to use those tools to be profitable.

Your first step in technical analysis is finding out how to create a chart. We focus on the most popular type — bar charting. In Chapter 9, you discover the art of deciphering simple visual stock patterns and how to distinguish between trends and trading ranges, all so you're able to spot when a stock moves from a trading range into either an upward or downward trend and know when you need to act.

In Chapter 10, we show you how to use your newfound skill of identifying trends to locate areas of support and resistance within a trend that ultimately help you find the right times to make your move. You find out how to read the patterns in the charts to identify trading signals and what to do whenever you've acted on a failed trading signal.

Chapter 11 fills you in on moving averages and how to use them to identify trends. You also find out about oscillators and other indicators that traders use for recognizing trading signals. As a newby trader, you'll probably find that your greatest risk is paralysis of analysis. That's where you may find that you're having so much fun reading the charts or are just so confused about which chart has the right signal that you feel paralyzed by the variety of choices. We show you how to create and use a tiny subset of tools that is available in today's charting software packages to simplify your life and make your choices easier. You'll likewise discover how to use such odd-sounding but critical tools as an MACD indicator or a stochastic oscillator, and we help you take advantage of the powerful concept of relative strength.

Putting Trading Strategy into Practice

After you get used to using the tools, it's time to put your new skills into practice making money. In Chapter 13, we show you how to put your newfound affinities for fundamental analysis and technical analysis together to develop and build your trading strategy. Using fundamental analysis, you can

- Determine which part of the economic cycle is driving the market.
- Determine which sector makes the most sense for stock trading.
- Figure out which sectors are in the best positions to go up.
- Find out which stocks are leading in the ascending sectors.
- Evaluate where the Fed stands on the economy and which potential moves by the Fed can impact the strength of the market.
- Evaluate and hopefully anticipate potential shocks to the market. Although doing so may seem like gazing into a crystal ball, you really can pick up some signs by checking out the key economic indicators. We show you what they are.

After you complete your fundamental analysis, we show you how to use your new technical analysis skills successfully. Using them, you find out how you can

- Trade within the overall technical conditions.
- Confirm which economic cycle a market is in by using index charts.
- Determine whether an ascending sector is stuck in a range or ready to enter a new upward trend.
- Determine whether leading stocks are stuck in ranges or ready to break out in upward trends.

Finally, we show you how to use your newfound skills to manage risk, set up a stop-loss position, and choose your time frame for trading.

After honing your skills, you're ready to start trading. So in Chapter 14, we focus on the actual mechanics of trading by:

- ✔ Discussing how to enter or trade into a position.
- ✔ Explaining bid and ask prices.
- ✔ Discussing the risks of market orders.
- ✔ Explaining how to use limit and stop orders.

We also explore how to exit or trade out of a position and still stay unattached emotionally, when to take your profits, and how to minimize your losses, in addition to discussing potential tax hits and how to minimize them.

Now that you know how to research the fundamentals, effectively use the technical tools, and mechanically carry out a trade, the next step is developing and managing your own trading system. We explore the basic steps to developing the system, which include:

1. **Designing and keeping a trading log.**

2. **Identifying reliable trading patterns.**

3. **Developing an exit strategy.**

4. **Determining whether you'll use discretionary trading methods or mechanical trading. We explore the pros and cons of each.**

5. **Deciding whether to develop your own trading system or buy one of the ones available on the shelf.**

6. **Testing your trading systems and understanding their limitations before making a major financial commitment to your new system.**

   We also discuss assessing your results and fixing any problems.

After you've designed, built, and tested your system, you're ready to jump in with both feet. The key to getting started: Make sure you begin with a small sum of money, examining your system and then increasing your trading activity as you gain experience and develop confidence with the system that you develop.

Trading at Higher Risk

Some traders decide they want to take on a greater level of risk by practicing methods of swing trading or day trading or delving into the areas of trading derivatives or foreign currency. Although all of them are valid trading options, we steer clear of explaining even the basics of how to use these high-risk trading alternatives, and instead, we provide you with a general understanding of the ways these trading alternatives work and the risks that are unique to each of them.

If you decide, however, that you want to take on these additional risks, don't depend on the information in this book to get started. Use the general information that we offer you here to determine what additional training you need to feel confident in moving into these trading arenas.

Remember: Have Fun!

Although you are without question considering the work of a trader for the money you can make, you need to enjoy the game of trading. If you find that you're having trouble sleeping at night because of the risks you're taking, then trading may not be worth all the heartache. You may need to put off your decision to enter the world of trading until you're more comfortable with the risks or you've designed a system that better accommodates your risk tolerance.

You may find that you need to take a slower approach by putting less money into your trades. You don't need to make huge profits with your early trades. Just trading into and out of a position without losing any money may be a good goal for you when you're just starting out. If you notice your position turning toward the losing side, knowing that you can trade your way out of it before you take a big loss may help you build greater confidence in your abilities.

Remember, making a losing trade doesn't mean that you're a loser. Even the most experienced traders must at times face losses. The key to successful trading is knowing when to get out before your portfolio takes a serious hit. On the other side of that coin, you also need to know how to get out when you're in a winning or profitable position. When you're trying to ride a trend all the way to the top, it sometimes starts bottoming out so fast that you lose some or possibly even all your profits, causing you to end up in a losing position.

Trading is a skill that takes a long time to develop and is perfected only after you make mistakes and celebrate successes. Enjoy the roller coaster ride!

Chapter 2

Discovering the Markets and the Stock Exchanges

In This Chapter

▶ Discovering the markets

▶ Understanding the exchanges

▶ Reviewing order basics

*B*illions of shares of stock trade in the United States every day, and each trader is looking to get his or her small piece of that action. Before moving into the specifics of how to trade, we first want to introduce you not only to the world of stock trading, but also to trading in other key markets — futures, options, and bonds. In this chapter, we also explain differences and similarities among key stock exchanges and how those factors impact your trading options. After providing you with a good overview of the key markets, we delve into the different types of orders you can place with each of the key exchanges.

Introducing the Broad Markets

You may think the foundation of the United States economy resides inside Fort Knox where the country holds its billions of dollars in gold, or possibly that it resides in our political center, Washington, D.C. Nope, it's neither of them. The country's true economic center is Wall Street, where billions of dollars change hands each and every day, thousands of companies are traded, and millions of people's lives are affected.

Stocks are not the only things sold in the broad financial markets. Every day, futures, options, and bonds also are traded. Although we focus on stock exchanges in this chapter, we first need to briefly explain each type of market.

Stock markets

The stocks of almost every major U.S. corporation and many major foreign corporations are traded on a stock exchange in the United States each day, and none of the money involved in these trades goes directly into the companies being traded. Today numerous local and international stock exchanges trade stocks in publicly held corporations; moreover, the only major corporations not traded are those held privately — usually by families or original founding partners — that chose not to sell shares on the public market. *Forbes* magazine's top privately held corporation is Cargill. Mars, Bechtel, and Publix are three others on the *Forbes* top 20 list. Many of the large private corporations that are not traded publicly do have provisions for employee ownership of stock and must report earnings to the SEC, so they straddle the line of public versus private corporations.

A *share of stock* is actually a portion of ownership in a given company. Few stockholders own large enough stakes in a company to play a major role in decision-making. Instead, stockholders purchase stocks, hoping that their investments rise in price, so that those stocks can be sold at a profit some time in the future.

For the majority of this chapter, we focus on the three top stock exchanges in the United States: the New York Stock Exchange (NYSE), NASDAQ (the National Association of Securities Dealers Automated Quotation system), and the American Stock Exchange (Amex). We also introduce you to the newly-evolving world of electronic communications networks (ECNs) on which you can trade stocks directly, thus bypassing brokers.

Futures markets

Futures trading actually started in Japan in the 18th century to trade rice and silk. This trading instrument was first used in the United States in the 1850s for trading grains and other agricultural entities. Basically, futures trading means establishing a financial contract in which you try to predict the future value of a commodity that must be delivered at a specific time in the future. Yup, if you had a working crystal ball, it would be very useful here. This type of trading is done on a commodities exchange. The largest such exchange in the United States today is the Chicago Mercantile Exchange. Commodities include any product that can be bought and sold. Oil, cotton, and minerals are just a few of the products sold on a commodity exchange.

Futures contracts must have a seller (usually the person producing the commodity, a farmer or oil refinery, for example) and a buyer (usually a consumer). You also can speculate on either side of the contract, basically meaning:

✔ When you buy a futures contract, you're agreeing to buy a commodity that is not yet ready for sale or hasn't yet been produced at a set price at a specific time in the future.

✔ When you sell a futures contact, you're agreeing to provide a commodity that is not yet ready for sale or hasn't yet been produced at a set price at a specific time in the future.

The futures contract states the price at which you agree to pay for or sell a certain amount of this future product when it's delivered at a specific future date. Although most futures contracts are based on a physical commodity, some futures contracts also are sold based on the future value of stock indexes.

Unless you're a commercial consumer who plans to use the commodity, you won't actually take delivery of or actually provide the commodity for which you're trading a futures contract. You'll more than likely sell the futures contract you bought before you actually have to accept the commodity from a commercial customer. Futures contracts are used as financial instruments by producers, consumers, and speculators. We cover more about those players and futures contracts in much greater depth in Chapter 18.

Bond markets

Bonds are actually loan instruments. Companies sell bonds to borrow cash. If you buy a bond, you're essentially holding a company's debt or the debt of a governmental entity. The company or government entity that sells the bond agrees to pay you a certain amount of interest for a specific period of time in exchange for the use of your money. The big difference between stocks and bonds is that bonds are debt obligations and stocks are equity. Stockholders actually own a share of the corporation. Bondholders lend money to the company with no right of ownership. Bonds, however, are considered safer, because if a company files bankruptcy, bondholders are paid before stockholders. Bonds are a safety net and not actually a part of the trading world for position traders, day traders, and swing traders. While a greater dollar volume of bonds is traded each day, the primary traders for this venue are large dollar institutional traders. We wanted to explain them here but won't discuss them any further in this book.

Options markets

An *option* is a contract that gives the buyer the right, but not the obligation, either to buy or to sell the asset upon which it is based at a price specified in the contract on or before a date specified in the contract. Sometime before the options period expires, a purchaser of an option must decide whether to exercise the option and buy (or sell)) the asset (most commonly stocks) at the target price. If the options buyer decides not to buy (or sell) the asset, his or her initial investment in the option is lost. Options also are called *derivatives*. We talk more about this investment alternative in Chapter 18.

Reviewing Stock Exchanges

Most of this book covers stock trading, so we obviously concentrate on how the key exchanges — NYSE, NASDAQ, and Amex — operate and how these operations impact your trading activity.

New York Stock Exchange (NYSE)

The U.S. stock market actually dates back to May 17, 1792, when 24 brokers signed an agreement under a buttonwood tree at what today is 58 Wall Street. The 24 brokers specifically agreed to sell shares of companies among themselves, charging a commission or fee to buy and sell shares for others who wanted to invest in a company. Yup, the first stockbrokers were born that day.

A formalized exchange didn't come into existence until March 8, 1817, when the brokers adopted a formal constitution and named their new entity the New York Stock & Exchange Board. Brokers actually operated outdoors until 1860, when the operations finally were moved inside. The first stock ticker was introduced in 1867, but it wasn't until 1869 that the NYSE started requiring the registration of securities for companies that wanted to list on the exchange. Registration began as a means of preventing the over-issuance (selling too many shares) of a company's stock.

From these meager beginnings, the NYSE built itself into the largest stock exchange in the world with many of the largest companies listed on the exchange. Trading actually occurs on the floor of the exchange with specialists and floor traders running the show.

The specialist

Specialists are the workers who are responsible for matching buyers to sellers. On the NYSE, seven firms employ more than 400 specialists who trade more than 2,800 stocks. Most specialists manage stock trades for between five and ten companies, unless they're representing the stock of a particularly large company with huge trading volumes — then they may represent only one other small company.

The specialists' role is to be certain that the stocks for which they're responsible are traded in a fair, competitive, orderly, and efficient market, ensuring that all customers have an equal opportunity to buy shares while receiving the best prices. The specialist seeks to avoid large or unreasonable price fluctuations between consecutive sales and usually is fairly successful. In fact, according to NYSE statistics, 98 percent of all stocks trade within a range of ⅛ of a point or less on either side (plus or minus) of the previous sale.

Specialists actually work out of a particular location on the floor of the NYSE from which all shares of a particular stock are traded. The four critical roles that specialists serve on the floor of the exchange are

- ✔ **Auctioneer:** The specialist serving in the capacity of an auctioneer shows the best bids and offers throughout the trading day. This information is disseminated electronically through the NYSE systems and reaches a worldwide audience almost instantaneously. The specialist maintains order and interacts with agents whose customers want to buy the stock.

- ✔ **Agent:** The specialist is the agent for Super DOT (electronically routed) orders. We explain Super DOT in "The Super DOT (Designated Order Turnaround) System" section later in the chapter. Floor brokers also may leave an order with a specialist with instructions for the specialist to execute the order at a later time when the stock is available at a spec-ified price. When specialists take on this role, they have the same fidu-ciary responsibilities as a broker. By leaving such orders with a specialist, brokers can concentrate on other orders that need their immediate atten-tion. Fiduciary responsibility in this situation means that someone has voluntarily agreed to act as a caretaker of another person's assets and must carry out those responsibilities in good faith with honesty and integrity, and in a way that benefits the asset owner for which the agent has taken the responsibility.

- ✔ **Catalyst:** Specialists serving as catalysts actually become conduits for the flow of orders, keeping track of all known interest in the stock, because not all buyers and sellers are always represented on the floor of the exchange. Specialists call interested parties, letting them know about what's available. Playing the role of catalyst may help to keep the stock moving when sales otherwise might never occur.

- ✔ **Principal:** Specialists must place and execute all orders ahead of their own. Three out of four transactions at the NYSE actually take place between customers without the capital participation of the specialist. In the small minority of trades in which specialists do participate, their role is to provide capital and add liquidity to the market. This capital bridges temporary gaps in supply or demand, which in turn helps reduce price volatility.

You may not realize just how much the concept of supply and demand influ-ences the trading price of a stock. Price swings of a stock frequently are caused by shifts in the supply of shares available for sale and the demand created by the number of buyers wanting to purchase available shares.

Specialists buffer dramatic swings when news about a company breaks. If news breaks that has a major impact on a stock's price, specialists buy shares or sell the ones they hold in a company to make the trend toward a higher or lower stock price more orderly. For example, if good news breaks, creating more demand for the stock and overwhelming existing supply, the specialist becomes a seller of the stock to minimize the impact of a major price increase by increasing supply. The same is true when bad news strikes, creating a situation in which having more sellers than buyers drives the stock price down. In that situation, the specialist becomes a buyer of the stock, easing the impact of the drop in price.

The floor trader

The guys you see on the floor of the stock exchange waving their hands wildly to make trades are the *floor traders*. They're actually members of the NYSE who trade exclusively for their own accounts. Floor traders also can act as a floor broker for others and sell their services.

The specialist's book

You may wonder how a specialist keeps track of all this information. That one's easy: The specialist records all trades and quotation changes in the specialist's order book. Any questions that arise about trading activities can be researched using this book.

Open outcry

The NYSE uses what is becoming an outdated method of trading called *open outcry,* in which stocks are sold like a public auction with verbal bids and offers shouted in trading pits. These pits are centered on the specialist's location for particular stocks. Other exchanges use computer-based screen systems for trading.

The NYSE is the last big stock exchange to use open outcry, a system that may soon become history because the U.S. Securities and Exchange Commission (SEC) is pushing for changes in this system after bowing to pressure exerted by investor groups. Major players such as Fidelity, the mutual fund company, and AIG, the insurance company, have joined the voices of individual investors who want to see a change in this antiquated system to a more modern system similar to that used by NASDAQ. If the SEC succeeds, this change would be the biggest shake-up in the more than 200-year history of the NSYE.

The Super DOT (Designated Order Turnaround) System

Orders from brokers not on the floor of the exchange reach specialists through the Super DOT System. Super DOT is a stock order entering system that can handle daily trading volume that exceeds 2 billion shares. The system sends brokers messages through a common message switch to the proper specialist's trading-floor workstation. Specialists handle these trades as buyers or sellers as particular stocks and orders become available, and they send acknowledgements to the originating brokerage firms, using the same switching system.

NASDAQ

NASDAQ, which stands for the National Association of Securities Dealers Automated Quotation System, is the fastest growing stock market today. The market was formed after an SEC study in the early 1960s concluded that the sale of over-the-counter securities, in other words securities that aren't traded on the existing stock exchanges, was fragmented and obscure. The report called for the automation of the OTC market and gave the responsibility for implementing that system to the National Association of Securities Dealers (NASD).

NASD began construction of the NASDAQ System in 1968, and its first trades were made beginning February 8, 1971, when NASDAQ became the world's first electronic stock market.

Market makers

Unlike the specialist structure of the NYSE, in which one specialist represents a particular stock, NASDAQ market makers compete with each other to buy and sell the stocks they choose to represent. More than 500 member firms act as market makers for NASDAQ. All market makers are members of the NASD. Each uses its own capital, research, and system resources to represent a stock and compete with other market makers.

Market makers compete for customers' orders by displaying buy and sell quotations on an electronic exchange for a guaranteed number of shares at a specific price. After market makers receive orders, they immediately purchase or sell stock from their own inventories or seek out the other side of the trades so they can be executed, usually in a matter of seconds. The four types of market makers are

- ✔ **Retail market makers:** They serve institutional and individual investors through brokerage networks that provide a continuous flow of orders and sales opportunities.
- ✔ **Wholesale market makers:** They serve primarily institutional clients and other brokers or dealers who aren't registered market makers in a particular company's stock but need to execute orders for their customers.

✔ **Institutional market makers:** They execute large block orders for institutional investors, such as pension funds, mutual funds, insurance companies, and asset management companies.

✔ **Regional market makers:** They serve companies and individuals of a particular region. By focusing regionally, these market makers offer their customers more extensive coverage of the stocks and investors in a particular area of the country.

Listing stocks on the NASDAQ

To be listed on the NASDAQ stock exchange, a company must meet one of three listing standards related to:

✔ Stockholder equity ($15 million minimum) or market value ($75 million minimum)

✔ Income from continuing operations of at least $1 million before taxes

✔ Publicly held shares (at least $1.1 million must be issued)

✔ Market value of publicly held shares (at least $8 million)

✔ Minimum bid price of $5 after already having achieved a minimum bid price of $1

✔ A minimum of 400 shareholders

✔ A minimum of three market makers trading in the stock

Over-the-counter and bulletin-board stocks

Stocks that do not meet the minimum requirements to be listed on NASDAQ are traded as over-the-counter or bulletin-board stocks (OTCBB). The OTCBB is a regulated quotation service that displays real-time quotes, last-sale prices, and volume information for the stocks traded OTCBB. These stocks generally don't meet the listing qualifications for NASDAQ or other national securities exchanges, and fewer than two (and sometimes even no) market makers trade in these stocks, making buying and selling them more difficult.

The SOES system

NASDAQ's Small Order Execution (market) System (SOES) was introduced in 1985 and became mandatory for all market makers after the 1987 stock market crash. Small traders using this system can execute trades directly without worry or fear of market-maker misconduct. Available stocks are posted on an electronic bulletin board and trades are executed electronically. All market makers list the stocks they have available for sale with their *bid* (current price at which the market maker will buy) and *ask* (current price at which the market maker will sell) prices.

Traders pick the bid/ask price that looks best and execute their trades in a matter of seconds using the SOES system. We take a much closer look at how to do this in Chapter 14.

Amex

When the NYSE moved indoors, some stocks still weren't good enough to be sold on the exchange. Those stocks were called *curb traders* and ultimately made up what became known as the American Stock Exchange (Amex), which also moved indoors in 1921. Amex lists stocks that are smaller in size than those on the NYSE yet still have a national following. Many firms that first list on Amex work to meet the listing requirements of the NYSE and then switch over.

Trades on the Amex are executed using an automated or manual order processing system. In the automated system, orders are routed electronically to specialists, virtually eliminating the use of paper on the trading floor. Using an automated order routing system called Booth Automated Routing System (BARS), transactions are electronically captured and reports to member firms are generated. Rather than the specialist's order books, Amex uses a New Equity Trading System (NETS) to collect information about the trades and automate the process of updating and matching orders, quoting and reporting trades, and regulating and researching order details.

Orders also can be placed manually by calling the floor broker by phone. Manual order processes usually are initiated for large or complex orders. Specialists in a stock help to assemble the buyers or sellers for these orders.

Regional exchanges

Stock exchanges that focus on listing stocks of corporations from specific geographic regions of the country are called *regional exchanges*. In the United States, the major regional exchanges include Boston, Chicago, Pacific, and Philadelphia stock exchanges. These regional markets are smaller than the NYSE, NASDAQ, and Amex. Although they list mostly regional stocks not on the national exchanges, regional exchanges sometimes list stocks of companies located in their regions even if they're listed on one of the national exchanges.

Listing requirements

NASDAQ has the easiest minimum listing requirements of all the exchanges, followed by the American Stock Exchange (Amex). The New York Stock Exchange (NYSE) has the toughest requirements to meet for companies to be listed.

In addition to listing requirements, companies on the exchanges must conform to certain rules, including publishing quarterly reports, soliciting proxies, and publicly announcing developments that may affect the value of the securities.

Each regional exchange offers its own unique blend of services. Boston serves a financial community where trillions of dollars that are invested in mutual funds are managed, so that exchange focuses on serving those clients. Chicago trades stocks listed regionally, but also trades stocks from other exchanges, including the NYSE, Amex, and NASDAQ, so it also serves the needs of its regional financial institutions.

The Pacific Exchange focuses on buying and selling options, and thus is known as one of the world's leading derivatives markets. The Philadelphia Stock Exchange focuses on trading options of various sectors including oil service, precious metals (gold and silver), semiconductors, banks, and utilities. The exchange also manages a market structure for trading currency options.

Electronic communications networks (ECNs)

Many traders look for ways to get around dealing with a traditional broker. Instead they access trades using a direct-access broker. We talk more about the differences in Chapter 3. A new system of electronic trading that is developing is called the electronic communications network (ECN). The SEC reports that about 30 percent of the total share volume in NASDAQ-listed securities and 40 percent of the dollar volume is traded using ECNs. Likewise, about 96 percent of the trades on ECNs are shares of NASDAQ-listed stocks.

ECNs enable buyers and sellers to meet electronically to execute trades. The trades are entered into the ECN systems by market makers at one of the exchanges or by an OTC market maker. Transactions are completed without a broker-dealer, saving users the cost of commissions normally charged for more traditional forms of trading.

Subscribers to ECNs include retail investors, institutional investors, market makers, and broker-dealers. ECNs are accessed through a custom terminal or by direct Internet dial-up. Orders are posted by the ECN for subscribers to view. The ECN then matches orders for execution. In most cases, buyers and sellers maintain their anonymity and do not list identifiable information in their buy or sell orders.

Currently, nine ECNs operate in the U.S. securities markets, including Instinet, Island, Bloomberg Tradebook, Archipelago, REDIBook, BRUT, Attain, NexTrade, and Market XT. Individual investors primarily use Instinet, Island, or Archipelago.

  ✔ **Instinet** (www.instinet.com): Instinet, which was launched in 1969, is the oldest and largest ECN. It operates around the clock and serves a truly global clientele. Until a recent partnership with E*TRADE was established, Instinet allowed only institutional investors to access its network. Instinet also holds a minority stake in Archipelago.

✔ **INET** (www.inetats.com):The second oldest and largest ECN is Island (now INET ATS), which was founded in 1996 and grew from a day-trading system called Watcher. Instinet and Island combined their listings into one electronic marketplace, using Island's technology, but Instinet still serves institutional clients with its own set of value-added services. Island's majority owner is Datek, which uses it primarily for its NASDAQ trades. Island first attracted day traders, who liked its speed, liquidity, and flexibility relating to trading rules, but today many sell-side firms also use Island. Traders can access Island's order system for free on the Internet, but when you want to trade, you must do so through a direct-access broker.

✔ **Archipelago** (www.tradearca.com): Archipelago also has its roots in the day-trading arena. It was founded in 1997 as a joint venture between Terra Nova Trading and Townsend Analytics. Archipelago differs from other ECNs because it uses SmartBook technology, which actively looks for the best price based on historical success to rate and route orders. Day traders particularly like this ECN.

Understanding Order Types

Buying a share of stock can be as easy as calling a broker and saying that you want to buy such and such a stock, but you can place an order in a number of other ways that give you better protections. Most orders are placed as day orders, but you can choose to place them as good 'til canceled orders. The four basic types of orders you can place are market orders, limit orders, stop orders, and stop-limit orders.

Understanding the language and using it to protect your assets and the way you trade is critical to your success as a trader. The next few sections explain the nuances of placing orders so you don't make a potentially costly mistake by placing a market order when you intended to place a limit order. Putting a stop-limit order in place may sound like the safest way to go; however, doing so may not help you in a rapidly changing market.

Market order

When you place a *market order,* you're essentially telling a broker to buy or sell a stock at the current market price. A market order is the way your broker normally places an order unless you give him or her different instructions. The advantage of a market order is that you're almost always guaranteed that your order is executed as long as willing buyers and sellers are in the marketplace. Generally speaking, buy orders are filled at the ask price and sell orders are filled at the bid price. If, however, you're working with a broker who has a smart-order routing system, which looks for the best bid/ask prices, you sometimes can get a better price on the NASDAQ or Amex exchanges. Whenever the order involves the NYSE, you need a good floor broker. In most brokerage houses, market orders are the cheapest to place with the lowest commission level.

The disadvantage of a market order is that you're stuck paying the price when the order is executed and possibly not at the price you expected when you placed the order. Brokers and real-time quote services quote you prices, but because the markets move fast, with deals taking place in seconds, you'll probably find that the price you're quoted rarely is the same as the execution price. Whenever you place a market order, especially if you're seeking a large number of shares, the probability is even greater that you'll receive different prices for parts of the order — 100 shares at $25 and 100 shares at $25.125, for example.

Limit order

If you want to avoid buying or selling stock at a price higher or lower than you intend, you must place a *limit order* instead of a market order. When placing a limit order, you specify the price at which you'll buy or sell. You can place either a buy limit order or a sell limit order. Buy limit orders can be executed only when the price of the stock you're buying is at the limit price or lower. A sell limit order can be executed only when the selling price is at the limit price or higher. In other words, you set the parameters for the price that you'll accept. You can't do that with a market order.

The risk that you take when placing a limit order is that the order may never be filled. For example, a hot stock peaks your interest when it is selling for $10, so you decide to place a limit order to buy the stock at $10.50. By the time you call your broker or input the order into your trading system, the price already has moved above $10.50 and never drops back to that level, thus your order won't be filled. On the good side, if the stock is so hot that its price skyrockets to $75, you also won't be stuck as the owner of the stock after purchasing near the $75 high. That high will likely be a temporary top that quickly drops back to reality, forcing you to sell the stock at a significant loss at some point in the future.

Most firms charge more for executing a limit order than they do for a market order. Be sure that you understand the fee and commission structures if you intend to use limit orders.

Stop order

You may also consider placing your order as a *stop order,* which means that whenever the stock reaches a price that you specify, it automatically becomes a market order. Investors who buy using a stop order usually do so to limit potential losses or protect a profit. Buy stop orders are always entered at a stop price that is above the current market price.

When placing a stop sell order, you do so to avoid further losses or protect a profit that exists in case the stock continues on a downward trend. The stop price always is placed below the current market price. For example, when you have a stock that you bought for $10 that now is selling for $25, you can decide to protect most of that profit by placing a sell stop order that specifies that stock be sold when the market price falls to $20, thus cementing a $10 gain.

You don't have to watch the stock market every second; instead, when the market price drops to $20, your stop order automatically switches to a market order and is executed.

The big disadvantage of a stop order is that if for some reason the stock market gets a shock during the news day that affects all stocks, it can temporarily send prices lower, activating your stop price. If it turns out that the downturn is actually merely a short-term fluctuation and not an indication that the stock you hold is a bad choice or that you risk losing your profit, your stock may sell before you ever have time to react.

The bottom can fall out of your stock's pricing. After your stop price is reached, a stop order automatically becomes a market order and the price that you actually receive can differ greatly from your stop price, especially in a rapidly fluctuating market. You can avoid this problem by placing a stop-limit order, which we discuss in the next section.

Stop orders more frequently are used for stocks that trade on an exchange (rather than NASDAQ- or OTC-traded stocks). You can't place a stop order on a NASDAQ stock. If you want a stop, your broker must actually simulate a stop order by watching the market and entering the market or limit order you designate as a stop when the stock reaches your specified sale price. Some broker-dealers won't accept a stop order on some securities and almost never accept a stop order for OTC stocks. If you intend to use stop orders, make sure that you:

✔ Check with the brokers you're planning to use to ensure that they accept stop orders.

✔ Find out what your brokers charge for stop orders.

✔ Review how your brokers' stop orders work, so you don't run into surprises.

After all, you don't want to execute a stop order and end up selling a stock that you didn't intend to sell or at a price you find unacceptable.

Stop-limit order

You can protect yourself from any buying or selling surprises by placing a *stop-limit order*. This type of order combines the features of a stop order and a limit order. When your stop price is reached, the stop order becomes a limit order rather than a market order.

A stop-limit order gives you the most control over the price at which you will trade your stock. You can avoid a purchase or sale of your stock at a price that differs significantly from what you intend. But you do risk the possibility that the stop-limit order may never be executed, which can happen in fast-moving markets where prices fluctuate wildly.

For example, you may find that deploying stop-limit orders is particularly dangerous to your portfolio, especially when bad news breaks about a stock you're holding and its price drops rapidly. Although you have a stop-limit order in place, and the stop price is met, the movement in the market may happen so rapidly that the price limit you set can be missed. In this case, the limit side of the order actually prevents the sale of the stock and you risk riding it all the way down until you change your order. For example, say you purchased Nortel at $8 near its peak in early 2004. At the end of April, on the day its CEO and CFO were fired, it dropped to $4.05. You may have had a stop-limit order in place to sell at $5, but on the day of the firing, the price dropped so rapidly after the company announced the firing that your stop-limit order could not be met.

Stop-limit orders, like stop orders, are more commonly used when trading on an exchange than in an OTC market. Broker-dealers likewise can limit the securities on which stop-limit orders can be placed. If you want to use stop-limit orders, be sure to review the rules with your broker before trying to execute them.

Day orders

Unless you specify differently, orders that you place with your broker are entered as day orders. *Day orders* are good only during the trading day on which they're placed. If for some reason your order is not executed during the regular trading day, it won't carry over to after-hours trading or the next regular trading day. The *regular trading day* is from 9 a.m. to 4 p.m. Eastern time.

ECNs, on the other hand, now enable individual investors to participate in after-hours trading. You can place an order during after-hours trading. If you place an order after hours using an ECN, it can be executed only during the after-hours session and won't carry over to the next trading day.

If your day order isn't executed, you have to place it again the next day.

Good 'til canceled orders

You can avoid having to replace an order time and again by using a good 'til canceled (GTC) order. GTC orders are placed at a limit price and last until the order actually is executed or you decide to cancel it. A GTC order won't be executed until the limit price is reached, regardless of how many days or weeks it takes.

You can choose to use this type of order whenever you want to set a limit price that differs significantly from the current market price. Many brokerage firms limit how much time a GTC can remain in place, and most of them charge more for executing this type of order.

Other order types

Less commonly used order methods include contingent, all-or-none, and fill-or-kill orders. *Contingent orders* are placed on the contingency that another one of your stock holdings is sold before the order is placed. An *all-or-none order* specifies that all the shares of a stock be bought according to the terms indicated or none of the stock should be purchased. A *fill-or-kill order* must be filled immediately upon placement or killed.

Chapter 3

Going for Broke(r): Understanding Your Brokerage Options

As an individual, you can't trade stocks — or bonds, or options, or futures — unless you have a broker or are a broker yourself. That doesn't, however, mean you have to work with a human being to trade stocks. Online brokers and direct-access brokers enable you to make trades electronically, so you never have to speak with a human being unless you're having a technical problem.

The differences between brokers are based on prices, services, and special capabilities. High-volume swing traders and day traders typically require the services of a direct-access broker, while position traders can and do trade successfully with more traditional discount, online, and full-service brokers. In this chapter, we help you understand the brokerage options that are available, the types of accounts you can establish, and the basic trading rules you must follow.

Why You Need a Broker

Unless you plan to get your brokerage license from the National Association of Securities Dealers (NASD) and set up shop yourself (which is hard — and expensive — to do), you need to work with a broker to be able to buy and sell stocks. How you choose a broker is based on the level of individual services you want. The more services you want, the more you pay for your ability to trade.

As an individual, you open your account with a brokerage house, but if you work with a human being, that person is considered a broker. Brokerage houses or brokerage services are also usually referred to as brokers for short. Actually there are many levels of brokers, which we cover in greater detail in Chapter 20 when we talk about licensing.

On one side of the spectrum is the full-service broker who does a lot of hand-holding and offers stock research and advice and other human-based services. When using a full-service broker, you pay a significant commission for each stock trade. In the middle are discount brokers that offer fewer services, but you pay less per trade. On the opposite side of the equation are direct-access brokers, who offer few human-based services and instead provide extensive trading platforms so you can trade electronically and access the stock exchange systems directly on a real-time basis.

Understanding Types of Brokers and Brokerage Services

Before you can pick the type of broker that best fulfills your needs, you need to understand the kinds of services that each kind of broker provides. After you gain an understanding of your options and select the type of services you want, you then need to carefully research each of the brokers that match your needs. Within each classification are good and bad brokers. We give you the tools for researching brokerage firms in the sections that follow.

Full-service brokers

If you want someone to assist you with buying decisions and implementing those decisions, you need to check out the full-service brokers. They offer extensive research and other services. Usually, they call you with trading ideas. All you need to do is say yes or no. You pay a transaction fee for trades plus a commission percentage based on the dollar volume. You can invest in stocks, futures, options, bonds, mutual funds, money market funds, and variable annuities. You can work with a full-service broker by telephone, mail, fax, or using an Internet connection. Most have Web sites you can access online for information and many allow you to enter your own trades.

For example, here is the transaction fee schedule for one of the better-known full-service brokers (others can be as much as twice as high):

Transaction Size	Commission Rate
$0–$2,499	$35 plus 1.7% of principal
$2,500–$6,249	$65 plus 0.66% of principal
$6,250–$19,999	$85 plus 0.34% of principal
$20,000–$49,999	$115 plus 0.33% of principal
$50,000–$499,999	$170 plus 0.11% of principal
$500,000+	$270 plus 0.09% of principal

Minimum broker-assisted trade — $54.95 per trade. Maximums are determined by transaction size.

Alternatively, some full-service brokers do permit you to make all the trades you want per year for a fee of 0.30 percent to 2.5 percent of the total assets in your brokerage account. Using language common to traders, that's 30 to 250 basis points. You have to have more than $10 million in an account to get the lowest fee. Traders with less than $100,000 pay closer to the 2.5 percent of assets to access the unlimited trading features.

Just because you choose to use a full-service broker doesn't mean you can just sit back after placing your money into an account and let it grow. Brokers make money on commissions for the exchange of stocks. If they have no transactions during a given month, they don't get paid. Unscrupulous brokers recommend trades to their customers to generate new commissions even when those decisions are not necessarily the best investment advice for their clients.

Even the research arms of many full-service brokerage houses have come under scrutiny from the Securities and Exchange Commission (SEC) in the past few years, primarily because their analysts didn't accurately reflect the values of stocks in companies that used the firms' investment-banking capabilities. Analysts tend to see their clients through rose-colored glasses when providing research reports, especially when their firms make a lot of money by providing investment-banking services to those companies.

Just because you choose to work through a full-service broker doesn't mean you can sidestep doing your own research. You always need to perform due diligence, independently researching your stock purchases. Although you certainly can use the research arm of your brokerage firm, it shouldn't be your sole source of research on any stock you're thinking about buying or that you already hold.

If you're planning to be a trader, do your own research and implement your own trading strategies. Why pay for the services of a full-service broker? We really don't recommend that you waste your money on the additional costs of maintaining a full-service brokerage account or paying the high transaction fees and commissions.

Discount brokers

Many discount brokers offer the same services as full-service brokers, including research. The big exception is that you won't get individual attention or unsolicited advice on what to buy or sell. Some discount brokers send out monthly newsletters with stock recommendations; most don't trade futures or sell variable annuities. You can access a discount broker by telephone, mail, fax, or using an Internet connection. In order to get the lowest fees on trades, you need to do your own trades by accessing the brokers' Web site.

The big difference to you, as an individual trader, is that you can save a lot of money on trading costs, provided you know what you're doing and you understand the language of stock trading. Transaction fees for online trades can range from as low as $5 up to about $30 with a discount broker. If you want special services requiring a broker's assistance, you can work with a human being. Depending on the discount brokerage firm and the level of service required, fees can range from $25 to $50 per trade. Some discount brokers provide broker-assisted trades using a commission rate schedule similar to the ones offered by full-service brokers, but for lower fees per trade. If you get involved in more complicated trading transactions that require human assistance, costs can rise significantly. Anytime you're planning to use a broker's assistance, be sure you understand any additional costs that may be charged to your account for that assistance.

Direct-access brokers

If you want to bypass the traditional brokers and trade directly through an exchange or market maker, you need to open your account with a direct-access broker so you can use one or more of the electronic communications networks (ECNs) to make your trades. Traders usually download software onto their PCs so they can access the ECN directly using their Internet connections.

Traders using direct-access brokers typically get real-time NASDAQ Level I quotes, which show the latest bid and ask prices, quote size, the last trade, and volume.

Direct-access brokers also offer NASDAQ Level II. NASDAQ fees are higher for Level II, and the brokerage may also charge an additional fee for this type of access. In addition to what you see in a Level I quote, you also find the number of market makers participating in the market for any one stock.

A NASDAQ Level II quote screen shows the best bid price and the best ask price for specific stocks from participating market makers. All the bid and ask prices are ranked from best to worst. Some direct-access brokers combine NASDAQ Level II information and ECN book data to show the complete market depth for a specific stock. The ECN book is not a printed book like you would expect to find on a bookstore shelf. It's a compilation of all the trades and the bid and ask quotes available on all the electronic networks. Examples of Level I and Level II quote screens are shown in Chapter 14.

Traders can review the quotes and select which market maker or ECN to use for each transaction. Most full-service and discount brokers make that choice for you when you're working with them. A few discount brokers are providing access to ECNs.

When working with direct-access brokers, one key difference is that the software you use may reside on your own computer and not on your broker's server, which greatly accelerates the speed at which you can trade. Again, some discount brokers provide software to enable you to receive direct raw data on your home computer, but their software is not as sophisticated as what direct-access brokers have to offer. Software issues are covered in detail in Chapter 4.

We often talk about how you can miss trading at the prices you want, especially in fast-moving markets. Well, having direct access doesn't guarantee that you won't miss a price, but your chances of catching those prices are better, because you won't have to wait for pages to download from your broker's server. Of course, for this advantage to work for you, you must have high-speed Internet access, which can include DSL, cable, or satellite access.

Working with a direct-access broker gives you a steady stream of raw financial data — the actual trades, current bid and ask prices, trading volume, and market statistics. The trading software that you load onto your computer determines how this data is organized and presented on your computer monitor. Providing better access is how direct-access brokers distinguish their services from other brokers.

Software prices and access fees vary greatly and can cost you as much as $300 per month. The fees sometimes can be waived, especially if your trading volume is high enough — typically about 50 or more trades per month. As you can see, you have to make regular trades for a direct-access broker to be more cost effective than a discount broker. That said, even some discount brokers offer limited direct access using less-sophisticated software.

Proprietary trading firms

Proprietary trading firms enable traders to use at least some of the firm's capital in addition to or instead of their own. Depending on the firm, traders share the gains and may (or may not) share the losses. You can't just walk in and expect to trade with one of these firms. You must have an NASD Series 7 license combined with a proven history of trading in the equity markets. Proprietary trading is definitely not an alternative for beginners. These firms train you in their respective trading styles.

Futures brokers

Unless you're working with a full-service brokerage firm, you may have to open a separate account with a futures broker if you want to trade commodities or other types of futures. Futures brokers must be licensed by the NASD in a way that differs from stockbrokers. Many direct-access brokers provide futures brokerage services, but you rarely find them at a discount broker. We talk more about licensing in Chapter 20 and about trading futures in Chapter 18.

Exploring Services to Consider When Choosing Your Broker

You can't choose your broker purely on the basis of price. You need to know what types of services are offered to enable you to make the type of trades you want to make. When researching brokers, check out the types of orders supported, whether they can offer you a data feed, what types of charts they provide, and whether they can give you ECN access if you want to make your own trades electronically.

Types of orders supported

As we mention in Chapter 2, not all brokers provide stop orders for OTC and NASDAQ trades. The NASDAQ has no facility for handling stop orders, so the broker must monitor your stop prices and enter either market or limit orders if your price is triggered. Although monitoring stop prices usually is done automatically, not all brokers offer the service. If you know you'll be using stops with many of your trades, you need to find a broker who provides those services. Some discount brokers provide those services, provided you're willing to pay for them.

As such, you also need to compare not only prices for those services but also the respective brokers' reputations for effectively and efficiently providing those services. If you want to place contingent orders (see Chapter 2), you may discover that few discount brokers offer that service even for a price.

As you trade, you definitely need to steer clear of brokers who accept *payment for order flow,* a practice in which some exchanges or market makers pay brokerage firms for routing orders to them. Firms can make a penny or more per share, but the SEC requires the firm to inform you whether it receives payment for order flow when you first open an account and thereafter on an annual basis. Each time a firm receives a payment for order flow, it must disclose that information on the trade confirmation. If you see an indication on one of your trades that your broker received this type of payment, you have the right to request notification in writing about the source and type of payment related to that transaction. These payments may encourage unethical brokers to steer orders away from the best prices and toward the market maker offering such payments.

Data feed

The type of data to which you want to have access is crucial. Most brokers provide basic stock quotes, usually in real time, and some may even offer market data providing a much deeper look at the market that includes not only current sales information but also previous sales information. If you want access to a higher level of data, you need to be certain that you open your brokerage account with a firm that provides the level of data that you need, or you may buy it from a third party. Again, pricing for differing data feeds can vary among brokerage firms. Firms that offer you ways of getting this data feed through your home computer, as opposed to accessing it from their servers, charge more, but remember that you'll receive the information quicker. The faster your Internet connection, the more quickly and reliably you will receive this information. We cover data feeds in greater detail in Chapter 4.

Charts

Data fed into your home computer is raw stock market data. How this information is formatted on your computer and the charts you're able to build from it are dependent on the software that's provided by your broker. Charting software can be critical to your ability to make trading decisions. Your broker may charge you to use the software, but will usually discount or waive the fee based on the size of your portfolio or your volume of trading activity. There are also many free charting alternatives available online. We talk about charting capabilities in Chapter 4.

ECN access

If direct access to stock exchanges and market makers is important to you, then you need to find a broker that provides ECN access. You don't have to open an account through a direct-access broker; some discount brokers do provide ECN access. Be sure to check out the section on "Choosing the Right Broker for You," later in this chapter.

Understanding the Types of Brokerage Accounts

You can open your brokerage accounts in a couple different ways — as a cash account or a margin account. If you open a margin account, you also must open a cash account. You also may open separate accounts for retirement savings. Because retirement accounts have more restrictions, your trading alternatives are more limited in those accounts, but that isn't necessarily a bad thing. You shouldn't be risking your retirement funds on speculative trading anyway.

Cash accounts

The traditional brokerage account is a *cash account,* which also is known as a Type 1 account. With a cash account, you must deposit the full cost of any purchases by the settlement date of the transaction. At many brokerage houses prior to 2002, you were permitted to place an order to buy stock even if the cash was not yet in your account. As long as the money was deposited within three days of the completion of the transaction, you could make the purchase. Today, however, few brokers give you that kind of flexibility. Most brokers require funds to buy stocks to be in your cash account before you can place an order. The amount of cash you need to have on deposit varies by broker; some let you open an account for as little as $100 or $1,000, but others require as much as $10,000 or more to open a new cash account.

Margin accounts

You don't have to have as much cash on hand to buy stock when you open a *margin account,* which also is known as a Type 2 account. This type of account enables you to borrow certain amounts of money using cash or securities already in the account as collateral. Because using a margin account essentially is buying stocks, bonds, or commodities on credit, each respective brokerage firm has its own screening procedure to determine whether you qualify for the loan and can buy on margin.

The Federal Reserve requires a $2,000 minimum deposit to open a margin account, and currently limits the amount you can borrow on margin to 50 percent of the initial purchase price. Not all stocks can be bought on margin. Some brokerage firms enforce even stricter margin rules, especially if you choose to invest in volatile stocks. When buying stocks on margin, you pay an interest rate on the margin loans, but most brokerage firms charge relatively low rates to encourage the transaction business. Be sure to check out the "Margin requirements" section later in this chapter.

When opening a margin account, the firm also requires you to sign what's called an *hypothecation agreement,* which stipulates regulations for the account and permits the broker to have a lien on your account whenever the balance in your account falls below the minimum maintenance margin (more about that in a moment). The agreement also enables your broker to loan your shares to short sellers. That's where shorted stock comes from. We talk more about short selling and the mechanics of margin trading in Chapter 14.

You're taking a risk by purchasing shares of stock with borrowed money and using shares you own as collateral. If your stock holdings fall in value below the minimum maintenance margin requirement, your broker can force you to sell stock you don't want to sell and use other assets you may not want to use to cover the outstanding loan. The risks and regulations for using a margin account are described more fully in the section on margin requirements, found later in this chapter.

Options

If you want to trade options, your broker will require you to sign a special options agreement acknowledging that you understand the risks associated with trading options or derivative instruments. This practice became common after brokers were sued by some clients because they suffered huge losses when trading options and claimed they were unaware of the risks. The agreement protects the broker from being sued if you lose a lot of money, so you need to know what you're doing when dealing with derivatives (see Chapter 18).

IRAs and other retirement accounts

IRAs and other accounts in which you're saving for retirement — such as 401(k)s or 403(b)s — rarely allow you to trade options, and margin trading is not allowed at all. These limitations are for your protection to avoid risking major losses in your long-term investments that never should be put at such high levels of risk. The amount you can contribute each year to all retirement accounts is limited by the Internal Revenue Code.

Although you may be able to find a brokerage firm that allows you to trade using options — puts and calls, which are a type of option (see Chapter 18) — you nevertheless risk penalties for certain trading activities that occur in your retirement account whenever the IRS determines the account is being used for trading purposes rather than long-term investing. Officially, the Internal Revenue Code prohibits the "IRA or Keogh Plan account holder from loaning money to the account. Likewise, the holder cannot guarantee borrowing by the account or cover its losses." That's why margin accounts, which entail a type of borrowing, are not allowed.

Because these accounts are either tax-free or tax-deferred, you can't write off any losses in them against any gains from investments held outside of them — in other taxable accounts. In other words, you don't have the same tax-planning choices with IRAs or retirement accounts to offset gains and losses. All money taken out of an IRA at retirement is taxed at your current income tax rate. This differs from stocks held outside an IRA. For these stocks, you can use stock losses to minimize the tax you might have to pay on stock gains. If you hold the stock for longer than a year, you are taxed based on the lower capital gains rate of 15 percent for most taxpayers (some low-income taxpayers qualify for a rate as low as 5 percent) rather than your higher current income tax rate, which can be as high as 35 percent for some taxpayers.

Here are some additional trading limitations of retirement accounts:

✔ **Margin is not allowed:** Using funds within a retirement account as collateral for trading on margin is not permitted. It's against the law. You won't find a broker that will permit you to place retirement funds in margin accounts.

✔ **Short positions are prohibited:** Speculative trading using short positions, which is a common trading strategy for futures contracts and widely used by experienced stock and bond traders, requires a margin account. When someone shorts a stock, he or she borrows the stock and sells it in the hope of buying it back later for less. Selling short requires the use of margin, and is therefore not permitted in a retirement account. We talk more about short selling in Chapter 14.

✔ **Trading policies are more stringent:** All brokers have more stringent trading policies for retirement accounts. Before you open a retirement account, check with your broker about their trading limitations to be sure they match your intentions for the account.

✔ **Options trading may not be permitted:** If you're an experienced trader, you can find some brokerage firms that allow options trading in your retirement account. Not all types of options, however, can be traded in a retirement account. The ones that you most likely can trade are covered calls, long call and put positions, or cash-secured puts. We talk more about puts and calls in Chapter 18.

Choosing the Right Broker for You

Before beginning a search for the right broker, you must first decide what type of trader you want to be and what services you need. If you want to be a position trader, or one who trades infrequently, your best bet is either a full-service or a discount broker. Making the choice between full-service and discount brokers depends upon how independently you want to operate as a trader. If you want advice on your stock investing plans, you need to seek out a full-service broker, but we certainly don't recommend this expensive option. Before risking your money on trading, however, you need to be comfortable enough with the language and mechanics of trading and how to conduct your own research. If you don't need the services of a direct-access broker, your best bet is to select a discount broker.

Considering more than price

Your choice of brokers is much more than who can offer you the cheapest price. Although price definitely is a factor in your selection of broker, it is one of many factors you need to consider. The most important factors are the services that your broker offers and how effective and efficient the broker is in carrying out those promised services. Look for brokers that offer smart order routing capabilities, but steer clear of the ones that accept payment for order flow (see the "Types of orders supported" section, earlier in this chapter).

You may find a brokerage firm that provides all the bells and whistles at the cheapest price, but if its systems break down at a critical trading moment and you're not able to implement your trades when you want to, those bells and whistles mean nothing, and not being able to rely on them can result in huge losses.

Doing a little research

If you expect to become an active and successful trader and want full access so you can trade electronically through the exchanges, you more than likely need to research direct-access brokers. If, however, you believe that your volume of trades per month will be lower than 50, you may want to consider a discount broker that offers access to ECNs. Basically, your choice of brokers comes down to the types of services and accounts you need and which broker offers the best mix for what you want to do and pay.

 Your first step is to make lists of your financial objectives, the types of trading you want to do, and the services you know you're going to need. After committing those factors to memory, talk with other traders you know and be sure to find out what their experiences have been with various brokers.

You can also research and compare ratings of brokers on the Internet. Try these Web sites:

- **Gomez Internet Performance Management:** An excellent source. Go to www.gomezadvisors.com, pull down the "Benchmarks" menu, and click on "Scorecard." On that Web page you'll find a pull-down menu that takes you to the site's rankings of various discount and full-service brokers.

- *SmartMoney:* This site also conducts a yearly survey that can give you an excellent overview of broker performance. Go to www.smartmoney.com, click on "Stocks," scroll down to "Broker Ratings," and click on "Broker Survey." The survey lists rankings for basic and premium discount brokers and full-service brokers.

- *Barron's:* The Web site of the weekly financial magazine (www.barrons.com) does an excellent annual evaluation of online brokers and direct-access brokers, usually in March. A subscription to WSJ.com is required.

- *Active Trader* magazine (www.activetradermag.com) and *Stocks and Commodities* magazine (www.traders.com) also periodically review brokers and trading platforms. Subscriptions are required.

After narrowing down your choices, check out the disciplinary histories of the brokerage firms you're considering. You can easily do that by calling a toll-free hotline operated by the National Association of Securities Dealers (NASD) at 800-289-9999, or checking its Web site at www.nasd.com to find out what disciplinary actions (if any) have been taken by securities regulators or criminal authorities. You also need to call your state regulator to be sure the specific broker you're thinking about working with is licensed to do business in your state. This information can be crucial. If you work with an unlicensed broker who goes out of business, you may not have any way of recovering any lost funds even if an arbitrator or court rules in your favor.

Understanding how you'll be paying

After conducting your initial research into brokerage firms and narrowing down your choices, be sure you understand how the brokerage firms are paid by:

✔ Reviewing each firm's fee and commission schedule. The schedules should include the fees or charges you're required to pay when opening the account and what you pay to maintain and close the account.

✔ Finding out how your broker is compensated, if you're planning to work with a human being rather than trading online. Many brokers receive higher compensation when they sell their firm's own products, so they may try to steer you toward them rather than another product that may be a better match for your trading objectives. Rarely are brokerage products good trading vehicles.

One other level of protection that you need to check on is the broker's membership in the Securities Investor Protection Corporation (SIPC). Although SIPC membership won't insure you against losses caused by market declines, the SIPC does give you some protection if your brokerage firm faces insolvency. You can find out more about the SIPC at www.sipc.org.

Getting to Know the Rules

After you've picked your broker, you must be sure that you know the trading rules. Although federal law mandates margin requirements, sets trade settlement rules, and bans free riding (nope, we're not talking about horseback riding here), brokerage firms sometimes have even more stringent rules for their clients. We review the federal requirements here, but you need to check with your broker to find out any additional rules your chosen firm imposes.

Rules for stock trading fall under the jurisdiction of the Federal Reserve, which specifies its stock trading regulations in Regulation T. Rules spelled out under Regulation T encompass margin accounts, broker-dealer accounts, securities transactions, credit extended based on securities, and other factors related to securities markets. We won't review all the specifics here, but instead we home in on three key areas that impact your trading choices — margin requirements, trade settlement, and free riding.

Margin requirements

The Federal Reserve's Regulation T specifies how much you can borrow when you use a margin account to purchase new shares of stocks on margin. This *initial margin requirement* permits you to borrow up to 50 percent of the cost of the new shares. For example, if you open a new margin account with a $10,000 cash deposit, you can buy up to $20,000 worth of stock. After your $20,000 purchase, your account will have a cash balance of $0, an equity balance of $10,000, and a margin balance of $10,000. At this time, all your equity is committed to this trade, so you cannot enter any new positions unless you deposit additional funds.

If the stock price increases, your equity balance increases. If the stock price decreases, your equity balance decreases. In either case, your margin balance remains the same, $10,000. The only way to reduce the outstanding margin balance is to deposit extra cash into your account or sell the shares of stock.

When your stock price increases, your equity balance increases and you may use the increased equity as collateral to borrow additional money to buy additional shares of stocks. You may borrow up to the value of the increased equity balance. This will increase your margin balance.

However, if your equity balance decreases, NYSE and NASD rules (Rule 431 and Rule 2520, respectively) regulate the minimum equity position permitted in your account. Currently, the minimum is 25 percent of the total value of all margined securities. Some brokers may require more.

In the single-stock example earlier in this chapter, if the total value of the stock falls below $13,332, then the equity balance in your portfolio will be less than 25 percent of the total value. The math is simple: 25 percent of $13,332 is $3,333. Your cash balance is still $0 and your margin balance is still $10,000. Subtract $10,000 from $13,332 to determine your equity balance, which is $3,332. Your equity balance is less than 25 percent of your total account balance.

When this occurs, your broker will call and demand additional collateral to support the outstanding margin loan. This is a *margin call*. You may meet your margin call requirements by depositing more cash or you may deposit fully paid, unmargined securities from another account. If you do not deposit additional collateral, your broker is permitted to sell up to four times the amount of stock required to meet your margin call, and may sell any of the stocks in your portfolio.

If you have more than a few positions, margin calculations become complex. It helps to think about it like this: When initiating a new position, you can never borrow more than half of the value of the position. To maintain sufficient collateral, your broker will insist that the value of your stocks be more than enough to cover the loan. Therefore, if your equity balance falls below 25 percent of the total portfolio value, your broker will ask for additional collateral in the form of a margin call.

As a trader, you should never satisfy a margin call. Instead, you should close the offending position(s). It is possible that an extraordinary event may cause the value of your stocks to fall below the amount owned on your outstanding margin loan. If this happens, your broker will close your positions, but you must still repay the debt. Unlike a cash account, you can lose more than 100 percent of the money you deposit into a margin account.

Note: Not all stocks can be bought on margin and neither can all stocks be used as collateral. If you want to trade on margin, be sure you understand the margin requirements imposed by your broker. Some brokerage firms require even stiffer requirements to maintain a margin account, especially if you trade volatile or lightly-traded stocks.

NASD Rule 2520 was amended in 2001 to restrict day-trading activity. Your broker or the NASD will consider you a *pattern day trader* after you buy or sell any security on the same day in a margin account and execute four or more such trades during a five-day business period (excluding Saturdays, Sundays, and holidays). If you're pegged as a pattern day trader, you're required to maintain $25,000 in your margin account, which can seriously impact your day trading and other trading activities.

Settling trades

When you place an order to buy a stock, you must settle that transaction in three business days. This *settlement cycle* is known as *T + 3.* The brokerage firm must receive your payment for any securities you buy no later than three days after the trade is executed. If you're selling a stock, it's probably being held in your brokerage account and will be taken out of that account on the day of settlement.

Free riding

No, we're not talking about taking a free ride on a train. Free riding in the stock-trading world can get you in a bunch of trouble, so keep reading. Basically it means that you must pay for a stock before you can sell it, and because it takes three days to settle a stock transaction, that means, in theory, you can actually buy a stock and then place an order to sell it before the stock purchase actually settles.

This is a cash account problem. Although many swing and day traders actually turn around stock purchases and sales that quickly, they typically trade in a margin account and are able to sidestep the problem. Margin traders use the unsettled proceeds of a trade as collateral to borrow money until the trade is settled. Still, day traders and swing traders must have enough cash or buying power in their accounts to cover all purchases of stock.

Formally, this rule is found in Section 220 of Regulation T, which states that in a cash account, a brokerage firm may buy a security on your behalf — or sell a security — if either of the following applies:

✔ You have sufficient funds in the account.

✔ The firm accepts in good faith your agreement to make a full-cash payment for the security before you sell it.

If you do ever buy and sell a security before the settlement cycle (T + 3) is complete — or even on the same day — and without sufficient cash in your account, a brokerage firm can make what is called an *intraday extension of credit* (a loan), but that exposes the firm to increased risks — especially the risk that you may overextend your financial resources and may not be able to settle your trades. Most brokerage firms require active traders who buy and then sell securities within the settlement cycle to conduct those activities within a margin account.

If you take a free ride and haven't made some type of credit arrangement with your broker, your broker is likely to freeze your account for 90 days. During that 90-day period, the broker requires you to pay for any purchase on the date that you make the trade. In other words, you lose the option of settling your trades within three days. Some brokerage firms require you to have enough cash in your account to complete the transaction before you make the trade so you thus avoid even the risk of free riding.

We'll talk more about these rapid forms of trading (swing trading and day trading) in Chapters 16 and 17.

Chapter 4

Setting Up Your Business: Putting Your Computer to Work

In This Chapter

▶ Streamlining trading activities

▶ Selecting charting software, fundamental information sources, and research tools

▶ Choosing a trading platform

▶ Evaluating computer and Internet resources

*B*ack in the old days, you'd call your broker to enter an order and then wait for your broker to phone back and report the fill price. Active traders? They'd hang out in the broker's lobby, watching the ticker, boasting over winning trades, commiserating over losing trades, and shooting the breeze.

If you kept charts, you either made them yourself or had them delivered by postal carrier in book form. They arrived at the end of each week. If you couldn't afford that extravagance, you'd buy monthly summaries and update them yourself.

Every retail investor bought and sold stocks the same way. The pros had the advantage, but it was more or less a level playing field for the rest of us.

Today, you'd be hard-pressed to find a ticker-tape machine in any brokerage office. The Internet has changed everything. You can still buy chart books, but now they're delivered via the Internet, and so are stock prices, real-time intraday charts, and research reports. You can enter orders online, have your orders filled within seconds, and receive notification showing the order's price almost as quickly.

Online brokers provide a vast array of research and trading tools for their clients. Real-time streaming quotes, proprietary and third-party research, sophisticated charts, and extensive order-entry capabilities make today's traders better informed and better equipped than ever before.

If you're anything like us, you're going to spend plenty of time with your trading platform. It pays to spend a little time thinking about what information you need now, how you'll use it, and what you may need in the future. With just a little foresight, you can set up your trading platform so that it's effective today and yet still be able to upgrade it without completely disrupting your day-to-day activities.

In this chapter, we review the basic computer hardware you need to access all there is to offer for traders, explore the software options you'll want to consider for managing your trading activities, and discuss various trading platforms and data-feed alternatives. Finally, we give you a road map to the options available on the Internet.

Deciding How to Use Your Computer

Although tracking the market and charting stock prices by hand is an excellent learning exercise — it gives you a feel for the market that you can't get by reviewing computer-generated charts — we doubt that you'd want to travel to the local library or your broker's office to research the stocks that interest you. The wealth of online information that can help you improve your trading results is simply remarkable. Here are some of the things you can do with your computer:

Identifying trading candidates

With your computer, you can

- Display and interpret price charts
- Research stocks, bonds, IPOs, options, and futures
- Read analyst's reports and company reports to the SEC
- Screen stocks for technical or fundamental constraints
- Monitor economic reports, earnings reports, and business news
- Monitor market indexes, sectors, and trading statistics

Managing your account

Managing your account can involve some or all of the following:

- Entering and executing trades, and monitoring open orders
- Controlling and tracking order routing

✔ Receiving almost instantaneous fill reports

✔ Monitoring and analyzing your portfolio and all open positions

✔ Tracking profits and losses

✔ Analyzing your trading history

Improving your trades

You can become a better trader by doing the following:

✔ Evaluating trading systems and testing trading ideas

✔ Keeping trading logs to audit your trading performance

✔ Monitoring the tax consequences of your trades

✔ Staying in touch with other traders

Finding Price Charts

Price charts show the history of a stock's price over time. These charts conceal useful trading information that is revealed with careful analysis. Reading, interpreting, and understanding what you see in a price chart are described in Chapters 8 through 11.

Fortunately, price charts are easy to find. If your broker doesn't provide an adequate charting package, you can find excellent charting tools on dozens of online sites. If you have to go outside your broker's environment, you may have to put up with Internet banner ads and pop-ups. Most of the charts on free Web sites display 20-minute delayed prices. You may have to pay $9.95 to $19.95 a month for Internet charts that update in real time.

At a minimum, you need control over the time frame and the types of charts displayed. For example, you probably want 1-minute, 5-minute, 15-minute, and 60-minute charts to go with daily, weekly, and monthly charts. Other features to look for include

✔ Trading volume. (It's critical.)

✔ Moving averages to show average prices over time. You'll want at least two types, simple moving averages and exponential moving averages, and you'll want control over the period being averaged. Moving averages are discussed in Chapter 11.

- ✔ Indicators and oscillators to help evaluate a stock's direction and momentum. We use the MACD (Moving Average Convergence Divergence) indicator and the Stochastics Oscillator. Indicators and oscillators are discussed in Chapter 11.

- ✔ A variety of chart styles, including bar charts and candlestick charts. Bar charts are the most popular stock charts, and they're the ones we use throughout this book. We describe how to read and interpret them in Chapter 9. Candlestick charts display the price data using a slightly different format that is preferred by some traders. The analysis techniques in this book work for both styles.

- ✔ Ability to display data in a log or semi-log format. This allows equal percentage price changes to appear the same on the price chart, which is helpful for comparing the price movements of two differently priced stocks. For example, if a $10 stock rises to $20, that's a 100-percent price change. If a $50 stock rises to $100, that's also a 100-percent price increase, but it will look like a much larger price increase on a standard price chart. Use a log or semi-log format to show similar percentage changes so they look the same on the chart.

- ✔ Ability to group charts together so you can quickly scan open positions or trade candidates.

- ✔ Ability to show support and resistance levels, draw trend lines, and make annotations.

There are two kinds of online charts: real-time charts and delayed-price charts. While the charts may be identical, the prices shown in the charts are not. Real-time charts display current price data updated within a few seconds of the trade. Delayed-price charts do not show the most current trades. Instead, the prices shown on the chart are at least 15 to 20 minutes old.

Although many excellent online charting alternatives are out there, they typically aren't as flexible or configurable as the ones offered in stand-alone charting packages or integrated trading platforms. And you probably won't have access to trading-system development and testing software that is required to create and test your own trading system. The advantages and disadvantages of online charts, stand-alone charting packages, and integrated trading platforms are discussed in the following sections. Methods for developing and testing personalized trading systems are discussed in Chapter 15.

Internet charts, delayed prices

Although real-time charts are desirable, they're a necessity only for extremely active short-term traders. Analyzing the market and developing your trading plan is best done before the market in which you plan to make your trades opens, or after it closes. Delayed-price charts are more than adequate for these planning and analysis activities.

You can use delayed-price charts to identify support and resistance levels, display moving averages, find emerging trends, and select possible entry and exit points for tomorrow's trading day.

Here are a couple of sources for online charts:

- **BigCharts** (www.bigcharts.com): BigCharts is part of the CBS MarketWatch family. The site is free and offers an excellent charting package with plenty of options, including interactive charts, industry analysis, and stock screeners. You can define a list of favorite charts for quick review. News and market commentary are also provided.

- **Investor's Business Daily** (www.investors.com): Investor's Business Daily (IBD) publishes its proprietary ranking system online and in its daily paper. Using the stock-picking methodology developed by publisher William O'Neil, the site provides charts and rankings by relative strength and earnings growth. Available by subscription.

- **Decision Point** (www.decisionpoint.com): Decision Point is another subscription charting site, but it takes a different approach, providing chart books, hundreds of unique charts, and market commentary based primarily on technical analysis. If you're looking for a quick way to scan a large group of stocks, this site provides excellent tools. You may find that Decision Point is a nice complement to a more traditional charting site or charting software package.

Internet charts, real-time prices

Although most online brokers provide support for real-time prices, not all provide real-time charting capabilities. If your broker doesn't offer what you need, and you find delayed prices are just too frustrating, you can find a number of sites that offer real-time price charts. Real-time, browser-based Internet charts usually aren't free. You will generally find them priced between $9.95 and $19.95 per month.

Sites offering real-time charts include

- **StockCharts** (www.stockcharts.com): Chip Anderson started StockCharts early in Internet history. He's one of the few independents who are still around, and for good reason — the site is excellent. StockCharts offers many excellent free charting tools, but the best parts are available by subscription. Advanced features include real-time, intraday pricing, the ability to create and store chart annotations, the ability to create large lists of your favorite charts, the ability to define custom chart settings, and the capability of creating custom scans based on technical indicators. Make sure that you click on "SharpCharts Voyeur," which is listed under "Tools & Charts" on the StockCharts home page. It shows charts that are of interest to other traders.

- ✔ **FreeRealTime.com (**www.freerealtime.com**):** The free capabilities of the site are fairly limited, and you'll have to put up with banner ads and the occasional full-page ad that display before the page you actually want appears. The free portion of this site uses data from electronic communications networks (ECNs), not data from the major stock exchanges. Unfortunately, ECNs do not trade all stocks, so real-time charts and quotes may not always be available. And ECN prices may not always match prices on the major exchanges, but they'll be very close. If you can put up with these limitations, the charts and price quotes are in real time. And they're free.

Charting software

Before taking your step up toward a stand-alone charting application, make sure that you explore the tools provided by your broker and other brokers and by Web sites offering Internet charts. Some of these online tools are powerful and may be more cost effective than a stand-alone package.

Stand-alone charting software, however, often provides capabilities beyond what you can find online. For example, charting software packages offer system testing but rarely are they part of a Web site's tool set.

Several packages are available; some examples include

- ✔ **MetaStock (**www.equis.com**):** MetaStock comes in two flavors, a standard end-of-day trading package, and a professional version for intraday charts. Each offers a variety of analysis tools, technical indicators, system development and testing capabilities, and access to fundamental stock data.

- ✔ **TradeStation (**www.tradestation.com**):** TradeStation is the gold standard of charting software. It is powerful, flexible, and configurable, and it's designed to work the same way institutional trading platforms do. You can fully automate your trading system by programming your strategies into the system and then having TradeStation execute them in real time. (Whether you should do so, however, is open for discussion.) It also supports direct access to all ECNs and stock exchanges.

Many other charting packages are available, but these two packages are widely used and give you a good basis for comparing all the other available products.

The drawback to stand-alone charting software is the expense. In addition to the price of the software, you need a data provider to deliver end-of-day or intraday market prices. When selecting a charting software package, make sure that it supports the data service you plan to use. They must work together.

Data service vendors include

✔ Reuters DataLink (www.equis.com)

✔ QCharts (www.qcharts.com)

✔ eSignal (www.esignal.com)

Finding Fundamental Information

Fundamental data — corporate information such as revenue, earnings, and cash flow — isn't as perishable as price data or trading statistics, but accessing these numbers directly from your trading platform as they're updated is a nice feature. Analysis of fundamental data is discussed in Chapters 5, 6, and 7. Many brokers provide access to at least some fundamental data, but if you'd like to run the numbers yourself, many of these online sources can review the raw financial data:

✔ *The Wall Street Journal* (www.wsj.com): The Wall Street Journal Online is available by subscription. It provides access to a wide variety of information including stock quotes, stock valuation indexes, fundamental ratios, industry comparisons, insider transactions, earnings estimates, and stock analysis reports. Delayed-price charts also are available. The price for subscribers to the print version of the Wall Street Journal or Barron's is $39 annually, otherwise it's $79. They offer a free two-week trial.

✔ **Edgar** (www.sec.gov/edgar.shtml): All publicly traded companies are required to file 10-Q and 10-K quarterly and annual reports electronically with the Securities and Exchange Commission (SEC) through its Electronic Data Gathering Analysis and Retrieval system (EDGAR). These reports are available to everyone online at no charge.

Finding Analyst's Reports

Sometimes you can find these research reports at your local library, especially for big outfits like Standard & Poor's and Value Line. Many analysts sell research in the form of investment newsletter subscriptions. We've used several of the following subscription services through the years, with varying degrees of success:

✔ **Standard & Poor's** (www.standardandpoors.com): Registration is required, but access is free. You cannot access the full reports and recommendations on this site, but the *Business Week* magazine Web site (www.businessweek.com/investor) offers several complete S&P reports, stock screens, and industry reports at no charge.

✔ **Value Line** (www.valueline.com): The Value Line Investment Survey has been around for a long time. It profiles many of the major corporations and provides a variety of stock screens based on proprietary models. It also offers opinions on current economic and market climates. Some reports and updates are available on the site at no charge, but a subscription is required to access the complete site.

✔ **Briefing.com** (www.briefing.com): This site has free and subscription components. Advanced features include access to analysts' upgrades and downgrades as they're released, access to updated earnings guidance, an IPO calendar, notification of changes in stock indexes, and quite a bit more.

✔ **Reuters Investor** (www.investor.reuters.com): Access to Reuters's and third-party research, including reports from many brokerage companies and independent analysts, is available on this site. Some reports are free, some require payment. Tools include sector and industry analysis, stock and industry screening tools, comparison charting, and more.

✔ **Morningstar** (www.morningstar.com): Morningstar probably is best known for its analysis of mutual funds, but it also provides extensive stock analysis, editorial commentary, a stock screening tool, and a thorough snapshot tool that shows financial performance, fund ownership, and recent fund transactions. A subscription is required to access premium content.

✔ **Hulbert Financial Digest** (www.hulbertdigest.com): The Hulbert Financial Digest evaluates investment newsletters and provides insight into their actual performance results. If you think you must buy proprietary research, a subscription to Hulbert's may be a good place to start before buying research reports and stock tips.

Selecting a Trading Platform

You'll find as many different approaches to trading as you'll find traders. Fortunately, almost as many alternatives for setting up your trading environment also exist.

As technology develops and expands, online brokers provide increasingly powerful trading tools for their clients. These tools include market research, charting capabilities, and streaming prices and news services. If your broker doesn't offer a specific service, you probably can find it offered on the Internet.

When selecting a trading platform, look for the capabilities you need today with an eye toward future expandability. You may want to consider the features in the three lists that follow.

Trading tools to look for include

- ✔ Stock trading
- ✔ Support of sophisticated option trading strategies
- ✔ Futures trading, especially single-stock and index futures
- ✔ NASDAQ Level II access
- ✔ Direct-access trading and ECN book data
- ✔ Watch lists
- ✔ Automatic e-mail or text message notification when a stock hits your price point

Analysis tools to shop for include

- ✔ Sector analysis
- ✔ Proprietary and third-party analyst's reports
- ✔ News feeds (Dow Jones, Reuters, and so on)
- ✔ Real-time charting capabilities
- ✔ Time and volume sales reports

Account management tools that you may need include

- ✔ Real-time account balances
- ✔ Real-time updates of buying power and margin exposure
- ✔ Portfolio management tools
- ✔ Open-order status

Before putting your computer to work as a trading platform, you need to understand the two primary techniques for delivering trading tools and services. The first uses your Internet browser to enter orders and deliver all information. The other approach uses a stand-alone software program, an *integrated trading platform,* to interact with your broker and your brokerage account.

For the most part, integrated trading platforms are married to specific brokerage firms. Some brokers provide you with a choice. For example, Charles Schwab's CyberTrader offers two of the integrated software-based systems, CyberTrader Pro and CyberTrader X2, and one browser-based system, CyberTrader.com.

The approach that suits you best depends somewhat on your trading style, cost considerations, and your computer's configuration. You may find that the level of service offered by your broker depends on the size of your account or your trading volume. You have to balance your cost with your actual informational needs.

Integrated trading platforms typically are direct-access systems. We discuss both direct-access brokers and traditional online brokers in Chapter 3. Although direct-access systems are offered in browser-based configurations, active day traders and swing traders may require a completely integrated, direct-access trading platform.

Browser-based trading environment

For most new traders, trading volume starts out relatively small, perhaps five or fewer trades each month. Your time frame for holding a position probably is measured in days to weeks or weeks to months. You probably won't be making many intraday trades, except to automatically exit a position after a stop price is hit. In that case, a browser-based trading environment certainly is good enough to get you started and may be all you'll ever need.

These systems may be tightly integrated or somewhat disjointed, depending on the way the broker implements them. Some brokers, for example, automatically fill in order-entry screens with as much data as can be gleaned from your account. Others make you type all the data into the order screen by hand, which can be cumbersome and time-consuming. Some brokers provide pop-up order confirmation and fill reports, and others make you continuously tap the enter key while waiting for a trade execution to show in your account.

Pros

For the most part, almost any Internet-ready computer can support a browser-based trading platform. Although Windows is most often used for trading platforms, even Apple Macintosh or Linux systems can be used for browser-based applications.

Much of the browser-based information offered by your broker is available to all clients, regardless of account size or trading volume. If your broker doesn't offer something you want, you usually can find it elsewhere on the Internet, either free or for a modest fee.

Cons

When compared to an integrated software solution, browser-based trading is relatively slow, requiring you to open many browser windows and manually update account information. Depending on how well your broker implements these systems, a bit more typing may be necessary to enter and execute your orders.

On some browser-based trading platforms, your Internet session may be disconnected whenever your screen is inactive for an extended period of time. At best, this kind of interruption can be frustrating. Similarly, some configurations depend on your using a specific browser, or may require that you download and install a special browser plug-in to operate correctly.

Integrated trading platforms

For very active traders, especially day traders and swing traders, and for traders looking to develop personalized trading systems, an integrated trading platform that doesn't rely on your Internet browser can be a better solution. You typically download these software programs, install them on your computer, and then use them to access your brokerage account and trading tools. They range from rudimentary text-based applications with modest graphing capabilities to sophisticated technical-analysis programs that enable you to design and implement custom trading systems.

The most sophisticated of these platforms provides an institutional-level trading experience. Some, for example, permit trading baskets that enable you to simultaneously enter orders for a number of different stocks. Others help you to define hot keys for fast order entry.

You'll also find that integrated trading platforms provide support for sophisticated strategies. The most flexible among them give you the ability to enter contingent orders, where, for example, a stock's price may trigger an option order or the execution of one order automatically cancels another. Several brokers will notify you by e-mail or a cellphone text message when a stock hits a price you've specified or an indicator reaches a preset level. One broker even gives you the ability to automatically execute trades based on recommendations from well-known and reputable advisory services.

Pros

These trading platforms typically are faster and easier to use and customize than browser-based applications. The best among them have system-testing tools that help you fine-tune your personal trading strategies.

My hybrid trading platform

Mike here: My trading horizon is relatively long, and I don't execute enough trades each month to justify the cost of an integrated direct-access trading environment. My trading strategies don't depend on having access to NASDAQ Level II data or direct electronic communications network (ECN) access.

However, I prefer working with a charting package versus evaluating charts using a browser. I've used several popular packages, and a couple of homegrown applications. (Yes, I'll admit that I'm sort of a geek.)

My solution was to implement a hybrid approach that uses browser-based tools for account management and order entry alongside a software-based charting application. This approach provides me with access to more market data than I ever had when I worked as a broker, gives me tremendous flexibility, and minimizes my trading costs.

And it suits my trading style. For some reason, the world looks different when I'm sitting in front of a computer. I feel rushed, somehow, and I don't make my best decisions. That's one of the reasons I don't day trade. The pace works against me; I get caught up in the moment and end up making mistakes.

I think and plan better when I'm sitting by myself, in a quiet corner of my home, with a pen in my hand. I'll print the reports and charts that interest me, sit in a comfy chair, mark up my reports, and deliberately chart my trading course.

Only then am I ready to enter orders online.

Cons

Integrated trading platforms can be expensive. Unless you have a large account balance, your broker may charge you either a monthly fee or base the access on your making a minimum number of monthly trades.

Furthermore, these platforms often require up-to-date computer equipment with a fast processor and plenty of storage to run well. Older equipment will not run this software satisfactorily. And it's likely you'll need to use the Windows operating system.

Figuring Out Computer Requirements

Few new traders actually need a fully integrated direct-access trading platform to begin trading or to trade profitably. But if you're considering a new computer system, the hardware and software requirements for these high-powered platforms may be of benefit. Otherwise, you may be unable to upgrade your new computer to run these applications.

Decisions, decisions, decisions . . .

Most trading platforms are designed for Windows, but die-hard Mac and Linux fans aren't completely locked out. If you're starting with a browser-based approach, almost any modern, Internet-ready computer can handle the task. Browser-based Internet tools usually work equally well on any hardware or operating system. Sadly, some sites require functions provided by a specific browser, but that is becoming increasingly rare.

If you're planning to buy new computer hardware for trading, we'd recommend that you avoid Apple hardware or Unix/Linux operating systems. Although Apple and Linux support browser-based applications at least as well as Windows, you may be unable to upgrade if ever you want a more integrated trading platform. We don't know of any commercially available trading platforms for independent traders (as opposed to institutional traders) that run on Linux or either Mac OS9 or OSX.

Configuring your computer system

Regardless of whether you decide to employ a browser-based approach or an integrated trading platform, you're going to need a reliable computer with sufficient horsepower, memory, and storage space.

Some of today's high-powered, integrated trading software requires equally high-powered computer systems. We give you general hardware guidelines in this section, but if you decide you want a computer that can be upgraded to handle a high-performance integrated trading platform, you also need to check with specific software vendors to identify any special hardware requirements. You also need to be certain that your hardware supports your software.

Software vendors often claim their products can run on relatively modest hardware configurations; however, you'll probably be disappointed and frustrated with system performance under such conditions. These software packages run much better on a computer that surpasses the system requirements. Trading platforms — especially testing applications and multichart, multi-window, multimonitor displays — consume considerable amounts of system resources and can make many computers run unbearably slow.

The minimum configurations that follow easily support browser-based solutions. Upgraded configurations, however, may be required to adequately support fully integrated trading environments.

✔ **Central processing unit (CPU):** At a minimum, you need a 500 MHz processor. Ideally, something much faster works better. Trading applications tend to rely on making many mathematic calculations, so you want either an Intel Pentium or AMD Athlon processor. Avoid Intel's Celeron and AMD Duron chip sets, because they're not designed to handle these kinds of applications.

   The slowest machines being sold today are rated in gigahertz multiples, and most modern machines have enough CPU horsepower to run charting application programs. However, high-end programs like TradeStation take advantage of specialty hardware such as multi-CPU and hyperthreading configurations. Check with software manufacturers for specific details.

✔ **RAM memory:** 128MB of RAM is the absolute minimum, but you probably want much more. Memory is inexpensive compared with other hardware upgrades, and having too much of it is next to impossible. Error-correcting memory may buy only extra peace of mind, but it doesn't cost much more than standard memory.

✔ **Available disk space:** 100MB of free disk space should be enough when starting out, but you'll need much more for long-term storage of real-time price data, which will be useful for developing and testing your own trading system. Chapter 15 discusses methods to personalize a trading system.

✔ **Operating system:** If you're running a Windows environment, you need to be running at least Windows XP. Although browsers and software applications will run on older versions of Windows, XP gives you more stability and reliability than earlier versions of Windows. For trading applications, you want the most reliable system you can find and afford. XP may not be bulletproof, but it's so much better than its predecessors that you definitely want to upgrade if you haven't already.

✔ **Video card:** Although you may be able to squeak by using a shared-memory video system (it shares some of your RAM), you'll be better off with a stand-alone video card that relies on its own video memory. A minimum configuration for a single monitor requires at least 16MB of video memory, but 32MB of video RAM is better. You may even want 64MB whenever you opt for a single video card that supports dual monitors.

✔ **Monitor size:** A 17-inch monitor probably is the smallest you should consider. Bigger is better. A cathode ray tube (CRT) type monitor may give you a sharper and crisper image. Liquid crystal display (LCD) monitors appear to blur moving images, which isn't helpful when you're looking at small squiggly lines on a price chart or a spreadsheet showing detailed historical price data.

✔ **Dual monitor configurations:** Some traders swear by the dual monitor configuration. The idea is to pull up your charts on one monitor and everything else on the other. Many video cards support dual monitors.

✔ **Network interface:** You need some way of accessing a high-speed Internet connection (see the next section). Many computers now come with either a built-in Ethernet port or an extra Ethernet Interface Card. Either works fine.

✔ **Power supply:** We recommend that you use an uninterruptible power supply (UPS). A UPS is relatively inexpensive and provides an extra measure of security. Some protect against lightening strikes. If you live in an area where power fluctuations are common, a UPS is a must.

Accessing the Internet

You must have reliable Internet access, and that means a high-speed connection — either DSL or cable Internet will work fine. Some very active day traders will spring for a fractional T1 or dedicated T1 line for an additional measure of reliability, but either approach is expensive. A dial-up connection is not fast enough or reliable enough for trading.

If dial-up is your only alternative, you may be able to squeak by with it, but we suggest that you look for an alternative as soon as possible.

Connecting to the Internet

Depending on where you live, you may have several good high-speed alternatives for reliably connecting to the Internet. Cable and DSL connections usually work well.

Because of security concerns, avoid wireless networks unless you're absolutely certain that you know how to configure the network to keep prying eyes from seeing your private trading and account information.

Picking a browser

Any modern browser probably will do. Although stumbling across a site that uses some browser-specific functions is a possibility, that scenario is becoming increasingly rare. Microsoft's Internet Explorer is bundled with the XP operating system at no additional charge. It will serve your needs well enough.

Securing your computer

The Internet is a dangerous place. You must protect your computer system and its data against attacks by vandals, hackers, and thieves. Make sure that you have modern virus scanning software, and keep your virus definitions up to date.

Norton's AntiVirus program gets good reviews and seems to do the job just fine. It can automatically update its virus definitions. You can get more information about Norton's program at www.symantec.com. McAfee Security's VirusScan also gets high marks from those in the know. Additional information is available on the Web at www.mcafee.com.

We also recommend that you use a firewall. A software firewall like the free Zone Alarm firewall from Zone Labs (www.zonelabs.com) works well. Unlike the free Windows XP firewall, Zone Alarm monitors your connection to the Internet and is able to detect trojans and worms that are trying to call home. This is an increasingly critical requirement. Or you may choose to install a hardware firewall, which is more secure than a software firewall and may allow you to share your Internet connection with multiple computers.

Finally, keeping up to date with your operating system's security patches, especially when you're running Windows, is important. More viruses are written for Windows than for any other operating system, so staying current with your system patches is important.

You can configure Windows XP to automatically check for system updates. To do so, go to System Properties in the Windows Control Panel. It is under Performance and Maintenance. Select the Automatic Updates tab, and check the appropriate settings to keep your Windows system up to date. You can also go to the Windows Update site (windowsupdate.microsoft.com) to make sure all your system patches have been applied.

Part II
Reading the Fundamentals: The Basics of Fundamental Analysis

The 5th Wave   By Rich Tennant

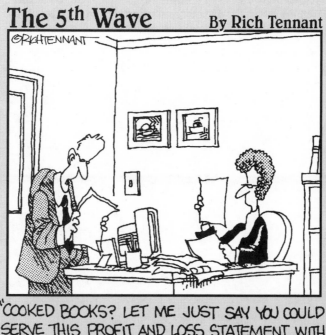

"COOKED BOOKS? LET ME JUST SAY YOU COULD SERVE THIS PROFIT AND LOSS STATEMENT WITH A FRUITY ZINFANDEL AND NOT BE OUT OF PLACE."

In this part . . .

We show you what you need to know to analyze the fundamental health of stocks and the markets. You'll need that information, because this part is where you discover how the economy and the business cycle affect your trading activities and how you can dig into the financial statements of a company to unearth good trading candidates. We also explain the roles played by stock analysts and how you can leverage their efforts as you trade.

Chapter 5

Fundamentals 101: Observing Market Behavior

*Y*ou hear plenty about recession and inflation. You know both can mean bad economic news, but do you really understand what they mean and why they happen? Regardless of what the economic gurus do, the economy cycles between periods of economic growth and recession. If growth becomes overheated, periods of inflation are likely.

The Board of Governors of the Federal Reserve (Fed) oversees moves that are made in monetary policy in the United States, and the legislative and executive branches of government are responsible for tax changes and other fiscal policy moves. The actions of the Fed and the government can minimize the impact of inflation or recession and spur economic growth, but nothing can be done to erase economic cycles. Markets and traders try to anticipate these cyclical moves with an eye toward recording gains. This chapter will help you understand which economic indicators tend to lead these cycles and how you can use them to understand the current state of the markets and the economy.

The Basics of the Business Cycle

The old adage, "What goes up must come down," is as true for the economy as it is for any physical object. When a business cycle reaches its peak, nothing is wrong in the economic world; businesses and investors are making plenty of money and everyone is happy. Unfortunately, the economy can't exist at its peak forever. In the same way that gravity eventually makes a rising object fall, a heated up economy eventually reaches its high and begins to tumble.

The peak is only one of the four distinct parts of every business cycle — peak, recession, trough, and expansion/recovery (see Figure 5-1). Although none of these parts are designated as the beginning of a business cycle, here are the portions of the business cycle that each represents:

- ✔ **Peak:** During a *peak,* the economy is humming along at full speed, with the Gross Domestic Product (GDP — more about that later in the chapter) near its maximum output and employment levels near their all-time highs. Income and prices are increasing, and the risk of inflation is great, if, for that matter, it hasn't already set in. Businesses and investors are prospering and very happy.

- ✔ **Recession:** As the old adage goes, "All good things must come to an end." As the economy falls from its peak, employment levels begin to decline, production and output eventually decline, and wages and prices level off, but more than likely won't fall unless the recession is a long one.

- ✔ **Trough:** When a recession bottoms out, the economy levels out into a period called the *trough.* If this period is a prolonged one, it can become a depression, which is a severe and prolonged recession. The most recent depression in the United States was in the late 1920s and early 1930s. Output and employment stagnate, waiting for the next expansion.

- ✔ **Expansion/Recovery:** After the economy starts growing again, employment and output pick up. This period of expansion and recovery pulls the economy off the floor of the trough and points it back toward its next peak. During this period, employment, production, and output all see increases, and the economic situation again looks promising.

Figure 5-1:
The basic business cycle.

How do you know which part of the business cycle the economy is in? Officially, you don't usually find out until months after that part of the cycle has either started or ended. The National Bureau of Economic Research (NBER) officially declares the peaks and troughs. The NBER is responsible for formally announcing the ends of peaks and troughs and signaling when a recession (end of a peak) or expansion (end of a trough) starts. You can see a table explaining the peaks and troughs since 1857 at www.nber.org/cycles/cyclesmain.html.

The time lag between events and when the NBER makes its announcements can be lengthy. For example, the NBER declared on November 26, 2001 that the peak of the current business cycle was reached March 21, 2001. Yikes, that's eight months after the economy peaked. But then, in January 2004, the NBER revised its position by announcing that the peak may have actually occurred as early as November 2000. The end of the trough for this cycle, November 2001, wasn't announced until July 17, 2003. In other words, the economy was in a period of expansion/recovery for 20 months before the NBER made it official.

Unfortunately for all concerned, information that the NBER needs to make its official announcements isn't always immediately available. The process of collecting economic data and revised preliminary estimates of economic activity takes time. Estimates and data don't become available immediately after a particular part of any business cycle ends. As a result, before drawing any conclusions, the NBER must wait until it sees a clear picture of what's happening with the economy. Recessions and expansions traditionally are based on at least two quarters (six months) of economic data. A growth spurt that lasts one full quarter won't indicate the start of an expansion nor will a decline that lasts a quarter indicate the start of a recession. Bearing that in mind, a time lag of at least six months is required before the NBER even considers declaring a recession or a recovery, which effectively renders the official announcement useless for traders.

The peak of a business cycle occurs during the last month before some key economic indicators begin to fall. These indicators include employment, output, and new housing starts. We talk more about economic indicators and which of them are critical for traders to watch in the "Understanding Economic Indicators" section, later in the chapter. However, because neither a recession nor a recovery can be declared until after two full quarters, finding a way around the time lag in official information is impossible.

In reality, clear signs that the economy was headed toward a recession were seen as early as the spring of 2000, which is when the NASDAQ index hit its peak and began its downward spiral. The effects of the recession took a bit longer to hit the other major exchanges, but they started a downward trend by the summer of 2000. Job losses also started mounting by mid-2000, and many economists already were sending alarms that the economy was headed into a recession.

Even though the NBER announced the official beginning of that recession as March 21, 2001, and the official end of the trough and beginning of the recovery as November 2001, no significant recovery was seen in the markets until October 2002. Job growth remained anemic as of early 2004. The first sign of job growth was seen during the fourth quarter of 2003, after nearly three years of job losses.

Identifying periods of economic growth and recession

Considering the type of lag time between events and official pronouncements, we're sure you're wondering how you can determine which part of the cycle the economy is in and how you can use this information as a trader. Most economists attribute changing business cycles to disturbances in the economy. Growth spurts, for example, result from surges in private or public spending. For example, during a war, government spending increases and companies in industries related to the war effort prosper. They often need to increase hiring to fulfill government orders. Employees at these companies usually receive increases in their take-home pay and start spending that extra money. As consumer optimism increases, other companies must fulfill consumers' wants and needs, so production and output also increases in companies that are unrelated to national defense.

When these same factors work in reverse, the start of a recession is sure to follow. For example, a cut in government spending will likely result in layoffs at related industrial plants, reduced take-home pay, and finally declines in output and production to cope with reduced spending.

In addition to government spending, a decision by the Fed to either raise or lower interest rates is another major disturbance to the economy. When interest rates rise, spending slows, and that can lead to a recession. When interest rates are cut, spending usually goes up, and that can aid in spurring an economic recovery.

Another school of economic thought disagrees with the notion that government policy or spending is responsible for changes in the business cycle. This second group of theorists believes differences in productivity levels and consumer tastes are the primary forces driving the business cycle. From this point of view, only businesses and consumers can drive changes in the economic cycle. These economists don't believe that governmentally-driven monetary or policy changes impact the cycle.

Which camp you believe is not critical; the key is picking up the signs of when the economy is in a recession and when it's in an expansion. Peaks and troughs are flat periods (periods where the high or low stays primarily even before moving in the opposite direction), and are impossible to identify until months after they end. As a trader, you can identify shifts in buying and spending behavior by watching various economic indicators. By doing so, you can discover when the economy is in the early stages of a recovery or recession or if it's fully into a recession or recovery.

Relating bull markets and bear markets to the economy

You've probably heard the terms bull market and bear market. To find out what they mean, you first need to understand how economic cycles affect the stock market. *Bulls* are people who believe that all is right with the world and the stock market is heading for an increase. They definitely think the economy is expanding. *Bears* are people who believe the economy is heading for a downturn, and stocks will either stagnate or go down. A *bull market* is a market in which a majority of stocks are increasing in value, and a *bear market* is a market in which a majority of stocks are decreasing. Bears definitely believe the economy is either in a recession or headed that way.

Regardless of whether the bulls or the bears are right, you can make money as a trader. The key: Identify the way the market is headed and then buy or sell into that trend. During a bear market, traders make their money by selling short, or taking advantage of falling prices (more about that in Chapter 14). Traders sell short by borrowing stock from their broker and then selling it with the hope of making a profit when the price falls.

Even during a bear market, some stocks offer opportunities for traders to make money, including oil and gas stocks and real estate investment trusts (REITs). Petroleum stocks and REITs pay higher dividends and, therefore, are most attractive when the rest of the market is falling or showing no growth potential. During a bull market, riding a stock through recovery but getting out before a fall is key. We'll talk more about trends and what they mean in Chapter 10.

Sector Rotation

In general, the markets are divided into sectors, and at any given time some of those sectors will be expanding, even during a bear market. Some traders are adept at rotating their investments from one sector to another that is more likely to be benefiting from the part of the business cycle that is driving the economy. This basic trading strategy is called *sector rotation*.

The guru of traders who want to take advantage of sector rotation is Sam Stovall, chief investment strategist for Standard & Poor's, who wrote the classic on sector rotation, *Sector Investing*, in 1996. Although the book is out of print, you can still follow his advice about sectors on *Businessweek*'s Web site at www.businessweek.com/investor/list/stovall_toc01.htm.

Stovall developed the Sector Rotation Model shown in Figure 5-2. As you can see, he found that market cycles tend to lead business cycles. Markets tend to bottom out just before the rest of the economy is in a full recession. The start of a bull market, on the other hand, can be seen just before the rest of the economy starts its climb toward recovery. Markets reach their tops first and enter a bear market before the general economic indicators show a peak.

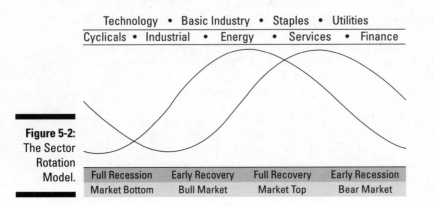

Technology • Basic Industry • Staples • Utilities
Cyclicals • Industrial • Energy • Services • Finance

| Full Recession | Early Recovery | Full Recovery | Early Recession |
| Market Bottom | Bull Market | Market Top | Bear Market |

Figure 5-2:
The Sector
Rotation
Model.

As a trader, you can take advantage of this knowledge by knowing which sectors are more likely to rise during the various parts of a market cycle. You need to buy into the sectors with stock prices that are likely to rise, or you can sell short the sectors in which prices are expected to fall. We discuss short selling in Chapter 14.

Early recovery

You can spot an early recovery when consumer expectations and industrial production are beginning to rise while interest rates are bottoming out. That scenario was evident during a recent economic cycle discovered during the fall and early winter months of 2003. During the early stages of recovery, Stovall found that industrial, basic industry, and energy sectors tend to take the lead.

Full recovery

When the economy has fully recovered, you start seeing signs that consumer expectations are falling and productivity levels and interest rates are flattening out. These factors were seen during the economy's recent period of full recovery from late 2000 until the early signs of recession in late 2001. During that period, companies in the staples and services sectors exhibited a tendency to take the lead. As knowledgeable investors know, when that happens, it's only a matter of time before a recession follows. Investors know that the staples of life are needed even in times of recession, so the stocks of those companies tend to benefit.

Early recession

When the economy reaches the earliest part of a recession, consumer expectations fall more sharply and productivity levels start to drop. Interest rates also begin to drop. Most of the 2.5 million job losses during the recent economic downturn occurred when the recession was just beginning in late 2001 and early 2002. During 2001, the Federal Reserve cut interest rates 11 times to try to ease the concerns about the upcoming recession. Rates still were at their bottom as of January 2004. Utilities and finance sector stocks are the most likely to see rising prices during the first part of a recession, because under those circumstances, investors seek stocks that provide some safety (because owning them involves less risk) and pay higher dividends. Gold and other valuable mineral stocks also look good to investors seeking safety.

Dissecting sector rotation

Some wag once said that the stock market predicted 15 of the last 8 recessions. And although it's true that the market isn't a terribly precise economic prognosticator, that's sort of beside the point. Economic indicators can help you understand the big picture, which, in turn, can help you make better trading decisions.

Of all the economic tools available, sector rotation analysis is probably the most valuable. Even if the sector rotation model can't help you identify an economic cycle, it can identify sectors and stocks that are ripe for further study.

When we trade, we want the strongest stocks in the strongest sectors, which is why we monitor sector performance carefully. Knowing the sectors that are performing best enables you to anticipate which sectors are likely to begin outperforming and which are likely to fade. Using those projections, you can start monitoring stocks in those up-and-coming sectors. For a sector to outperform, the stocks within it must also outperform. You need to be monitoring those stocks before they begin their runs.

Plenty of data is available to help you separate the strongest sectors from the ones that are underperforming. *Investor's Business Daily,* for example, ranks nearly 200 industry groups by price performance. Stockcharts. com provides a similar capability with its Performance Charts (stockcharts.com/charts/performance). You can also monitor sectors by following Exchange Traded Funds (ETFs), such as the Select Sector SPDRs (Standard and Poor's Depository Receipts) at www.spdrindex.com.

Full recession

Although it may not make much sense intuitively, during a full recession is when you first start seeing indications that consumer expectations are improving, which is seen by increased spending. However, industrial productivity remains flat, and businesses won't increase their production levels until they believe consumers actually are ready to spend again. Additionally, interest rates continue to drop, because both business and consumer spending are slow, so demand for the money weakens while competition for new credit customers grows between banks and other financial institutions. During a full recession, cyclical and technology stocks tend to lead the way. Investors look to safety during a recession, so companies that satisfy that need tend to do best.

Understanding Economic Indicators

The key to knowing where, as a trader, you are during the business cycle is watching the economic indicators. Every day that you open your newspaper, you see at least one story about how the economy is doing based on various economic indicators. Popular indicators track employment, money supply, interest rates, housing starts, housing sales, production levels, purchasing statistics, consumer confidence, and many other factors that indicate how the economy is doing.

Economic indicators are useful to your trading. Some are definitely more useful than others. We don't have the space here to describe each of the indicators; so instead, we focus on the ones that can provide you with the most help in making your trading decisions.

Fed watch: Understanding how interest rates affect markets

Watching the Federal Open Market Committee (FOMC) of the Federal Reserve (which includes the seven members of the Board of Governors, the President of the New York Federal Reserve Bank, and presidents of 4 of the other 11 Federal Reserve Banks) and tracking what it may or may not do to interest rates is almost a daily spectator sport in the business press. Although members of the FOMC meet only eight times per year, discussions about whether the Federal Reserve will raise or lower interest rates serves as fodder for stories published on at least a weekly, if not daily, basis. Every time Fed Chairman Alan Greenspan speaks, people look for indications of what the Fed may be thinking. Speeches by other members of the Fed likewise are carefully dissected between FOMC meetings. Most press coverage will short-cut all this by saying the Fed may raise or lower interest rates.

The key reason for you to be concerned: A change in interest rates can have a major impact on the economy and thus on how you make trades. An increase in rates is likely to slow down spending, which can lead to an overall economic slowdown. For the most part, when the Fed raises interest rates, it's because the board believes the economy is overheated, which can fuel the risk of infla-tion. An increase in interest rates can reduce spending and thus ease overheat-ing. If, on the other hand, the Fed fears an economic downturn or is trying to fuel growth during a recession, the board frequently decides to cut interest rates to spur spending and growth.

In addition to following press reports covering speeches and Congressional testimony by members of the Fed, you can also get a good hint about what the Fed is thinking by reading the Beige Book, which is a report compiled by the 12 Federal Reserve Banks. Summaries about current economic con-ditions in each of the 12 districts are circulated to Federal Reserve Board members two weeks prior to the FOMC meeting, at which monetary policy, including interest rates, is set. The summaries are developed through inter-views with key business leaders, economists, market experts, and others familiar with each individual district. You can read the Beige Book online at www.federalreserve.gov/FOMC/BeigeBook/2004. You can find out about past FOMC statements at www.federalreserve.gov/fomc. These links give you access not only to current issues of the Beige Book and FOMC statements but also to information from those two sources dating back as far as 1996. They can provide an excellent overview of economic trends and possible shifts in Federal Reserve monetary policy.

Money supply

The money supply is a key number to watch, because growth in money supply can be a leading indicator of inflation in situations when the money supply is greater than the supply of goods. When more money than goods is around, prices are likely to rise. Commodities and money traders will want to keep close watch over these three aggregates — money supply, inflation, and goods and services.

The Fed tracks three monetary aggregates — M1, M2, and M3. *M1* includes money used for payments, such as currency in circulation plus checking accounts in banks and thrifts. Currency sitting in bank vaults and bank deposits at the Fed are not part of M1, but instead are part of the monetary base. *M2* includes M1 money plus retail nontransaction deposits, which is money sitting in retail savings accounts and money market accounts.

M3 takes the aggregates one step further and includes money from M1 and M2 and adds in wholesale deposits and institutional money market funds. You can follow the money stock measures at `www.federalreserve.gov/releases/h6/Current`. When one totals the money base, M1, M2, and M3, you can track the total amount of money sitting in someone's account or circulating in the economy.

The Fed decided in July 2000 that it no longer would set target ranges for growth rates of the monetary aggregates. In the late 1970s, money supply drove the Fed's decision-making process. As money supply grew to what was considered out of hand, the Fed kept raising interest rates until they were so high that many believe the Fed moves actually caused the recession in the early 1980s. After that time, managing interest rates became a higher priority than managing money aggregates. The Fed didn't kill the idea of target ranges for the money supply until it was certain that managing interest rates alone would help stem inflation. Now that the Fed has proved interest-rate management works, it decided it no longer needed to set a target for monetary aggregates.

Inflation rate

Several key economic indicators point you toward ways of identifying the risk of inflation. The primary overall indicator is Gross Domestic Product; it's released quarterly by the United States Department of Commerce's Bureau of Economic Analysis (BEA). You can also follow monthly trends by keeping your eye out for the Consumer Price Index, the Producer Price Index, Retail Sales Data, and the Employment Status Report, as described in the list that follows.

- **Gross Domestic Product (GDP)** represents the monetary value of goods produced during a specific period in the economy. GDP is released quarterly in three different versions. The first version, which includes advance data, is released at 8:30 a.m. on the last business day of the months January, April, July, and October for the previous quarter. Preliminary data is released a month later, and the final numbers are released a month after that. GDP is important to traders because it indicates the pace at which the economy is growing. In the GDP, you'll find numbers for consumer spending, private domestic investment, government or public spending, and the net exports. Essentially, it includes all information about labor and property involving business activities inside the confines of the United States. If GDP fails to meet expectations set by the analysts or exceeds market expectations, stock prices will be affected at least temporarily. For a glimpse of what may be in store for the future, pay attention to the rate that inventories are increasing. It can be a leading indicator that growth is slowing or consumer demand is changing. Even though the final official numbers are released quarterly, the advance reports and preliminary reports give you a good indication of what to expect in the final numbers. You can get full details about the GDP reports at www.bea.doc.gov/bea/dn1.htm. You can track the release schedule for the GDP reports, as well as other government statistical reports, at www.bea.doc.gov/bea/newsrel/news_release_sort_national.htm. Often the report is posted at the Bureau of Economic Analysis early in the morning before the actual release and embargoed until the official release time, so as a trader you may be able to get a heads up before the news is actually reported by the press.

✔ **Consumer Price Index (CPI)** measures the cost of a representative basket of goods and services, including food, energy, housing, clothing, transportation, medical care, entertainment, and education. Each type of cost is weighted. For example, medical costs are weighted more highly in recent years, because they are rising at a faster pace, especially as the current population ages. In addition to the broad CPI, a core rate is issued that excludes food and energy, which are considered more volatile. The core rate is an indicator you can watch for general price shifts. The financial markets, in general, look for a rate of increase in the range of 1 percent to 2 percent; anything higher may be a sign of inflation and can cause at least a temporary shock to stock prices. Any shock to stock prices obviously can be an opportunity for traders. The CPI is released by the Labor Department about 8:30 a.m. around the 15th of each month and reflects data from the previous month. You can track the CPI at the Web site of the U.S. Department of Labor's Bureau of Labor Statistics at www.bls.gov/cpi/home.htm.

✔ **Producer Price Index (PPI)** is thought of more as a basket full of other indexes that affect domestic producers, including goods manufacturing, fishing, and agricultural and other commodities. The Labor Department collects more than 100,000 prices each month from 30,000 production and manufacturing firms to calculate this basket. The markets pay close attention to the index, because even though it isn't as powerful an inflation index as the CPI, it gives traders clues about what to expect in the next CPI release. The PPI is released a couple of days before the CPI, at 8:30 a.m. usually around the 13th of each month, and it reflects data from the previous month. You can track PPI data at www.bls.gov/ppi.

✔ **Retail Sales Data** tracks information about (you guessed it) retail sales by large corporations and by small mom-and-pop retail outlets. The U.S. Census Bureau, which is a part of the Department of Commerce, surveys hundreds of firms each month using a random sampling of retail outlets that make federal insurance contributions to collect this data, which is particularly important whenever you're trading stocks in the retail sector. The survey looks at changes in retail numbers from month to month. When the number is a negative number, it means sales levels decreased from the previous month. This type of negative news can be a shock to stock prices, especially for companies in the retail sector. The data is released about two weeks after it's collected, or at 8:30 a.m. about the 12th of each month. You can track it online at www.census.gov/svsd/www/advtable.html.

Deflation

In addition to watching the economic indicators discussed in the previous section for inflation, traders also need to watch the numbers for signs of deflation. Serious concern about the possibility of deflation takes center stage when prices start falling. *Deflation* occurs when a sustained period of falling prices takes place. The Great Depression of the 1930s was a classic period of deflation. Many economists believe that printing more money cures deflation, because (as mentioned earlier in the "Money supply" section) increases in the money supply normally lead to increases in prices when more money is around than goods to be purchased.

During periods of deflation, increasing the money supply isn't necessarily the answer. Some economists believe injecting more money into the economy is risky, especially when production capacity is in excess, and producers continue to produce goods even though prices are falling. Whereas, in other economic situations, producers commonly stop producing when prices fall.

In early 2004, Japan faced a continuing period of deflation even though its central bank had lowered rates to an effective negative interest rate and continued printing money in attempts to prop up its sagging pricing structure, and yet prices were continuing to drop. Some economists believe the Japanese are experiencing a liquidity trap. No matter how much money Japan prints, prices continue downward in a deflationary spiral. Although some are concerned that the United States may be headed in a similar direction, the Fed doesn't believe the country, at least for now, faces the danger anymore, because signs of growth continue to strengthen and prices no longer are dropping. In fact, while we were writing this book early in 2004, members of the Fed were signaling that interest rates may soon be increased because early signs of inflation were being seen in some economic indicators.

Jobless claims

The Employment Situation Summary, another report from the BLS, is one of the most important leading indicators to watch. This report is the first critical economic indicator released every month and frequently sets the expectations for the rest of the reports that month. For example, signs of a weak labor market reported in the Employment Situation Summary usually are a strong indication of poor retail sales and other possible negative reports later in the month. The summary also breaks down data by industry, such as construction manufacturing. For example, a significant drop in employment numbers for the construction sector is a strong sign that the housing starts report will also be negative.

This report can send shockwaves through the financial markets, especially if the numbers that are released vary greatly from expectations. Stock prices definitely fall whenever the report doesn't meet expectations or employment statistics show signs of weakness. On the other hand, stock prices can rise dramatically whenever the report indicates better than expected numbers. As is true with any shock to the market, changes in prices are temporary unless other indicators also exhibit the same trend or tendency.

The reason why the employment report can drive markets so strongly is that the information it contains is a timely assessment of the overall market, because it includes data that is only a few days old. This report is widely recognized as the best indicator of unemployment and wage pressure. Rising unemployment can be an early sign of recession, while increased pressure on wages can be an early sign of inflation. The report also is a broad-based snapshot of the entire labor market, covering 250 regions of the United States and every major industry.

The Labor Department releases the report at 8:30 a.m. on the first Friday of each month with data for the previous month. The two key parts of the report that traders need to watch are

- Unemployment and new jobs created
- Average weekly hours worked and average earnings

Another employment indicator traders like to watch is the Employment Cost Index (ECI). It's especially relevant during actual times of inflation or when fear exists that an inflationary period may be imminent. The ECI is a quarterly survey of employer payrolls that tracks movement in the cost of labor, including wages, benefits, and bonuses. Wages and benefits make up 75 percent of the index. The Bureau of Labor Statistics (BLS) surveys more than 3,000 private-sector firms and 500 local governments to develop the index. The ECI, which reports data from the previous quarter, is released on the last business day in January, April, July, and October.

Consumer confidence

Keeping an eye on consumer confidence is another way of casting a glance into the future of the market. When confidence is high, consumers are more likely to spend. The best overall index for monitoring consumer confidence is the Consumer Confidence Index (CCI), which is put out by The Conference Board. This index is compiled through a sampling of 5,000 households and is widely respected as the most accurate indictor of consumer confidence.

Although minor changes in the CCI are not strongly indicative of a problem, major shifts can be a sign of rocky waters ahead. Most people who watch the CCI look for three- to six-month trends. The Fed, as an example, looks closely at consumer confidence when determining interest rate policy, which as you know can greatly affect stock prices. When confidence is trending lower, the Fed is more likely to lower interest rates. Stock markets love to hear about the Fed lowering interest rates. Confidence levels that are trending higher can be a warning of a pending inflationary period. A rapidly rising trend in consumer confidence can lead the Fed to raise interest rates to cut off inflation; moreover, a rise in interest rates can send stock prices lower.

The Conference Board releases the CCI at 10 a.m. the last Tuesday of each month. The biggest weakness of this index is that it isn't based on actual spending data. Instead, it's a survey of planned spending. You can track the CCI online at `www.conference-board.org/economics/consumerconfidence.cfm`.

Business activity

A number of key economic indicators can give you a good idea of what business is doing and how that information may impact the stock markets. Key business indicators to watch include

- **The National Association of Purchasing Managers report (NAPM):** One of the first economic indicators released each month is the NAPM report, which surveys purchasing managers and provides reviews of new orders, production, deliveries, and inventories. This report is released at 10 a.m. the first business day of each month and reflects data compiled from the previous month. You can track this report online at `www.ism.ws/ISMReport/index.cfm`.

- **Durable Goods Orders:** The Commerce Department releases another critical economic indicator of business activity in the area of Durable Goods Orders. This indicator measures the dollar volume of orders, shipments, and unfilled orders of durable goods, or types of merchandise that have a lifespan of three years or more. This report serves as a leading indicator of manufacturing activity and can move the stock market, especially when its numbers vary from expectations. You can track the Durable Goods Orders online at `www.census.gov/indicator/www/m3/index.html`.

- **Housing Starts and Building Permits:** This report is another that's released by the Commerce Department. It can be a leading indicator of the direction the economy will take. When the number of permits rises, a positive economic indicator results. About 25 percent of investment dollars are plowed into housing starts, and that makes up about 5 percent of the overall economy. The report is broken down by regions —

Northeast, Midwest, South, and West — so you can also get a strong indication of the strength of the economy on a regional basis. You can track this indicator online at www.census.gov/const/www/C40/table2.html.

You can also track other reports on myriad industries at www.census.gov/cir/www/alpha.html.

✔ **Regional Manufacturing Surveys:** Each Federal Reserve Bank district compiles data from regional manufacturing surveys that can help you find a score of indicators including new orders, production, employment, inventories, delivery times, prices, and export and import orders. Positive reports indicate an expanding economy. Negative reports indicate a contracting economy. The two most closely watched are the Philadelphia survey at www.phil.frb.org/econ/bos/bosschedule.html and the Chicago survey at www.chicagofed.org/economic_research_and_data/cfmmi.cfm. If you're trading in regional stocks, following the manufacturing surveys from the Federal Reserve Banks in key regions that you follow can help you determine the direction of the economy for the areas most relevant to the stocks you're trading.

Using the Data

You can see that plenty of data is available, but not all of it is relevant to the types of stocks you want to trade. Organizing your data collection and tracking the trends can make choosing economic signs and analyzing which part of the business cycle is driving the markets easier for you. Here are a few steps that can make this task much easier:

1. **Maintain a calendar of the release dates for the key economic indicators you decide to follow.**

    The markets may move in anticipation of this data, so if you know a key economic indicator is about to be released, be sure to watch stock price trends for the possible impact the anticipated release may be having on the market.

2. **Know the parts of the economy that are most impacted by the economic indicators you're following.**

    For example, the GDP strongly suggests the path of economic growth, but PPI and CPI are strong measures of inflation.

3. **Know which economic indicators are most important to the market.**

    For example, in times of inflation, economic indicators that reveal key data regarding inflation are the biggest market movers. If the markets are worried about growth, the growth components of GDP and other indicators will have the greatest potential for moving the markets.

4. **Know what the market is expecting to see in the numbers.**

   The actual number is not as critical as whether that number was expected by the markets. Surprises are what move the markets.

5. **Know what parts of the economic indicator are important.**

   Newspapers may write headlines for shock value, but the parts of the index they cover may not be what are critical to your decision-making. For example, traders know that food and energy components of the CPI are volatile, so the more important number to watch is the core CPI, which doesn't include food and energy. The news media may focus only on the more volatile number.

6. **Don't overreact to a newly announced economic indicator that didn't meet market expectations.**

   Indicators frequently are revised after they're initially issued. The difference may merely be related to a revision and not an indication of a shift in the business cycle. However, be sure to check information about revisions to the previous month and how those revisions have impacted the current month's trend.

7. **Monitor the trends.**

   On your calendar, keep track of key components of each economic indicator that you watch. Follow the trends of the most important data components to get a good idea of where the business cycle is headed.

Keeping a tight watch on economic indicators is the best way for you to determine at what point the economy is in a new business cycle. Waiting for official pronouncements is much too late. By the time they're released, that phase of the cycle may be over and a new cycle may be driving the markets.

Chapter 6

Understanding the Critical Parts of Fundamental Analysis

Most traders don't worry about the fundamentals. These numbers include the general economic and market conditions that impact a stock, as well as the financial information known about a company's activities and its financial successes and failures. Instead, traders tend to focus entirely on technical analysis and trends that can be seen using that type of analysis.

Taking the time to analyze the fundamentals of a stock puts you one step ahead of the trading crowd. Using fundamental analysis, you can determine how a stock's price compares with those of similar companies based on earnings growth and other key factors, including business conditions. This chapter helps you understand critical parts of fundamental analysis and how you can use the information gathered from it to make better trading decisions.

The first step you take in conducting fundamental analysis usually is selecting an industry or business sector that interests you for possible stock purchases. Sometimes, a particular company peaks your fancy, and you start your research by looking at the major players in that company's sector or by turning to the sector's fundamentals. Regardless of how you start, you need to narrow down your list of the companies you want to compare to the ones that are in similar businesses within the sector, so you can find the best opportunity.

Most of the tools used in fundamental analysis require you to compare at least two companies operating in similar business environments to understand the meaning of the information. For the purposes of discussion in this chapter, we look at two big players in the home improvement retail sector — Home Depot and Lowe's. If you've followed the business conditions in this sector, you know that both are vying for market share in the expanding home improvement market with major investments in new store construction.

Before discovering the tools of fundamental analysis, you first must understand how to read key financial statements, including the critical parts of the income statement, cash flow statements, and the balance sheet.

Checking Out the Income Statement

The *income statement* is where a company periodically reports its revenues, costs, and net earnings. It's basically a snapshot of how much a company is earning from its operations and any extraordinary earnings that may have impacted its bottom line during a specific period of time. From the income statement, you'll be able to determine the impact of taxes, interest, and depreciation on a company's earnings and to forecast earnings potential.

Every income statement has three key sections: revenue, expenses, and income. The revenue section includes all money taken into the company by selling its products or services minus any costs directly related to the sale of those products or services (cost of goods sold). The expenses section includes all operating expenses for the company not directly related to sales, as well as expenses for depreciation (writing off the use of equipment and buildings — tangible assets), amortization (writing off the use of patents, copyrights, and other intellectual property or intangible assets), taxes, and interest.

The income section includes various calculations of income. Usually you'll find one calculation that shows income after operating expenses and before interest, taxes, depreciation, and amortization called EBITDA. This will be followed by net income, which is the bottom line showing how much a company earned after all its costs and expenses have been deducted. Public companies must file financial reports with the SEC on a quarterly and annual basis. You can read any company's financial reports at the Edgar Web site (www.sec.gov/edgar.shtml).

A year's worth of figures won't show you much, so you need to look at the trends throughout a number of years to be able to forecast growth potential or assess how well a company is doing compared with its competitors. We discuss a number of good sources for finding fundamental information in Chapter 4.

Both quarterly and annual reports are important. Comparing a company's results on a quarter to quarter basis gives the trader an idea of how well the company is meeting expectations. Also, for example, looking at results for the first quarter of 2003 versus the first quarter of 2004, you can see whether a company's earnings are increasing or decreasing in a similar market environment. While for some types of companies the first quarter is generally productive, other types of companies, such as retail stores, are dependent mostly on fourth-quarter holiday results, so you need to know what is expected in earnings for the various quarters. Quarterly results allow you to monitor results at similar time periods.

Annual statements give you a summary for the year. You can also compare current year results to the results over a number of years to see at what rate the company is growing.

Revenues

The first line of any income statement includes the company's sales revenues. This number reflects all the sales that have been generated by the company before any costs are subtracted. Rather than go to all the trouble of showing their math — gross sales – any sales discounts, adjustments for returns, or other allowances = *net sales* — most companies show only net sales on their income statements. From these figures, you want to see obvious signs of steady growth in revenues. A decrease in revenues from year to year is a red flag that indicates problems and probably not a good potential trading choice.

Cost of goods sold

The *cost of goods sold* (also known as cost of merchandise sold or cost of services sold — depending on the type of business) is an amount that shows the total costs directly related to selling a company's products or services. The costs included in this part of the revenue section include purchases, purchase discounts, and freight charges or other costs directly related to selling a product or service.

Gross margins

The gross margin or gross profit is the net result of subtracting the cost of goods sold from net sales. This figure shows you how much money a company is making directly from sales before considering other operating costs. The gross profit is the dollar figure calculated by subtracting costs of goods sold from net revenue. The gross margin is a ratio calculated by dividing gross profit by net revenue. Watching year-to-year trends in gross margins gives you a good idea of a company's profit growth potential from its key revenue sources.

You can calculate a gross margin ratio by dividing a company's gross profit by its net sales:

Gross margin ratio = Gross profit ÷ Net sales

The *gross margin ratio,* expressed as a percentage, considers revenue from sales minus the costs directly involved in making those sales and is a good indicator of how well a company uses its production, purchasing, and distribution resources to earn a profit. The higher the percentage, the more efficient a company is at making its profit.

By comparing gross margin ratios among various companies within the same industry or business sector, you can get an idea of how efficient each company is at generating profits. Investors favor companies that are more efficient.

To give you an idea of how to use this ratio and others in this chapter, we compare figures from two of the leaders in the home improvement retail sector — Home Depot and Lowe's. Tables 6-1 and 6-2 present the gross profits section from the past three annual income statements (information taken from Yahoo! Finance) for each respective company. Table 6-3 compares the gross margin ratios for the two companies.

Table 6-1	Home Depot Inc. Gross Profits (All Numbers in Thousands)		
Fiscal Year Ending	*Feb 2, 2003*	*Feb 3, 2002*	*Jan 28, 2001*
Net Revenue	58,247,000	53,553,000	45,738,000
Cost of Goods Sold	40,139,000	37,406,000	32,057,000
Gross Profit	18,108,000	16,147,000	13,681,000

Table 6-2	Lowe's Companies Inc. Gross Profits (All Numbers in Thousands)		
Fiscal Year Ending	*Jan 31, 2003*	*Feb 1, 2002*	*Feb 2, 2001*
Net Revenue	26,491,000	22,111,108	18,778,559
Cost of Goods Sold	18,465,000	15,743,267	13,487,791
Gross Profit	8,026,000	6,367,841	5,290,768

Table 6-3	Comparing Gross Margin Ratios by Year		
Fiscal Year	*2003*	*2002*	*2001*
Home Depot	31.1%	30.2%	29.9%
Lowe's	30.3%	28.8%	28.2%

You can see that Home Depot is slightly more efficient at using its production, purchasing, and distribution resources than Lowe's, because Home Depot has consistently higher gross margin ratios. Both corporations, however, show a trend toward improvement. The advantage of using this ratio, rather than the actual revenue and profit numbers for comparison, is that it makes comparing large companies with small companies within the same business or industry sector much easier. Even though Home Depot has more than twice the sales volume, the ratio enables you to compare how efficiently each company uses its resources.

Expenses

The next section of the income statement shows the expenses of operating the business, including the sales costs and administrative costs of business operations. When comparing a company's year-to-year results, you need to watch for signs of whether expenses are increasing faster than a company's gross profits, which can be an indication that a company is having a problem controlling its costs and won't bode well for future profit growth potential.

When you see expenses drop from one year to the next, while gross margins increase, that's usually a good sign and means a company likely has a good cost control program in place. The potential for growth in future profit margins is good.

Gross profits and expenses that are rising at about the same rate is neither a significant positive nor negative sign. When that happens, the best way to get a reading on how a company is controlling its expenses is to compare its expenses with the expenses of other companies in similar businesses.

Interest payments

The interest payments portion of the expense section of an income statement gives you a view of a company's short-term financial health. Payments shown here include interest paid during the year on short- and long-term liabilities (more about those in the "Looking at debt" section, later in the chapter). These payments are tax deductible expenses, which help reduce a company's tax burden.

To determine a company's fiscal health, use the *interest expense number* and the earnings before interest and taxes (EBIT) number, which is usually shown on the income statement. If not, you can calculate it by subtracting interest and tax expenses from operating income (which will be gross profit minus expenses, also usually shown on the income statement). You can use this figure to determine whether the company is generating sufficient income to cover its interest payments using the interest coverage ration. You can calculate the company's *interest coverage ratio* (expressed as a percentage, this ratio provides a clear-cut indicator of company's solvency) using this formula:

Interest coverage ratio = EBIT ÷ Interest expenses

Companies with high interest coverage ratios won't have any problems meeting their interest obligations, and their risk of insolvency (going belly up) is low. On the other hand, a low interest coverage ratio is a clear sign that a company has a problem and may face bankruptcy. Whether an interest coverage ratio tends to run high or low depends a great deal on the type of industry or business a company is in. Comparing the interest coverage ratios of several companies in the same industry or business is the best way to gauge, or judge, the value of the ratios.

Table 6-4 shows annual EBITs and interest expenses from three successive annual income statements for Home Depot, and Table 6-5 shows the corresponding numbers for Lowe's.

Table 6-4	Home Depot Inc. Interest Payments (All Numbers in Thousands)		
Fiscal Year Ending	*Feb 2, 2003*	*Feb 3, 2002*	*Jan 28, 2001*
EBIT	5,909,000	4,985,000	4,238,000
Interest	37,000	28,000	21,000

Table 6-5	Lowe's Companies Inc. Interest Payments (All Numbers in Thousands)		
Fiscal Year Ending	*Jan 31, 2003*	*Feb 1, 2002*	*Feb 2, 2001*
EBIT	2,541,000	1,856,219	1,402,265
Interest	182,000	231,968	120,825

Table 6-6 shows the respective interest coverage ratios for Home Depot and Lowe's.

Table 6-6	Comparing Interest Coverage Ratios		
Fiscal Year	*2003*	*2002*	*2001*
Home Depot	159	178	202
Lowe's	14	8	12

Home Depot obviously is in a much stronger position to make its interest payments, but Lowe's isn't in trouble either. Lowe's has 14 times more income than it needs to make its interest payments. Analysts generally consider a company in trouble whenever its interest coverage ratio falls below 3.

Tax payments

Corporations are always looking to avoid taxes, just like you. The *income tax expense* figure on the income statement shows the total amount that a company paid in taxes. A corporation pays between 15 percent and 38 percent of its income in taxes, depending on its respective size; however, corporations have many more write-offs they can use to reduce their tax burdens than you have as an individual taxpayer. Most large corporations have teams of tax specialists who spend their days looking for ways to minimize taxes. When looking at tax payments, reviewing how well the company you're interested in manages its tax burden compared with other similar companies is important.

Dividend payments

Companies sometimes pay a *dividend,* or part of the company profits, for each share of common stock that an investor holds. This dividend is distributed to shareholders usually once every quarter after the company's board of directors reviews company profits and determines whether to pay and how much the dividend will be. Paying dividends is not a tax-deductible expense for companies that pay them. In the past, traders have preferred growth stocks that do not pay dividends. However, recent changes in the way dividends are taxed may have altered the way traders view dividend-paying stocks.

Testing profitability

You now can use the income statement to quickly check your company's profitability by using one or both of two ratios — the operating margin and net profit margin. The *operating margin* looks at profits from operations before interest and tax expenses, and the *net profit margin* considers earnings after the payment of those expenses.

You calculate operating margin using this formula:

Operating margin = operating income ÷ gross profit or net sales

You calculate net profit margin using this formula:

Net profit margin = earnings after taxes ÷ gross profit or net sales

Table 6-7 shows the gross profits, operating incomes, and earnings after taxes from three successive annual income statements for Home Depot, and Table 6-8 shows the corresponding numbers for Lowe's.

Table 6-7	Home Depot Inc. Profitability (All Numbers in Thousands)		
Fiscal Year Ending	*Feb 2, 2003*	*Feb 3, 2002*	*Jan 28, 2001*
Gross Profit	18,108,000	16,147,000	13,681,000
Operating Income	5,909,000	4,985,000	4,238,000
Earnings After Taxes	3,664,000	3,044,000	2,581,000

Table 6-8	Lowe's Companies Inc. Profitability (All Numbers in Thousands)		
Fiscal Year Ending	*Jan 31, 2003*	*Feb 1, 2002*	*Feb 2, 2001*
Gross Profit	8,026,000	6,367,841	5,290,768
Operating Income	2,541,000	1,856,219	1,402,265
Earnings After Taxes	1,471,000	1,023,262	809,871

Table 6-9 compares the respective profitability margins for Home Depot and Lowe's.

Table 6-9	Comparing Profitability Margins		
Fiscal Year	*2003*	*2002*	*2001*
Operating Margin			
Home Depot	32.6%	30.9%	31.0%
Lowe's	31.7%	29.1%	26.5%
Net Profit Margin			
Home Depot	20.2%	18.9%	18.9%
Lowe's	18.3%	16.1%	15.3%

You can see from the numbers in Table 6-9 that each is improving its respective profitabilities, although Home Depot shows a slightly stronger profit picture than Lowe's. The reason that checking operating and net profit ratios is a good idea: Doing so shows you the impact of taxes and interest on a company's profits.

Looking at Cash Flow

When you review income statements, you're looking at information based on accrual accounting. In *accrual accounting,* sales can be included when they're first contracted, even before revenue from them is collected. Sales made on credit are shown even if the company still needs to collect from the customer. Expenses are recorded as they're incurred and not necessarily as they're paid. However, the income statement definitely does not show a company's cash position. A company that's booking a high level of sales can have a stellar income statement but nevertheless be having trouble collecting from its customers, which may put that company in a cash-poor situation. That's why cash flow statements are so important.

You can get an idea of your favorite company's actual cash flows from the adjustments shown on its *cash flow statement.* The three sections to this statement are operating activities, investment activities, and financial activities. Cash flow statements are filed with the SEC along with income statements on a quarterly and annual basis.

Operating activities

Looking at cash flow from *operating activities* gives you a good picture of the cash that's available from a company's core business operations, including net income, depreciation and amortization, changes in accounts receivable, changes in inventory, and changes in other current liabilities and current assets. We talk more about these accounts in the "Scouring the Balance Sheet" section later on.

Calculating cash flow from operating activities includes adjustments to net income made by adding back items that were not actually cash expenditures but rather were required for reporting purposes. Depreciation is one such item. Similarly, expenses or income items that were reported for accrual purposes are subtracted out. For example, changes in accounts receivable are subtracted out, because they represent cash that has not been received. Conversely, changes in accounts payable represent payments that have not yet been made, so the cash still is on hand.

The bottom line: This section of a company's cash flow statement shows actual *net cash from operations*. Table 6-10 compares three successive years of cash flow from operating activities at Home Depot and Lowe's.

Table 6-10	Total Cash Flow from Operating Activities (All Numbers in Thousands)		
Fiscal Year	*2003*	*2002*	*2001*
Home Depot	4,802,000	5,963,000	2,796,000
Lowe's	2,696,000	1,613,049	1,129,709

Looking at the numbers in Table 6-10, you can see Lowe's cash position is steadily improving, while Home Depot's cash position took a drop between 2002 and 2003. If you're thinking about purchasing Home Depot stock, you'd certainly want to look more closely at cash flow changes in operating activities to find out why it dropped in 2003.

Depreciation

For all companies, one of the largest adjustments to cash flow is depreciation. Depreciation reflects the dollar value placed on the annual use of an asset. For example, if a company's truck will be a useable asset for five years, then the cost of that truck is depreciated over that five-year period. For accounting purposes on its income statement, a company must use a method called *straight-line depreciation,* a method of calculating depreciation in which the company determines the actual useful life span of an asset and then divides the purchase price of that asset by that life span. Each year depreciation expenses are recorded for each asset using this straight-line method. Although no cash is actually paid out, the total amount of depreciation is added back to the cash flow statement.

For tax purposes, companies can be more creative by writing off assets much more quickly and thus reducing their tax burdens at the same pace. One type of write-off — dealing with Section 179 of the Internal Revenue Code — enables a company to deduct the full cost of an asset during its first year of use. Other methods enable a company to depreciate assets sooner than the straight-line method, but not as soon as the 100 percent permitted by Section 179. How a company depreciates its assets can have a major impact on how much that company pays in taxes.

Although you won't know how a company depreciated its assets by looking at its cash flow statement, you will know the adjustment made for depreciation for cash purposes. Remember that depreciation is an expense that must be reported on an income statement . . . and not a cash outlay.

Financing activities

The financing activities section of a cash flow statement shows any common stock that was issued or repurchased during the period the report reflects, and any new loan activity. The financial activities section gives you a good idea whether the company is having trouble meeting its daily operating needs, and as a result, is seeking outside cash. You won't, however, find that new financing always is bad. A company may be in the process of a major growth initiative and may be financing that growth with cash flow from issuing new debt or common stock.

The bottom line: This section of the cash flow statement shows a company's total cash flow from financing activities. Table 6-11 compares three successive years of cash flow totals from financing activities at Home Depot and Lowe's.

Table 6-11	Total Cash Flow from Financing Activities (All Numbers in Thousands)		
Fiscal Year	*2003*	*2002*	*2001*
Home Depot	(2,165,000)	(173,000)	737,000
Lowe's	(64,000)	929,466	1,084,488

A negative cash flow from financing activities usually means that a company has either paid off debt or repurchased stock. A positive cash flow here usually means new stock or debt was issued. Obviously, many combinations of various financing activities can affect the bottom line, but the key for traders is to gain an understanding of why the change occurred and whether the company's reason for making the change was solid enough to improve its profit and growth picture.

Investment activity

This section of the cash flow statement shows you how a company spends its money for growing long-term assets, such as new buildings or other new acquisitions, including major purchases of property, equipment, and other companies. It also shows you a company's sales of major assets or equity investments in other companies. Tracking investment activities gives investors a good idea of what major long-term capital planning activities have taken place during the period.

The bottom line: This section shows a company's total cash flow from investing activities. Comparing three successive years of investment activities by Home Depot and Lowe's, Table 6-12 indicates that both companies had significant capital outlays that more than likely were for opening new stores. If you've followed the news about these two major home-improvement players, you know they're expanding the numbers of their stores around the country in a battle for market share.

Table 6-12	Total Cash Flow from Investing Activities (All Numbers in Thousands)		
Fiscal Year	*2003*	*2002*	*2001*
Home Depot	(2,934,000)	(3,466,000)	(3,530,000)
Lowe's	(2,578,000)	(2,199,334)	(2,249,661)

Scouring the Balance Sheet

The balance sheet gives you a snapshot of the company's assets and liabilities at a particular point in time. This differs from the income statement, which gives you operating results of a company during a particular period of time. A *balance sheet* has three sections, including

✔ An *assets* section that details everything the company owns

✔ A *liabilities* section that details the company's debt or any other claims on the company's assets made by debtors

✔ A *shareholder's equity* (also called owner's equity) section that lists all the claims made by owners or investors

The balance sheet gets its name because the total assets of the company are supposed to equal the total claims against it — total liabilities plus total equity.

Assets and liabilities are listed on the balance sheet according to their liquidity, or how quickly and easily they can be converted into cash. Assets or liabilities that are more liquid appear first on the list, while the ones that are increasingly more difficult to convert to cash — long-term assets or liabilities — appear later. The asset section is divided into current assets (the ones that are used up in one year) and long-term assets (the ones whose life spans are longer than a year), and so is the liabilities section — current liabilities and long-term liabilities.

Current assets include cash and other assets that can quickly and easily be converted into cash — marketable securities, money market mutual funds, accounts receivables, and inventories. Long-term assets include holdings such as buildings, land, and equipment. Similarly, on the liabilities side, current liabilities include any claims against assets that are due during the next 12 months, such as accounts payable and notes payable. Long-term liabilities are claims due in more than 12 months, such as mortgage or lease payables.

Equity accounts include outstanding (read remains on the market) preferred and/or common stocks and retained earnings. Retained earnings reflect the profits that are reinvested in the company rather than paid out to owners or shareholders.

Analyzing assets

In analyzing assets, two key ratios look at and measure how quickly a company is collecting on its accounts receivable — the *accounts receivable turnover* — and how quickly inventory is sold — the *inventory turnover*.

A two-step process is used to find the accounts receivable turnover. First you must find out how quickly a company turns its accounts receivables into cash using this formula:

Accounts receivable turnover = sales on account ÷ average accounts receivable balance

Then you need to find out how quickly a company collects on its accounts by dividing the accounts receivable turnover into 365 to find out the average number of days it takes to collect on accounts.

Testing for inventory turnover uses a similar two-step process. First you must find out how quickly inventory turns over during the year using this formula:

> Inventory turnover ratio = cost of goods sold ÷ average inventory balance

Then you need to divide the inventory turnover ratio into 365 to find out the average number of days it takes a company to turn over its inventory. Comparing these results for the companies you're considering can help you determine how well each company is handling the collection of its accounts receivable and the sale of its inventory. Obviously, the faster a company collects on accounts or sells its inventory, the better that company is doing in managing its assets.

Whenever you see accounts receivable rising rapidly, and the number of days to collect on those accounts also is rising, that signals a red flag that indicates cash problems likely lie ahead. Whenever you see inventory numbers rising, a company can be having a hard time selling its product, which also raises a red flag indicating problems ahead.

We're summarizing these two common ratios, so that you know what they mean whenever you see them mentioned by analysts. As a trader, you aren't likely to take the time to do these calculations yourself.

Looking at debt

When considering debt, or what a company owes, the two primary ratios you want to look at are the current ratio and acid or quick ratio. You can quickly calculate the *current ratio,* which tests whether a company can make its payments, by looking at the balance sheet and using this formula:

> Current ratio = current assets ÷ current liabilities

Again, like the other ratios in this chapter, you must compare the ratio of one company to that of other companies in the same industry. A current ratio that's lower than most other companies in the industry can indicate the company is having a problem paying its short-term debts, which, in turn, is a strong sign that bankruptcy may be just around the corner. A current ratio that's significantly higher can be a bad sign too, because it can mean the company isn't using its assets efficiently. For these reasons, traders like to see companies with current ratios that are close to the industry average.

Luckily, you won't have to calculate current ratios, because they're easily found on any Web site that includes fundamental statistics. Using Yahoo! Finance, we found that Home Depot's current ratio is 1.431 and Lowe's is 1.526.

The acid test, or quick ratio, is almost the same as the current ratio; however, the key difference is that inventory value amounts are subtracted from current assets before dividing that result by current liabilities. Many financial institutions take this extra step because inventories aren't as easy to convert to cash. The acid test ratio is calculated by:

Acid test ratio = (current assets − inventory) ÷ current liabilities

The acid test ratio is primarily of interest to financial institutions thinking about making a short-term loan to a company. They look for an acid test ratio of at least 1 to 1 before considering a company a good credit risk. Even though as a trader you're not likely to be in the business of making loans, a company that has problems getting short-term debt is likely to have problems meeting its short-term obligations in the near future. As the market recognizes the problem, the company's share price is likely to drop.

Reviewing goodwill

Goodwill is not a tangible asset but rather is usually collected through the years as companies are bought and sold. Goodwill reflects a competitive advantage, such as a strong brand or reputation. When one company buys another and pays more than the tangible assets are worth, the difference is added to the acquirer's balance sheet as goodwill. In other words, it's the premium in price that one company pays for another.

Determining Stock Valuations

By now the key question you're probably asking is, "How do I use all this data to decide how much I should pay for a stock?" Basically, the value of a stock is the amount buyers are willing to pay for the stock and the amount for which sellers are willing to sell the stock under current business conditions. The actual value of a stock shifts throughout the day and usually in a matter of seconds when the trading volume is high.

Fundamental analysis is one of the tools that investors and some traders use to analyze earnings, revenue growth, market share, and future business plans so they can determine the value of the stock and the price they're willing to pay for or sell it. Earnings and earnings growth are key factors and considered a part of fundamental analysis. Common ratios used to determine a stock's value include the price to earnings multiple, or P/E ratio; price to book multiple, or price/book ratio; return on assets (ROA); and return on equity (ROE). We talk more about how these ratios are calculated in the sections that follow.

After considering all this data, investors decide whether a company's stock is undervalued or overvalued. Although past performance is no guarantee about a company's or stock's future success, fundamental analysts believe collecting and analyzing the appropriate data enables investors to make more of an educated guess about a stock's value.

Earnings

Using the income statement, we've talked extensively about a company's earnings. Remember the three types of earnings figures to consider are

- ✔ **Gross profit,** which is calculated after considering the direct costs related to sales

- ✔ **Operating income,** which shows a company's profit after subtracting operating expenses

- ✔ **Net income,** which is the bottom-line earnings after all expenses, taxes, and interest are subtracted

When you encounter discussions about earnings figures, be certain that you know which types of earnings are being discussed for the stock you're eyeing. To be able to compare apples with apples, you must know that you're using the same type of earnings figures.

Earnings growth rate

The earnings growth rate, which shows how quickly the company is expected to grow, isn't something you'll calculate. What you will find in the fundamental analysis statistics for stocks are earnings growth rate projections made by industry analysts based on their analysis of a company's potential earnings. The earnings growth rate is included on all the Web sites that we mention in Chapter 4 that provide fundamental statistics. When looking for this data, be sure to check out the earnings growth rate potential at a number of those sites.

Continuing the comparison of Home Depot and Lowe's, Yahoo! Finance projected

- ✔ Home Depot's earnings growth rate at 20.4 percent

- ✔ Lowe's earnings growth rate at 43.8 percent

Clearly, at this point in time, analysts believed Lowe's was in a much better position to improve its earnings growth. Looking at another analyst's opinion on Morningstar.com, Lowe's growth rate was projected in the low 20 percent range. Morningstar's (which is a global investment research firm) analyst wrote on January 12, 2004: "Lowe's has produced some powerful results over the past five years. The company has been expanding rapidly; its store base has swelled from 500 units to more than 900 during the past five years. Along the way, sales increased an average of 20 percent per year, while net income surged 30 percent annually. These tremendous gains were the result of an ambitious, somewhat risky, and successful foray into Home Depot's HD prized regions." The analyst's fair value estimate for the stock is $56 per share.

Morningstar's analyst doesn't set a target earnings growth rate for Home Depot but expects average earnings to be about 10 percent per year with earnings growth being a bit higher. The key problem the analyst points out for Home Depot: "The biggest obstacle Home Depot faces is a deteriorating shopping experience at its aging stores. Merchandise is messy and hard to find at too many stores, and employee help is inconsistent. The result has been a dramatic slowdown in comparable-store sales growth, or comps (sales at stores open at least a year), from 10 percent in 1999, 4 percent in 2000, and 1 percent in 2001, to flat in 2002." His fair value estimate for the stock is $36 per share.

Eyeing the most fundamental data of all

If we were allowed to choose only one piece of fundamental data to guide our trading, we'd choose the earnings growth rate (you'll sometimes see this called the EPS Growth Rate — EPS stands for earnings per share). You can use it as a quick summary of a company's performance. Evaluating the entire financial condition of a company isn't necessary when its earnings aren't up to par.

We don't put much faith in analyst's estimates and don't use them when evaluating trading candidates. We're much more interested in actual earnings reported than we are in the analyst's estimates for future earnings. And we're interested only in companies whose earnings are growing and growing at a faster rate than most other companies. Those companies typically outperform the broad market.

Investor's Business Daily is an excellent source for EPS growth rate data. A proprietary ranking that shows which companies are growing earnings fastest is published in it.

As much as we like this tool, we don't follow the rankings blindly. (And we don't believe the good folks at IBD recommend that you do so, either.) IBD doesn't distinguish between companies that are earning more and companies that are losing less. That companies can and do turn from losing money to making money is a fact, and that situation can be lucrative for the knowledgeable trader. Call us old-fashioned, but we prefer companies that actually have a history of reporting real, positive earnings.

Just looking at the difference between earnings growth rate projections from Yahoo! Finance (based on projections from analysts at Multex, which was an investment and research information Web site now gobbled up by Reuters news services) and from Morningstar, you can see why researching information from more than one analyst is important when collecting fundamental data about a stock.

Figuring Your Ratios: Comparing One Company's Stock to Another

In this section, we show you how to calculate four key ratios — P/E, Price/Book, ROE, and ROA — but luckily you can find all these where fundamental statistics are reported (newspapers, Web sites, and so on — see Chapter 4 for more). Each of these ratios gives you just one more piece in the puzzle of determining how much you want to pay for a stock. By comparing each of the ratios for each of the companies you're considering, you can make a more educated case about the price you want to pay for any stock.

Price/earnings ratio

The *P/E ratio* is probably the one that's quoted more often in news stories. This ratio reflects a comparison of a stock's earnings with its share price. You calculate this ratio using this formula:

P/E ratio = stock price ÷ earnings per share

You'll probably find two types of P/E ratios for a stock. The *trailing P/E* is based on earnings reported in previous quarters, and the *forward P/E* is based on projected earnings. At Yahoo! Finance, the trailing P/E for Home Depot was 19.87, and its forward P/E, expectations as of February 2, 2005, was 17.37. Lowe's trailing P/E was 23.61, and its forward P/E, expectations as of January 31, 2005, was 18.81. Because the market is willing to pay more per dollar per earnings for Lowe's, its P/E ratio is higher. Historically, market analysts believed a P/E ratio of 10 to 15 was reasonable. Today, however, much higher P/Es are tolerated. When comparing companies, you can get a good idea of how the market values each stock by looking at its P/E ratio. While the P/E ratio is actually a percent, it is rarely stated that way. However, you will sometimes hear it called a price multiple because the P/E ratio represents how much you are paying for each dollar of a company's earnings.

Price/book ratio

The *price/book ratio* compares the market's valuation of a company to the value that the company shows on its financial statements. The higher the ratio, the more the market is willing to pay for a company above its hard assets, which include its buildings, inventory, accounts receivable, and other clearly measurable assets. Companies are more than their measurable assets. Customer loyalty, the value of their locations, and other intangible assets add value to a company. Investors looking to buy based on value rather than growth are more likely to check out the price/book ratio. Price/book ratios are calculated using this formula:

Price/book ratio = stock price ÷ (book value − total liabilities)

Lowe's price/book ratio at Yahoo! Finance was 4.23 and Home Depot's was 3.62. As we saw with the P/E ratio, the market is willing to pay a higher premium for Lowe's stock.

Return on assets

Return on assets (ROA) shows you how efficiently management uses the company's resources. ROA, however, doesn't show you how well the company is performing for its stockholders. To calculate return on assets, use this formula:

Return on assets = earnings after taxes ÷ total assets

Home Depot's ROA at Yahoo! Finance was 12.23 percent; Lowe's was 10.33 percent. Home Depot is doing a more efficient job using its resources based on those two ROA numbers.

Return on equity

Investors are more interested in *return on equity* (ROE), which measures how well a company is doing for its shareholders. This ratio measures how much profit management generates from resources provided by its shareholders. Investors look for companies with high ROEs that show signs of growth. You calculate ROE by using this formula:

Return on equity = earnings after taxes ÷ shareholder equity

Home Depot's ROE was 19.27 percent, and Lowe's was 20.22 percent.

Although Home Depot's ROA was higher, the ROEs show that Lowe's is doing a better job for its shareholders, which, again, is reflected in the price investors are willing to pay for its shares.

As a trader, you may not make your buy and sell decisions based on fundamental analysis, but collecting and having access to this information as part of your arsenal certainly helps you to make better and more informed stock choices. Knowing a company has strong fundamentals helps to back up what you're seeing in the technical analysis (see Part III). If you're trying to decide between two stocks whose technical charts are positive, you can use the fundamental analysis to tip the scale toward your best trading opportunity.

Chapter 7

Taking the Analyst Call

· ·

· ·

Stock analysts are supposed to be independent oracles who help mere mortal traders understand a company's financial future. Don't count on them, however, because they're not always looking to protect the small investor's pocketbook.

Scandals exposed by New York Attorney General Eliot Spitzer show how analysts recommended stocks to the public to help their companies land lucrative investment banking deals, while at the same time privately writing and sending e-mails calling those same stocks junk. Whenever you read recommendations from an analyst, you must determine whether that analyst is a buy-side analyst, sell-side analyst, or independent analyst before you ever consider using the information he or she is providing.

Analysts get much of their information from conference calls sponsored by companies when they report their earnings or make other key financial announcements. Today, individual investors are invited to listen in on more and more of these calls. You can find out a great deal about a company's prospects by listening in on analyst calls, but the language of these calls can be confusing. This chapter explains the types of analysts, their importance, and the language unique to what they do. We also introduce you to resources on the Internet that can make listening in on analyst calls easier.

Getting to Know Your Analysts

If you watch any of the financial news cable television stations, you've probably seen numerous industry analysts frequently touting certain stocks and panning others. Do you know who those analysts represent? Do you know whether they're independent analysts, buy-side analysts, or sell-side analysts? Before deciding whether to follow an analyst's recommendations, be sure that you understand who pays his or her salary and what's in it for him or her.

Buy-side analysts: You won't see them

You rarely come in contact with a buy-side analyst, because they work primarily for large institutional investment firms that manage mutual funds or private accounts. Their primary role is analyzing stocks that are bought by the firm for which they work and not necessarily the ones bought by individual investors. Their research rarely is available outside the firm that hired them. Buy-side analysts focus on whether an investment that's under consideration is a good match for the firm's investment strategy and portfolio. In fact, buy-side analysts frequently include information from sell-side analysts as part of their overall research on an investment.

Sell-side analysts: Watch for conflicts

When you read stock analyses from brokerage houses, you're more than likely reading information from sell-side analysts. These analysts work primarily for brokerage houses and other financial distribution sources where salespeople sell securities based on the analysts' recommendations.

The primary purpose of sell-side analysts is providing brokerage salespeople with information to help make sales. As long as the interests of the investor, the broker, and the brokerage house are the same, sell-side analyst's reports can be useful sources of information. A conflict arises, however, when sell-side analysts also are responsible for helping their brokerage houses win investment-banking business.

New York State AG Spitzer exposed why this conflict is a primary reason for all the scandals you've read about regarding star analysts, such as Henry Blodget of Merrill Lynch, whose e-mails privately called stocks "dogs," "toast," or "junk" at the same time he and his team were publicly recommending that their customers buy the same stocks. Why do this? Well, according to Spitzer's charges, Blodget's recommendations brought in $115 million in investment banking fees for Merrill Lynch, and Blodget took home $12 million in compensation.

Merrill Lynch was only the first to be exposed. Similar charges were raised against many other firms, including Morgan Stanley, Dean Witter, and Credit Suisse First Boston. Few firms that sell stocks and have an investment banking division avoided the scandal.

At one time in the distant past, analysts were separated from investment banks by what companies called a "Chinese Wall." Analysts' work supposedly was kept completely separate from deals that were being generated in a company's investment banking business. At some point, the lines between the two broke down and analysts actually were included in the process of generating deals for mergers, acquisitions, and new stock offerings. By writing glowing reports, analysts helped their companies sign more lucrative investment banking deals, all the while putting their small investors at great risk of losing all their money by buying the recommended stocks. When the market bubble burst in 2000, many of the stocks that were recommended because of these deals, particularly in the Internet, telecommunications, and other high tech industries, dropped to being worthless, and investors lost billions.

Merrill Lynch, in trying to settle their problems with Spitzer, agreed to publicly disclose its investment banking connections and list its clients. As of June 2002, Merrill Lynch began stating in all its research reports whether it received or will receive fees for investment banking services from any company that was followed by the Merrill Lynch analysts in the prior 12 months. Other companies followed Merrill Lynch's lead in settling their disputes with Spitzer.

The United States Securities and Exchange Commission (SEC) finally stepped into the fray in April 2002 and announced it was broadening the investigation into analysts' roles and was developing new regulations regarding analyst disclosure. The SEC ultimately endorsed rulemaking changes recommended by the New York Stock Exchange and the National Association of Securities Dealers, including

- ✔ Structural reforms that increase analysts' independence. These reforms include a prohibition on investment banking departments supervising analysts or approving research reports.

- ✔ A prohibition on tying analyst's compensation to specific investment banking transactions.

- ✔ A prohibition on offering favorable research to induce business for the firm.

- ✔ Increased disclosures of conflicts of interest in research reports and public appearances. These disclosures include information about business relationships with or ownership interests in companies that are the subjects of analysts' reports.

> ✔ Disclosure in research reports of data concerning a firm's ratings, such as the percentage of ratings issued in each of the buy, hold, and sell categories, and a price chart comparing the rated security's closing prices and the firm's rating or price targets over time.
>
> ✔ Restrictions on personal trading by analysts in securities of companies that they analyze and/or report on.

These rule changes should help investors identify conflicts of interest that can compromise the objectivity of the sell-side analyst's report. Pay close attention to the disclosures and the relationships between the brokerage houses and the companies that their analysts' reports cover. Take these connections into consideration when including their buy or sell recommendations in your plans for future stock transactions.

Independent analysts: Where are they?

You are probably wondering where these *independent analysts* — people who you can trust who don't have investment banking connections — really are. Although they do exist, most work for wealthy individuals or institutional investors and provide research for people who manage portfolios of much more than a million dollars and pay fees of at least $25,000 per year.

No one really knows exactly how many independent analysts are out there. Estimates range from 100 to several hundred, but their ranks surely will grow now that independent research will be a required part of selling to individual investors.

In addition to independent research that you probably see distributed by your brokerage house, as a small investor you can turn to some of the major investment research firms such as Morningstar (www.morningstar.com) and Standard & Poor's (www.standardandpoors.com). They offer services to individual investors through their publications and Internet sites at more reasonable fees than many of the small independent analyst firms. Nevertheless, you need to bear in mind that even these analysts are answering to the companies or wealthy individuals that pay the greatest share of their costs.

The Importance of Analysts

No matter which analyst's report you're reading, you must remember that the analyst's primary income is coming either from the brokerage house or the large institutional clients that he or she serves. Analysts rate stocks on whether you need to consider purchasing them, but no standardized rating system exists. The three most common breakdowns that you can expect to see are shown in Table 7-1.

Table 7-1	Common Stock Recommendations from Analysts	
Analysis by Company A	*Analysis by Company B*	*Analysis by Company C*
Buy	Strong Buy	Recommended List
Outperform	Buy	Trading Buy
Neutral	Hold	Market Outperformer
Underperform	Sell	Market Perform
Avoid		Market Underperformer

You can see from this table that you must understand how a company's analysts rate stocks for that company's recommendations to have any value. Company A's "Buy" recommendation is its highest, but Company B uses "Strong Buy" for its highest rating, and Company C uses "Recommended List" for its top choice. Merely seeing that a stock is recommended as a "Buy" by a particular analyst means little if you don't know which rating system is being used.

Unfortunately, when it comes to stock analysts, if the information is free, it's probably no better than that free lunch you're always looking to find. Someone has to pay the analyst, and if it isn't you, you must find out who is footing the bill before you use that advice to make decisions.

The best way to use analysts' reports is to think of them as just one tool in your bucket of trading tools. Analysts are one good way to find out about an industry or a stock, but they're not the final word about what you need to do. Only your own research using fundamental and technical analysis can help you make your investment decisions. We discuss fundamental analysis tools in Chapters 5 and 6 and technical analysis tools in Part III.

Tracking how a company's doing

Analysts are good resources for finding historical data about how a company or industry is doing. Their reports usually summarize at least five years of data and frequently provide a historical perspective for the industry and the company that goes back many more years. In addition, analysts make projections about the earnings potential of the company they're analyzing and indicate why they believe those projections by including information about new products being developed or currently being tested at various stages of market development.

These reports help you track how a company is doing so you can find the gems that may indicate when to expect a company to break out of a current trading trend. For example, if an analyst covering a pharmaceutical company mentions that a new drug is under consideration by the Food and Drug Administration, you may look for news stories about the status of that drug and monitor the stock for indications that drug approval may soon be announced. Watching the technical charts may help you jump in at just the right time and catch the upward trend as positive news is announced.

Providing access to analyst's calls

In addition to reading reports, you can track companies by listening in on *analyst calls*. Some calls are sponsored by the companies themselves to review annual or quarterly results, and others are sponsored by independent analysts.

Company-sponsored calls

Analyst calls sponsored by companies more often are earnings conference calls primarily for institutional investors and Wall Street analysts. They occur on either a quarterly, semiannual, or annual basis, and can be the richest sources of information concerning a company's fundamentals and future prospects.

Senior management, which usually includes the chief executive officer (CEO), president, and chief financial officer (CFO), talk about their financial reports and then answer questions during these calls. The calls sometimes are scheduled to coincide with announcements of major changes in a company's leadership or other breaking news about the company. After a formal statement, senior management answers questions from analysts. That's when you usually can get the most up-to-date information about the company and how management views its financial performance and projections. We discuss how to read between these lines and get the most out of these calls in the next section of this chapter.

Access to these calls used to be limited to professional analysts and institutional investors, but today more than 80 percent of companies that sponsor analyst calls open them to the media and individual investors, according to a survey conducted by the National Investor Relations Institute. This change primarily is credited to the SEC's new Fair Disclosure (FD) Regulation, which requires companies to make public all major announcements that can impact the value of the stock within 24 hours of informing any company outsiders. This rule helps level the information playing field for individual investors.

Analysts no longer can count on getting two or three days of lead time on major announcements, which heretofore helped them inform major investors about company news. Often that amount of lead time enabled analysts to recommend buy or sell decisions to their key clients, but that same practice hurt small investors and traders who weren't privy to the news. Some complain this new rule actually hurt the flow of information, because companies clammed up in private conversations with analysts, making it harder for the analysts to write their investigative reports. Since the regulation first took effect in 2000, the jury is still out on the effectiveness of the fair disclosure rule in leveling the information playing field and how much it will cost stock investors and traders.

Independent analyst–sponsored calls

Firms that provide independent analysis also sponsor calls primarily for their wealthy and institutional clients. During these calls, analysts often discuss breaking news about a company or an industry that they follow. Doing so gives their clients an opportunity to discuss key concerns directly with the analysts. Unless you're a client, opportunities for listening in on these calls are rare.

Seeking insider information

Investors began seeking insider information about companies long before the scandals that you now read about almost daily. In fact, one of the first stories ever told about trading on insider information involved the start-up of one of today's leading financial information services — Reuter's. Julius Reuter started his news service in response to the desire investors had for insider information and how it could impact stock prices. In 1849, Reuter used trained homing pigeons to fly information about closing stock prices from Europe's mainland across the English Channel to England, thus giving his subscribers a jump on news about a stock so they'd be able to react before other, less informed investors received the information. This story highlights a simple but powerful secret of investing: *Information is power.* Investors with privileged access to information hold a distinct advantage over other investors who don't have the same access.

Just to give you an idea of how insider information was used by analysts more recently, here are a couple of examples. In February 1999, during a tour of the headquarters of Compaq Computer Corporation, the company's treasurer told a group of big-time investors that he was concerned about softness in the software industry. Compaq shares dropped 14 percent before most individual investors ever discovered such a concern existed. In September 1999, executives at Apple Computer, Inc., called analysts to alert them that an earthquake in Taiwan disrupted the production of iBook and Powerbook notebook computers. The Apple execs wanted to warn analysts that the company would not meet its numbers for the quarter. The stock fell 7 percent in four days, and again, by the time most investors found out, it was too late. The new SEC fair disclosure rule prevents this kind of favored treatment for insiders.

Listening to Analyst Calls

Most company conference calls start with a welcome to all call participants that's followed by a discussion of the financial results being released or the purpose the company has designated for the call. After the CEO, president, and CFO make their statements, other key managers may comment on the results before the call is opened to questions from the listening audience.

The question-and-answer portion of the call usually is the most revealing and enables you to judge just how confident senior managers are with their reporting. The question-and-answer part of the call is when you're most likely to hear information that hasn't been revealed in press releases or formal annual or quarterly reports. Analysts and institutional investors usually are given the first shot at asking questions, meaning before other listeners, the press, or individual investors get their turn. Not all companies permit individual investors to ask questions. Even when you can't ask any questions, listening to responses to the questions posed by analysts, institutional investors, and the media still is worthwhile.

Be sure to listen closely to how the company's senior managers answer those questions. Chances are good that any question you may have will be answered during the question-and-answer period. If not, you can always write or call the company's investor relations division to get an answer to your specific question.

Understanding the analysts' language

Before ever listening to your first call, you must familiarize yourself with the language used during the calls. Most of the common terminology is discussed in Chapter 6, including earnings per share (EPS), EPS growth, net income, cash, and cash equivalents, but not other terms that are unique to the analyst call world. These include:

- *Hockey stick* — When companies say their revenues come in like a hockey stick, company officials are not exactly talking about getting hit with a puck. Instead, they're talking about the shape of a hockey stick. What they mean is that because most of their revenues are booked in the final days of the quarter, revenue charts take on the appearance of a hockey stick. Most companies, in fact, book revenues this way, because sales incentives are designed to encourage the sales force to close their contracts before the end of a quarter. Sales people have to meet their quotas, and companies that are planning purchases frequently delay those decisions until near the end of a quarter so they can negotiate the best deals when the sales people are most desperate to make a deal. You've probably done the same thing yourself when buying a car or other major item.

✔ *Lumpy* — Nope, the CEO isn't talking about poorly cooked oatmeal whenever he or she says revenues or orders were lumpy. This term means that sales were uneven during the quarter, with some weeks having low order rates and others having high order rates. The key is finding out why sales were lumpy and whether lumpy sales are normal for the company.

✔ *Run-rate* — Don't worry, you won't be asked how fast you can run a race. The run-rate is the way senior management talks about how its current performance can be projected over a period of time. For example, if the current quarter's revenues show a $1 million monthly run-rate, then you can expect annual revenues to total close to $12 million. This concept may work for companies with steady earnings but not for companies whose products primarily are seasonal. For example, if a retail company reports a run-rate of $1 million per month during the fourth quarter, which of course includes holiday sales, you won't expect that performance to be indicative of a full 12-month performance. You must be certain that you understand a company's revenue picture before counting on run-rate numbers.

If you hear other terminology that you don't understand, write it down so you can research it and thus be ready for the next time you hear it.

Developing your listening skills

In addition to *what* senior management is saying, you also need to listen to *how* they're saying it. If management is happy with the results, they'll probably be upbeat and talking about a rosy future for the company. On the other hand, if management isn't so happy with the results, the mood probably will be downbeat and apologetic as they try to explain why the company didn't perform as expected and, of course, make excuses for their failure to meet expectations.

Learn to listen and read between the company lines. Try to listen in on every earnings call. The first one you hear may not mean much unless you know how the results differ from previous reports and projections. Before that first call, you need to read analysts' reports and become as familiar as possible with the company's earnings history. After you've followed a certain company's calls for a while, the information presented will mean much more to you. Among the many indicators that may help you determine your trading activity are signs relating to earnings expectations, revenue growth, analysts' moods, company facts, and future projections.

Earnings expectations

Whether a company is meeting its own projections and analysts' expectations is the most important clue about how a company is doing and how the stock market will react to its periodic reports. If the company fails to meet expectations, the market will likely punish the stock by driving the price down, and that can point to a good trading opportunity. If you believe the setback is temporary and the company's long-term prospects look good, you may want to wait for the stock to bottom out before buying it. If you think failing periodic expectations is a sign of long-term bad news, and you hold a position in the stock, you may want to sell it as soon as possible. If you don't own it, you may want to consider shorting the stock. We discuss shorting a stock at length in Chapter 18.

Revenue growth

Listen for information that indicates whether revenue growth kept pace with earnings growth. This factor becomes even more critical whenever the economy slows down, because a company may play with or manipulate the numbers in a practice that's known as *window dressing,* or making sure that earnings meet expectations. However, manipulating revenues is much more difficult. Growth in revenues is the key to continued earnings growth in the future.

Although manipulating earnings may be difficult, we've seen companies do it successfully for a least a few quarters and, in some cases, a few years. A number of companies caught in recent Wall Street scandals successfully manipulated these numbers with creative methods of booking revenue. One account that you may want to watch for signs of revenue manipulation is accounts receivable. If receivables rise dramatically above historical balances, one of two things are likely — the company is having a hard time collecting on its accounts or the company is booking fictitious revenue. Manipulation may also be detected when a company reports revenue for items sold that actually is greater than the company has the capacity to produce.

You may notice analysts questioning revenue-growth figures in great detail. This examination by analysts can be a sign that they may suspect problems with the numbers. Detecting any of these signs while listening to a call can be a sign of possible trouble ahead, and you need to take a closer look before buying the stock or holding what you already have.

Analysts' mood

You can find out a great deal about how analysts are responding to a company's report by merely listening to the tone of their questions. Listening to how analysts are asking questions and what questions they are asking, you can judge whether the analysts are downbeat on company prospects, especially if they're asking increasingly probing questions. On the other hand, you may notice that analysts are upbeat and encouraging senior management to talk even more positively about their results and future plans. When you've followed the analysts' calls for a company during several quarters, recognizing whether the mood has changed won't be difficult. When analysts receive news positively, they often start their questions with some kind of congratulatory remark.

Be sure to jot down the names of analysts, especially the ones making positive remarks. The positive remarks from analysts with sell-side orientation may not be as good a sign as the positive remarks from buy-side analysts. If you don't know what type of analyst is commenting, research his or her affiliations and leanings after the call.

Buy-side analysts carry the most weight whenever they're indicating a positive reaction to the company's financial news. Many buy-side analysts who attend analyst calls already have a stake in the company, so they have a vested interest in putting a positive spin on the news. If they're positive, they'll likely revise their earnings estimates upward, which can be the first indication that they'll recommend additional buys and the stock may be getting ready to enter an upward trend. This positive spin can give you the first sign of a good trading opportunity, so watch your technical analysis for any signals of a potential breakout. We discuss more about breakouts in Chapter 10.

Just the facts, ma'am

The best way to judge whether senior management is confident in their reporting is determining how quickly they respond to questions. If senior managers are confident with their numbers, they respond to questions quickly, taking little time to think their responses through. If senior managers are unsure of their reports, they're more likely to take a good deal of time checking through their papers to answer even the simplest questions. You definitely need to think twice about buying or holding stock in a company whose management shows a lack of confidence in reporting their numbers.

The future

You're likely to get a good reading about how senior managers view the company's future prospects by listening to their vision for the company and whether the results actually demonstrate that they are fulfilling that vision. When managers are successfully fulfilling their vision, they clearly articulate their view of the company's future and how they plan to get there. Ask yourself whether management inspires you with its vision. If not, managers most likely are not inspiring their employees, which can be an early sign that the company is heading on a downward trend.

Employee satisfaction

Happy employees are a good sign that a company will be able to meet its future expectations. If, during the call, you hear that the company is having trouble attracting new employees or retaining its existing staff, you may be looking at a sign of trouble on the horizon. High employee turnover is bad for future growth, and so is having trouble finding and recruiting qualified employees.

Analyst conference calls are best used as a research tool and not for taking an immediate action based solely on the information you gather from them. You need to consider them as just one more way of gaining more knowledge about a stock that you're thinking about buying, or tracking stocks after you've already bought them. Day traders and swing traders sometimes use the information from analyst calls to trade after hours, but such trades can be highly risky. We talk more about these two trading strategies in Chapters 16 and 17.

Locating Company Calls

Many companies list information about their upcoming earnings reports and analyst calls on their company Web sites, while others simply post an audio version after the event. Some companies offer their investors a service that alerts them to upcoming events. If these services are not available for the companies you plan to follow, your best way of tracking upcoming calls is through one of two online sites — VCall (www.vcall.com) and Best Calls (www.bestcalls.com).

VCall is the leading Webcaster for official investor relations events. Many companies use its services to run their events online. This Web site offers you free access to live and archived corporate communications. In addition to the calls, you can find copies of financial information released by the company. VCall also enables you to set up e-mail alerts for the companies you track that are served by VCall.

Best Calls is the leading resource site for locating earnings conferences on the Internet. Although VCall is the leading provider for companies that play host to calls, the only company calls that are listed on VCall's site are for companies that use its services. Best Calls, on the other hand, is the largest single source for tracking analyst call schedules with links to the location for these calls and access to archived calls. Thousands of companies list their conferences and analyst calls on this site, and you can set up an e-mail alert for any company you want to follow. Best Call charges membership fees to access the entire site and fees for transcripts of older calls.

Identifying Trends in the Stock Analyst Community

The new regulatory climate in Washington now drives changes in the stock analyst community following disclosures of the abuses exposed after the stock bubble that ended in 2000. The Financial Disclosure Regulation of 2001

(Regulation FD) controls the flow of information between companies and analysts and ultimately what information makes its way to you as an outside investor or trader.

Some traders believe that the new restrictions that ban selective disclosure to friendly analysts or key investors actually hurt the flow of information to the general public. Regulation FD requires that any information disclosed to analysts or key investors that can affect the value of the company must be disclosed to the general public within 24 hours, even if the information wasn't part of a planned report.

The preference is for making announcements about material information at the same time for everyone, but sometimes during meetings with an analyst or institutional investor information is shared inadvertently. For example, if analysts find out information during a company tour, the company then is required to put out a press release disclosing the same information to the general public. Some analysts believe this is making the preparation of their reports much more difficult than it needs to be.

Regulation FD, however, halted some commonplace industry practices, including closed meetings with analysts and institutional investors. Lawyers for many companies warn senior managers to be careful about responding to calls from individual analysts. Some companies require that any contact with analysts first be evaluated and approved through their legal advisors.

Regulations also impact *roadshows,* which are marketing tours that introduce a company's new securities offerings. The SEC permits these events but gives clear guidance that they now need to be more like oral offers that are designed to avoid the prohibition against written or broadcast offers made outside the official prospectus of the offering. The SEC believes these roadshows are best conducted in the open to all investors and has voiced objections to having two separate roadshows, one for institutional investors and another, more sanitized version, for retail investors. Some legal experts also advise companies to be careful about whether they include outside analysts, those not employed by the underwriter of the offering, as part of the roadshow. Including outside analysts, some believe, can be viewed as selective disclosure, which violates Regulation FD.

The biggest regulatory changes you'll see as an individual investor or trader relate to disclosures that must be made in research reports, including a requirement that securities firms must disclose any compensation they receive for investment banking services they provide during the three months following the public offering for a covered company. In addition, firms that are members of the New York Stock Exchange or the National Association of Securities Dealers must disclose when they stop coverage of a public company. Many times this type of news generates unfavorable publicity for the company and can result in a drop in stock prices. In addition to these big disclosures, analysts' research reports now must include information about the relationships between the analysts, underwriters, and stock issuer.

Operating in this type of fish bowl may make companies and analysts nervous, but it nevertheless should level the playing field for individual investors. Look carefully for these disclosures as you read analysts' reports and take advantage of your newfound access to information by attending analysts' earnings conferences and being part of the insider pool rather than a passive outsider waiting to be fed information by the financial media or professional analysts.

Part III
Reading the Charts: The Basics of Technical Analysis

The 5th Wave   By Rich Tennant

"OUR GOAL IS TO MAXIMIZE YOUR UPSIDE AND MINIMIZE YOUR DOWNSIDE WHILE WE PROTECT OUR OWN BACKSIDE."

In this part . . .

You discover how to read and interpret stock price charts as we describe the virtues and usefulness together with the weaknesses of chart analysis. We cover the basics of constructing a stock price chart, and then delve into identifying distinct patterns that lead to profitable trades. In addition, we talk about trends, how to spot them, and why they're so important, and we explore how computer-generated indicators and oscillators can enhance your analytical skills.

Chapter 8

Tarot Cards, Tea Leaves, and Trend Charts: Does Technical Analysis Work?

In This Chapter

▶ Revealing truth beyond the mythology

▶ Understanding technical analysis procedures

▶ Deciding whether it works

▶ Determining whether technical analysis is for telling fortunes or trading

*E*veryone knows that foretelling the future is a tough thing to do, especially when money is involved. Whether your prognosticating tool of choice is a Ouija board or a Magic 8 Ball, knowing exactly what the future holds is difficult.

Investors and traders always are looking for an edge in forecasting stock prices to improve their trading results. The method of choice for many investors is *fundamental analysis,* which we describe in Chapters 5, 6, and 7. For traders, on the other hand, *technical analysis,* as described in Chapters 9, 10, and 11, is the way to go.

Although some overlap exists between fundamental and technical analyses, you find dyed-in-the-wool, true believers in both camps, and they argue that their way is best, even going so far as to say the opposite way is worse than useless. For our money, the truth lies somewhere in between these two extremes.

Understanding the Mythology

A *technician* — that's someone who reads charts — believes that you can use price charts and market statistics to develop a profitable trading plan. Some technicians even say that price charts foretell where a stock's price is heading simply by showing where it has been. Detractors argue that technical analysis is merely another name for fortune telling, a charlatan's moniker that avoids entanglements with local authorities and the Federal Trade Commission (FTC).

Had Miss Cleo, that recently-deposed temptress of tarot cards, made her living foretelling stock prices, she might still be in business. Likewise, had she lived in earlier times, she might have been revered by the masses and the high priests for her fortune-telling skills instead of being scorned as a fraud.

In ancient Rome, tracking the stars, the planets, and the behavior of birds was popular, and so was inspecting the entrails of sacrificial animals. Although a bit gruesome, the *haruspex* — that's the expert gut checker — was highly regarded. As an *augur,* an official diviner in ancient Rome, Miss Cleo would have been consulted to foretell events and reveal the gods' reactions to any future courses of action. She would have been in the limelight and riding as high as she was right before the FTC brought her into check. Although it may have been bogus, Miss Cleo couldn't have hoped for more.

In spite of Miss Cleo's fate, fortune-tellers still ply their trade. Are the most successful the ones who divine future price movements by reading the entrails of stock price charts? That's what a cadre of academic financial experts thinks. To the uninitiated, price charts are merely squiggles and lines on a page. The academics apparently believe, just like augurs of old, that technicians track those squiggles and lines as a means of predicting price behavior and attempting to divine a particular stock's future course of action.

Thankfully, the market entrails viewed by technicians aren't as gruesome as the ones analyzed by the haruspex. Nevertheless, academics and fundamental analysts often regard technicians in the same light as *haruspices* — little more than an expert gut checker — but the analogy isn't really valid. Technical analysis is not a forecasting tool. It is a trading tool and nothing more.

Understanding the Methodology

Although technicians try to anticipate the future and make trading plans based on price-chart squiggles, technical analysis is a far cry from reading tea leaves or tarot cards. Instead of predicting the future, technical analysis is used to identify events that are likely to occur, and to make trading plans in case they do, and alternative plans in case they do not. Technicians use a logical framework to identify price trends, turning points, trading ranges, and breakouts. These important trading concepts are covered in Chapters 9 through 11.

To understand the technical analyst's methods, you need to be familiar with these technical analysis concepts:

- ✔ Everything is in the price.
- ✔ Price movements are not (always) random.
- ✔ Price changes are caused by an imbalance between supply and demand.

Finding everything in the price

The stock market is so efficient that everything that's currently known about a company is priced into its stock. In other words, the current price reflects the combined wisdom of everyone in the market, including corporate insiders, pension funds, mutual funds, individual investors, stock analysts, fundamental analysts, technicians, and you.

Technical analysis provides a synopsis of all the fundamental and psychological factors that affect the price of a stock. Although we personally think putting all your eggs in the price basket is taking the point to an extreme, that's why some technicians don't even try to evaluate the fundamentals. Why bother trying to outsmart the smartest when everything's in the price?

The technician's understanding of why a stock's price moves is not important. Technicians don't care whether the price movement was caused by the most recent analyst's report or by the flapping of a butterfly's wings somewhere in China. They are concerned only with

- ✔ What the price is now
- ✔ What the price history is

Technical analysts examine current prices relative to the histories of price movements to understand and plan for what may happen next. Fundamental analysts ask why, trying to understand what piece of news causes a particular rise in price or what bit of insider knowledge causes a sell off. Technicians try to see everything the price represents and base their trades only on what they see.

You can't know what causes every ripple in the price continuum. So why try?

Price movements are not always random

Sometimes, prices move higher. Sometimes, they move lower. And sometimes, prices move back and forth within a tight trading range. When prices move higher or lower, we say prices are trending. The trading-range periods between trending periods often appear to be random price movements, and at times, they may actually be random. But when you zoom in to view the price movements within those seemingly random trading-range periods, you will find the trading range is made up of many mini trends. The closer you look, the less random these price movements appear, and that is the crux of technical analysis. These are important concepts for trading and are covered more fully in Chapter 10.

At its simplest, technical analysis identifies the periods of time during which trends occur. In general, technicians want to base their trades on trending markets. The idea is determining when trends are beginning and when they're ending. But which trend? Are you the type of trader who is interested in the little mini trends that make up a trading range? Or are you most interested in trading longer lasting trends?

The trick to technical trading, therefore, is identifying a stock's price trend within the time frame during which you want to buy or sell it. Depending on the length of time you plan to hold the stock, you want to base your trades on analyses done in the corresponding time frame. We are primarily concerned with long-lasting trends that span many weeks or months. In that case, you'll want to analyze charts showing daily and weekly prices. If, instead, you plan to hold your stock for no more than a few hours or a few days, you'll want to analyze charts showing intra-day prices. When looking at intra-day price charts, you will see many examples of mini trends and trading ranges. However, if you're buying a stock and holding your position for weeks or months, those mini intraday trends and trading ranges are meaningless. These concepts are discussed more fully in Chapter 9.

Balancing supply and demand

If you've ever watched the nightly business news, you've probably heard reporters claim that stocks rose because more buyers were looking for stocks than sellers were willing to part with them. At some level, that's hogwash. Even novice investors realize that every trade must have a buyer and a seller.

What the reporter really means is that the supply and demand were out of balance and that price is a function of supply and demand. In macroeconomics, this concept is illustrated using a freely traded commodity like wheat.

When farmers grow more wheat than bakers need, the price of wheat falls. When bakers need more wheat than farmers grew, bakers bid higher prices to get the wheat they need.

In many ways, the price of a stock works just like the price of wheat. When buyers want to buy more shares of a stock than sellers are willing or able to sell, buyers bid the stock price higher until they find sellers willing to part with their shares. Conversely, when sellers can't find enough buyers, they offer their shares at lower and lower prices until enough buyers can be found.

Changes in a company's business plan, a new competitor, anything really, can throw the balance between supply and demand out of whack. Realizing that imbalances cause prices to move — and not the news itself — is the point where technical analysis is concerned.

Understanding where you've been

Technicians examine price history, trading volume, and additional market statistics to evaluate the balance between supply and demand. The conceptual framework is easy to understand. As long as prices are rising, demand exceeds supply, and buyers are more interested in buying than sellers are in selling. The reverse is equally true. When prices are falling, supply exceeds demand, and sellers are more interested in selling than buyers are in buying. When a stock trades within a tight range of prices, a balance between supply and demand has been achieved. This situation is evident on the price chart when a stock trades within a trading range. Examples are shown in Chapter 9.

Technical analysis helps identify these kinds of scenarios. Technicians examine charts in search of the price levels where buying pressure stops a stock's price from falling further or where selling pressure squashes a rally.

Here's a hypothetical scenario to illustrate that point. A high-profile investment advisor issues a recommendation to buy shares of XYZ, which closed at $18.50 the day before and has traded in a tight price range of $17 to $18.75 during the past four months. The recommendation to buy is in effect only if the stock trades for less than $19 a share. The idea is not necessarily to buy the instant that a recommendation is made, but rather to buy at a good price.

Taking the hypothetical example a step further, say that the investment advisor has a wide following. Invariably, the recommendation is quickly followed by a surge in the volume of buyers purchasing shares of XYZ that ultimately pushes the price of the stock to $21.

Buying surges based on these kinds of recommendations have a tendency to stall out and return to the buy-under price (in this case $19) after all the early buyers make their trades. Patient subscribers of this advisor have seen this movie many times before, so they wait for a pullback, and place either a limit order or a buy-stop order near the $19 price. (Limit and buy-stop orders are discussed in Chapter 2.) Enough patient subscribers usually are in the market for the stock to keep its price from falling further.

Now imagine that you're watching this stock without knowledge of the investment advisor's recommendation. The steps that you'd likely see the price of XYZ shares take during the course of a week or two include

1. **XYZ breaking out of its trading range and rallying on high volume**

2. **XYZ pulling back on low volume**

3. **High-volume buying of XYZ resuming as the price falls near $19**

This type of market activity is what technicians wait for. You will see this scenario play out over and over again, both in individual stocks and in the general market indexes. Chapter 9 covers this technique in more detail, but for now, know that it is a textbook example of a *trading-range breakout* defined by:

✔ A high-volume breakout after a long period of range-bound trading

✔ A low-volume pullback

✔ High-volume rally to new highs

If you were interested in this stock, you may have taken a position. In fact, given this setup, the three logical places where a technician takes a position are

✔ **At the breakout:** Buy as soon as the stock trades through the resistance at the upper end of the trading range.

✔ **At the pullback:** Buy immediately as the stock begins trading higher after the low-volume pullback.

✔ **At the double top:** When the stock retraces the move from the pullback to its high price, it's called a *double top*. Buy when the stock makes a new high for the move.

Of these three alternatives, our favorite is the middle one, because buying at the pullback is a relatively low-risk, high-reward trade. Our least favorite is the last one, trading the double top as the stock makes a new high, because it is the riskiest of the three alternatives. Both the breakout and the pullback trades are covered in much more detail, including example charts, in Chapter 9.

As long as technical analysis helps you get a good entry price on your trade and keep your losses small, you'll have a powerful trading tool at your disposal.

Understanding where you're headed

Technical analysis helps you find out where in the ups and downs of the market buyers took action in the past. If you have a hint where buyers have stepped in before, you can reasonably expect that they will do so again in the future. When they do as you expect, you need to be able to trade on that information profitably.

If they don't do as you expect, you may have to bust your trade, and yet you've still discovered a great deal of valuable information. You hope that the price you pay for that knowledge isn't too great, but you nevertheless know more now than you did before. You know that the last wave of buying exhausts demand, and thus you need to begin looking for further evidence of a reversal.

You don't have to adhere to arguments that technical analysis is a good forecasting tool merely to recognize that it's a useful trading tool.

Answering the Detractors

A few arguments against technical analysis actually make some sense, but an entire category of lame complaints also exists. For example, some people lamely argue that no technicians have been successful over the long run and that no technician has mustered the stature or success of illustrious market moguls like Warren Buffet, Benjamin Graham, or Peter Lynch.

As if to further this argument, they point to some infamous technician who blew up his portfolio in a spectacular fashion. Then a few years later, they harp on another well-known technician who made a boneheaded call, and then it happened again, and therefore, technical analysis is useless.

The impulse to counter these arguments with a list of high-profile fundamental analysts who also blew client portfolios, however, is misguided. Even a litany of disasters wouldn't disprove the usefulness of fundamental analysis any more than a list of high-profile successes proves that fundamental analysis is the only way to make money in stocks. Why, then, should anyone accept that either proves technical analysis is useless?

In fact, many successful technicians have long, profitable trading careers. While most toil in self-imposed obscurity, some are prominent and outspoken. For example, John W. Henry, who owns the Boston Red Sox, made his fortune as a trend-following technician. Additional examples include Ed Seykota, a trader with 35 years experience and one of the original *Market Wizards,* and Bill Dunn of Dunn Capital Management, Inc. This is just a tiny sample of the many successful independent traders and fund managers who employ technical analysis tools to make trading decisions.

A related argument about a chart-reading challenge that no technician ever has attempted (or would even consider) works like this: The technical analyst is given one half of a price chart with all identifying information removed. From that information, the technician is supposed to tell whether the stock's price was higher or lower at any point in the second half of the chart.

Of course, nobody ever claims the prize for having accomplished this feat, and that, therefore, is supposed to be proof that no technician ever has enough confidence in technical analysis to even try. Accomplished technicians aren't any better at telling the future than a haruspex or tarot-card reader — and neither, for that matter, are fundamental analysts. Technical analysis is not fortune-telling, it's simply a trading tool.

Walking randomly

The *Random Walk Theory* has nothing to do with hiking without a map, but instead, is an academic theory that says the stock prices are completely random. What happened to a stock yesterday has nothing to do with what happens to its price tomorrow.

Furthermore, this theory claims that the market is so efficient that consistently outperforming broad-based market indexes is impossible. In other words, any edge that you may gain from fundamental analysis, technical analysis, or tea leaves is useless and expensive. After all, transaction costs far outweigh any performance improvement that your analysis provides.

Armed with computer models and reams of study results, academic experts cling to these efficient-market hypotheses as gospel. Several challenges oppose their argument. No less an authority than the Federal Reserve Bank of New York published a study showing that using support and resistance levels (see Chapter 9) improved trading results for several firms. Additionally, articles published in the *Journal of Finance* suggest that trading based on moving averages and head and shoulder reversal patterns outperformed the market averages. Reversal patterns are discussed in Chapter 9, and moving averages are discussed in Chapter 11.

So do you think this is proof that technical analysis is effective all the time? Of course not. But it casts doubt about the validity of the Random Walk Theory, especially the part that technical analysis cannot be used to consistently improve results compared to the market averages.

Debating these arguments to a logical conclusion is nearly impossible. Even when you use technical analysis successfully, random walkers claim your performance is the result of random chance — nothing more than good luck. Don't believe them. Instead, believe that luck favors the prepared mind.

Trading signals known to all

Anyone who cares to look can see exactly the same patterns and has access to the same indicators as every other trader. Nothing is new under the sun — or in the markets.

While some traders create proprietary indicators to gain a trading edge, many more use well-known off-the-shelf trading tools. The patterns and indicators described in Chapters 9, 10, and 11 are all well-known. Some are freely available on the Internet for anyone to use. Thus, if everyone sees the same thing, how can you use those trading signals profitably? The question is perfectly legitimate.

Although everyone sees the same patterns and the same indicators, this equality is a strength rather than a weakness. Technical analysis gives you insight into what future actions you can expect from your fellow market participants. With practice, you can use that information to construct a consistently profitable trading plan.

After you become familiar with traditional patterns and indicators, you can incorporate your experience and market knowledge into your trading plans and thus come to an understanding about when to use specific tools and when results are meaningless. From these plans, you can find out when a trading signal works and when it fails. You can make trades based on indicators and patterns that help and ignore the rest.

Many widely known indicators and trading patterns exist, but personally, we use only a handful of the simplest ones. Your results will differ from mine. You may trade in a different time frame than we do, or you may choose a different set of tools altogether. As long as your tools improve your trading, continue using them.

Telling Fortunes or Planning Trades

Cutting to the chase, you probably guessed by now that you're never going to foretell the future with technical analysis. Technical analysis, instead, is simply a useful trading tool.

Successful trading does not mean that you have to be right all the time or even half the time. You don't have to tell the future. Technical analysis is an excellent tool for managing your money, controlling your losses, and enabling your profits to run (see Chapter 12 for more money management information).

Even people who base their trades on fundamental factors can use chart analysis to help them time market entry and exit points and gauge price volatility and risk. Using technical analysis successfully means

✔ Being patient

✔ Finding out how to identify and use a small number of patterns and indicators

✔ Becoming proficient at finding these patterns and profitably trading on them

✔ Adding methodically to your tool kit to improve your trading results

Remember that no method is foolproof. Nothing ever ensures successful trades 100 percent of the time. But technical analysis is an excellent tool for improving your trading results.

Chapter 9

Reading Bar Charts Is Easy (Really)

• •

In This Chapter

▶ Creating a bar chart

▶ Deciphering simple visual patterns

▶ Distinguishing between trends and trading ranges

▶ Pinpointing transitions from trading range to trend

• •

*S*tock charts come in many flavors. Some prominent ones include point-and-figure charts, candlestick charts, and the ever-popular bar charts, which are used throughout this book.

Bar charts are easy to create, interpret, and maintain. Furthermore, charting tools and analysis techniques for bar charts apply to stocks, bonds, options, indexes, and futures, and are applicable across any time frame in which you may want to trade. In addition, most chart patterns work for *long* (buy first, sell later) and *short* (sell first, buy later) *trades.*

This chapter shows you how to draw price charts for a single stock, or for an index such as the S&P 500 or NASDAQ Composite, and recognize simple single-day trading patterns. In addition, you find out how to identify trends and trading ranges and how to look for key transition points that often lead to good trading opportunities. Charting is a visual methodology, so you'll find many example charts used throughout this chapter. Examine them carefully. You'll want to quickly identify the patterns we describe here when evaluating charts for your own trading.

Creating a Price Chart

Traders used to create their charts by hand. Today, however, many charting alternatives and options are available, including easy-to-use computer software and easily accessible Internet sites, both of which are discussed in Chapter 4. You may, of course, still want to create charts by hand; that's something we encourage you to do — at least for a little while. Making your own charts is easy, a great way to discover charting concepts, and an excellent way of getting a feel for the markets.

A chart of stock prices shares characteristics with other charts with which you're probably familiar. These kinds of charts typically are made up of two axes; the *horizontal axis* represents time, and the *vertical axis* represents price. One unusual feature of a stock chart is that its vertical axis, the price axis, usually is shown on the right, as in Figure 9-1. The most current prices are shown on the right-hand side of the chart, and so are the newest trading signals. You always trade while those signals are on the right edge of a chart, so having the price axis closest to the most crucial part of the chart makes sense.

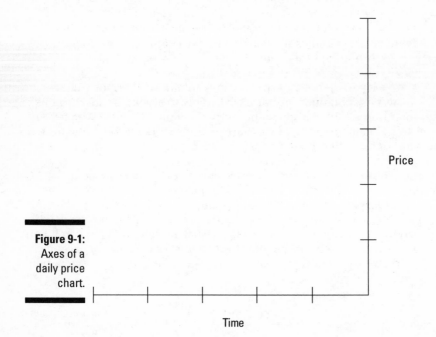

Figure 9-1:
Axes of a
daily price
chart.

Price

Time

Creating a single price bar

Regardless of whether your chart is an *intraday chart* (showing fluctuations throughout a trading day) or a chart of daily or weekly prices, the format of the price bar is the same. Each bar represents the results for a single trading period. On a chart that provides daily information, for example, each bar represents the results for a single trading day.

Most stock-price bar charts show four important prices on each bar:

 ✔ **Open:** The price recorded for the first trade

 ✔ **High:** The highest price trade during the trading period

 ✔ **Low:** The lowest price trade during the trading period

 ✔ **Close:** The price recorded for the last trade

By convention, a daily bar chart shows trades for the standard New York Stock Exchange (NYSE) trading day — from 9:30 a.m. to 4:00 p.m. — but some charting packages include optional after-hours results (prices from trades that occur after the market closes) as part of each daily bar. Likewise, some charting packages omit the opening prices on intraday charts. The opening price on an intraday chart (almost) always is the same as the closing price for the previous bar, so omitting it is of little consequence. However, omitting the opening price on daily, weekly, and monthly charts diminishes the usefulness of the chart, so avoid charts that don't provide all four prices.

Figure 9-2 shows a single price bar. The full range of prices traded throughout the period is shown by the vertical bar. The opening price is shown as a small line on the left-hand side of the bar, and the closing price is shown by a similar line on the right-hand side of the bar.

Figure 9-2:
A single
price bar.

This identical format is used for all time periods. For example, an intraday chart may use 1-minute bars, where each bar spans all the prices for your stock that occur during trades over a full minute. Common time frames for stock price charts are:

- **1-minute bars** — Each bar represents one minute of trading.
- **5-minute bars** — Each bar represents five minutes of trading.
- **10-minute bars** — Each bar represents ten minutes of trading.
- **15-minute bars** — Each bar represents 15 minutes of trading.
- **60-minute bars** — Each bar represents 60 minutes of trading.
- **Daily bars** — Each bar represents one full day of trading.
- **Weekly bars** — Each bar represents one week of trading.
- **Monthly bars** — Each bar represents one full month of trading.

In our own trading, we typically monitor weekly charts, daily charts, and one of two intraday charts, either 60-minute bars for stocks or 5-minute bars for indexes. We cover our chart selection and methodology more fully in Chapter 13.

Measuring volume

In addition to prices, bar charts often show the volume, or the number of shares traded during the given time period represented by each bar. On a daily chart, trading volume shows the total number of shares traded throughout the day. By convention, the volume is shown as a separate bar graph and usually is shown directly underneath the price chart. Figure 9-3 shows an example.

Volume (the number of shares sold) is used as a confirming indicator. In other words, if a price bar shows bullish activity (which is discussed later in the section on "Identifying Simple Single-Day Patterns"), that bullishness is confirmed by a higher-than-average trading volume. However, that bullishness may diminish if trading volume is lower than average.

Volume also is used to gauge institutional participation in a stock. Significant trading volume often signals that large institutional investors — mutual funds, pension funds, insurance companies, and others — are placing orders to buy or sell a stock. When prices rise and volume is strong, you usually can infer that institutions are accumulating positions in the stock. The reverse also is true. When prices fall and trading volume is high, large institutions may be liquidating positions, which is considered a bearish development.

Low-volume price changes are less meaningful, at least from a technical perspective, than high-volume changes. That's why technicians say, "Volume confirms price."

Price Bars

Figure 9-3:
A daily chart
shows price
and volume.

Volume

Coloring charts

Displaying price and volume bars in color is common on charts. When using color, be sure to use contrasting colors so you can distinguish up days from down days. One prominent charting package, for example, defaults to green for up days and red for down days. A prominent Internet site defaults to black for up days and red for down. Most charting services enable you to configure colors to suit yourself.

Identifying Simple Single-Day Patterns

The goal of chart reading is determining whether buyers or sellers are in control of the price. In a bull market, stockowners may be willing to sell, but only if they can coax higher prices from buyers. In a bear market, buyers are able to negotiate a better price when sellers are more eager to sell than buyers are to buy.

You're trying to infer the market's underlying psychology by looking at the history of price movements. Inferring that as prices rise, buyers are more interested in buying than sellers are in selling is a fair observation. In a rising market, buyers must continue bidding prices higher to convince sellers to part with their shares. Rising prices attract additional buyers, who must continue to bid prices higher to convince even more reluctant sellers to part with their shares.

Single-bar patterns

The most bullish thing that a market can do is go higher. Although technicians typically view each bar within the context of its neighboring bars, each individual bar has something to tell the careful observer. Figure 9-4, for example, shows a *bullish single-bar pattern.*

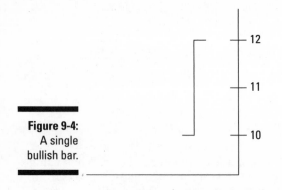

Figure 9-4:
A single
bullish bar.

In the example in the figure, buyers bid prices higher throughout the day. The opening price of $10 also is the lowest trade for the day. The daily range shown on the bar is $2, and the stock closed at $12, the high for the day.

If you're keeping score (and as a trader, believe me, you are), the bulls gained ground and clearly are ahead for the day. Bears holding short positions were hurt where it hurts the most — in their pocketbooks. A trader takes a short position by borrowing shares of stock and selling them in the hope of making money if the stock price falls. This trade loses money if the stock's price rises. The mechanics of selling short are described in Chapter 14. The example in Figure 9-4 shows the stock opening at the extreme low and closing at its extreme high, but the pattern nevertheless is just as bullish when the stock opens near its low and then closes near its high.

Figure 9-5 shows a *bearish single-bar pattern.* The stock opened at $11.75; traded to $12, the high for the day; fell to $10, the daily low; and then closed at $10.25. The stock doesn't have to close at the low for the day for it to be bearish. Closing near the low is good enough.

Figure 9-5:
A single bearish bar.

These single-day patterns are helpful to the trader who's trying to understand the underpinnings of the markets. Whether these patterns present a trading opportunity depends on the stock's recent history and whether its trading volume confirms the pattern (see the earlier section on "Measuring volume"). We give you several examples later in this chapter, in the section "Searching for Transitions," where a bullish single-bar pattern triggers a buy signal.

Reversal patterns

A *reversal bar* is another single-bar pattern that shows a stock opening and closing at the same end of its trading range. Figure 9-6 shows a *bullish single-bar reversal* where the stock opens at the high, trades lower through part of the day, and by the close, the stock regains all its losses and closes at its highest intraday price.

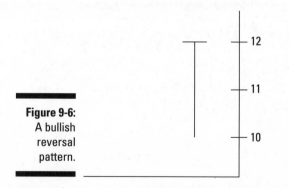

Figure 9-6:
A bullish reversal pattern.

During the early part of the trading sessions depicted in the bullish reversal pattern, buyers were willing to buy only if sellers lowered their offering (asking) prices. By the end of the day, the tide had turned and roles were reversed, with sellers willing to sell but only at higher prices. This situation is another win for the bulls, because they were able to stop the price slide and recover all the intraday losses.

Figure 9-7 shows a *bearish reversal pattern.* In this case, the stock opens at $10.25, rallies during the day to $12, but closes at the $10 low.

Figure 9-7:
A bearish
reversal
pattern.

Reversal patterns often represent a powerful single-bar trading pattern. Whenever a bullish reversal bar is preceded by several periods of falling prices, for example, its pattern represents a buying opportunity. On the other hand, when a bearish reversal bar is preceded by a rising trend, it may be a signal to close a long position or initiate a short position. Selling short is described in Chapter 14.

Not all price bars, however, present specific trading opportunities. Some bars are neutral by themselves, but add to a stock's history when viewed in context. Through charts, you can use a stock's visual historical record to develop your trading plan, as you'll see in the following sections.

Identifying Trends and Trading Ranges

Technical analysis helps you identify trends, discovering when one begins and when it ends. Our style of trading, *position trading,* looks for the persistent trend, a trend that lasts for at least several weeks to several months, perhaps even longer. Day traders and swing traders who buy and sell in the shortest of terms also look for trends to trade. In fact, the distinction between a day trader, a swing trader, and a position trader is the length of the trend that each is hoping to find. Swing trading and day trading are discussed in Chapters 16 and 17, respectively.

Following trends is an effective trading strategy, especially for new traders. To follow trends successfully, you first need to identify and distinguish between stocks and markets exhibiting trends and their counterparts, trading within specific price ranges.

Identifying a trading range

Stocks are either trending up or down or trading within a confined price range. The latter are said to be *range bound* or stuck in a trading range, never trading higher than the high nor lower than the low during a specific time frame. You also hear range-bound stocks described as consolidating or building a base. Although some subtle distinctions may exist among these terms, we nevertheless use them interchangeably.

In general, we're not interested in trading range-bound stocks. Trading ranges can persist for long periods of time. Some may even last for years. For a position trader, having money in a range-bound stock represents wasted opportunity. You won't lose money, but you won't make any either. Instead, we are interested in identifying range-bound stocks because they have the potential to begin trending. We patiently watch these stocks for a signal indicating the trading range may end and a trend may begin. Stocks that break out of a long-lasting trading range often begin trends that can be traded profitably.

Trading ranges are easy to spot after the fact, but anticipating when a stock is about to enter or exit a trading range is nearly impossible. For this and other reasons, range-bound stocks are difficult to trade, especially for new traders. Some short-term traders are able to trade range-bound stocks successfully, so it isn't impossible, but we encourage you first to become a proficient trend trader before attempting to trade stocks stuck in trading ranges. Tools you can use in trading-range situations are described in Chapter 11. In Chapter 10, we discuss what to do if a stock you own stops trending and becomes range bound.

Identifying a trading range is best done visually. Figure 9-8 shows a chart of Time Warner, Inc. (TWX) stock in a range-bound pattern.

Time Warner spent nearly six months trading between $14.75 and $17.00. Notice how the price moves up and down but always between those levels, never making much progress one way or the other. Also notice the lines drawn on the chart near $14.75 and just below $17.00. These lines show support and resistance levels, respectively, and are discussed in the "Support and resistance: Not just for undergarments" section, below.

Figure 9-8: Time Warner stock gets stuck in a trading range.

Spotting a trend

Now contrast the Time Warner chart in Figure 9-8 with the chart of Electronic Arts (ERTS) in Figure 9-9. ERTS appears quite different from the range-bound stock. Notice the steady stair-step march upward as the stock rises higher and higher.

Even in a strong upward trend, stocks rarely go straight up. You often see some reversals and mini-consolidations in a trend that cause the stair-stepped look.

That stair-stepped upward march is an identifying characteristic of an *uptrend*. Although defining it quantitatively is possible, seeing an uptrend on a chart is easy and that's the way it often is done. As long as a stock price continues to reach higher intermittent highs, and its new lows don't fall below previous lows, the uptrend remains intact. Chapter 10 discusses trends and these stair-step patterns in more detail.

Figure 9-9:
Electronic
Arts stock
exhibits and
upward
trend
pattern.

Stocks can also *downtrend;* a series of lower highs and lower lows is as much of a trend as its upward-bound counterpart. See Figure 9-10, a chart showing Kohl's Corporation in a downtrend.

Figure 9-10:
Kohl's
stock in a
downtrend.

Time frame matters

The time frame of your chart determines your trading perspective.

You may notice that the price lines of a range-bound stock are made up of many small trends. If you look at an intraday chart of Time Warner stock (TWX) that spanned the 19 or so days of trading from August 7, 2003, through September 3, 2003, TWX appear to be in an uptrend.

In fact, TWX was in a trend during that period. However, when you step back and observe a broader historical record of TWX's trading pattern by looking at the daily and weekly charts, you can easily see that the multi-day trend actually was confined within the prevailing trading range.

Although short-term swing traders and day traders make a living basing their trading on these mini- and microtrends, doing so isn't our cup of tea. We caution you that consistently trading range-bound stocks profitably is very difficult to do.

Searching for Transitions

A stock can transition from a downtrend to an uptrend in several different ways. It can, for example, fall precipitously, turn on a dime, and begin heading higher. Furthermore, a stock can fall, bounce around in a trading range for a while, and begin a new trend — up or down — as it breaks from the trading range.

Although turning on a dime from downtrending to upward trending sometimes presents profitable trading opportunities, these transitions are difficult to identify, much less base a trade on. Additional tools of technical analysis to unearth these transitions are explained in Chapters 10 and 11. Rather than trying to score big on such sharp transitions, we recommend that you search for stocks making the transition to trending after a period of range-bound trading lasting at least six to eight weeks, preferably longer.

Support and resistance: Not just for undergarments

The transition from range-bound to trending is relatively easy to identify visually and is the easiest to trade profitably. To find the transition, you must be familiar with the concept of support and resistance. You will see support and resistance used in many contexts. For example, they are used to identify a trading range, as discussed in this section. They are also used to help identify when a trend has reached its end, as we discuss in Chapter 10.

For an example of how support and resistance levels are shown on a chart, refer back to Figure 9-8, the chart showing TWX stuck in a trading range. The support line shown on this chart is at approximately $14.75; the resistance line is shown near $17.00.

Support is always the lower trading-range boundary; *resistance* is always the upper trading-range boundary.

When technicians talk about support, they mean the price where buyers are willing to buy enough stock to stop the price from falling. Said another way, when sellers see enough buying interest at the support price, they may still be willing to sell, but, as for now, they'll sell only if they can coax buyers to raise their bids. Buyers are now eager to buy, so they're willing to bid a little more to complete the transaction. The result: Prices end their descent and begin heading higher.

The reverse is true as the stock price approaches the resistance level. Buyers begin losing interest as the stock reaches elevated prices. Eager sellers must lower their offer (asking) price to complete the transaction, which causes prices to stop rising and begin falling.

Support levels and resistance levels often are determined visually by means of a chart. Knowing the exact price where lines of support and resistance need to be drawn is difficult, and traders may differ on where to draw these lines. Some choose the extreme, plotting intraday highs and lows of a trading range during a specific time frame to establish those levels. We prefer using closing prices on a daily or weekly bar chart to define the upper and lower boundaries within the trading range. If you're analyzing an intra-day chart, use the last trade price on each bar when drawing the support and resistance levels. In my opinion, closing prices (or last prices) have more significance and better represent the consensus of traders and investors. Ultimately, the choice is yours.

Let us caution you that technical analysis is not an exact science. And as such, thinking of support and resistance levels as areas of support or zones of resistance is probably better than viewing them in terms of specific prices or single lines on a chart, even though that's how they appear.

Finding a breakout

A stock remains stuck in its trading range as long as it bounces between zones of support and resistance. Short-term traders may be interested in these movements, but as a position trader, you're looking for a more substantial trend, so you must wait for something to change the status quo and cause the stock to break out of its trading range.

A *breakout* sometimes signals the transition of a stock trading within a range to a new uptrend or downtrend. When breaking out to the upside, we want to see the resistance zone violated by a significant amount, certainly by more than 5 or 10 cents. More important, we want to see the stock trade through its resistance zone on much higher volume than the average. Ideally, volume needs to be at least 50 percent higher than average. More volume is even better.

Figure 9-11 shows a chart of D.R. Horton stock (DHI) and is a textbook example of a stock breaking out of a trading range. DHI fell from its March 2002 highs and entered a trading range in late October 2002 that lasted through early April 2003. We drew the support line near $11.50 and the resistance line near $13.50. The support and resistance levels were tested several times from November 2002 to March 2003.

Figure 9-11: D.R. Horton stock breaks out of its trading range.

Breakout

April 7,2003

Bullish single bar pattern

Resistance

Breakout gap

Support

Higher than average breakout volume

Line showing average volume

On April 2, 2003, DHI opened well above its previous close, traded through the zone of resistance and closed at $13.93. This pattern — where a stock's opening price is well above its previous close and moves up, breaking out of its trading range — is called a *breakout gap,* which we discuss more fully in Chapter 10. Although not a requirement for a stock to break out of its trading range, a breakout gap does bolster the case for this rise in prices to be a transition from trading within a range to a new uptrend. Trading volume was 3 million shares, or almost double the average daily volume. Be sure to also notice the bullish single-bar pattern on the day of the breakout.

As the chart shows, DHI traded down a bit during the next two days, approached the zone of resistance, but then headed higher through April and May. Although you cannot see it in Figure 9-11, DHI continued its rally through the end of 2003 and closed the year close to $29, which was very near its all-time high. ***Note:*** All these prices were adjusted for DHI's January 12, 2004, stock split, which is the accepted practice and is often done automatically by your charting software or Web site.

The DHI breakout was a picture-perfect setup for a trading opportunity. D.R. Horton is a leading stock in a leading industry. The stock built a solid trading-range base and broke out on higher-than-average volume. Then, DHI went on to rally for the remainder of 2003. Nice. Your entry point for this trade would be either at the breakout or during the two-day pullback. We discuss ways to identify when a trend has come to an end, and when to close your trade to realize your profits, in Chapter 10.

Waiting patiently for winning patterns

I can hear the gears grinding from here. Yes, it's a nice trade . . . but you're probably saying to yourself, "Couldn't I have bought DHI for $11.50 several times between November 2002 and March 2003? Why wait until the breakout drives my entry price up?"

The answer: Finding a good trading signal is important, avoiding bad trading signals is more important.

Foretelling the future is hard. Of course hindsight is going to tell you that buying DHI at $11.50 would've earned you more money than buying it for $14. But when the price was $11.50, how could you know that DHI wouldn't stay in its trading range for many more months or years? Or how could you tell that DHI wasn't going to break out of its trading range to the downside, and start trending lower?

It happens. In fact, if the stock had traded below its zone of support, technical analysis would've suggested a resumption of the earlier downtrend and a potential opportunity to sell DHI short.

Another important reason for waiting for a breakout is that when you enter a trade, you need an exit strategy. Exit strategies are discussed more fully in Chapters 12 through 14, but for now, know that you need technical signals to show you when to exit your position, the same way you needed them to enter the position in the first place. If you're trying to buy stocks at the bottom and then sell them at the top, no signals are available to tell you whether your entry signal has failed.

Fine-tuning your trading-range breakout strategy

Three ways you can fine-tune your trading-range breakout strategy are

- Observing that breakouts from long trading ranges tend to result in more profitable buying and selling than breakouts from shorter trading ranges.

- Understanding that breakouts from tight trading ranges, where price fluctuations are confined to a relatively narrow price range, usually result in better trades than when trading-range price fluctuations are wide.

- Waiting for a short while — at least one day, possibly two or three — to confirm the trading range breakout can be helpful. Waiting to see whether the stock falls back into the trading range before you take a position can save you from a negative market reaction. Running into a wave of selling immediately after a breakout is not uncommon, and the way the stock reacts to that selling is just as important as the breakout itself.

Consistently snagging the lowest price is nearly impossible, regardless of whether you use technical analysis, fundamental analysis, a Ouija board, or follow the best prognosticators in the business. Technical analysis can help you find transitions, but it can't tell the future. As a technician, you never (almost never) buy your stocks at their lowest prices, and you rarely exit your positions at the highest prices.

However, if you wait for a solid trading signal, you can ride the middle part of the trend for a large portion of the move. Try not to be greedy. The middle part of the trend is a very profitable place to trade.

Sipping from a cup and saucer

Another widely followed transitional formation is called a cup and handle. In a *cup and handle formation,* a stock's price levels form a rounded curving bottom that looks a bit like a cup or a saucer, which often is followed by a modest shakeout formation that (use your imagination) looks a bit like the handle on a coffee cup.

Figure 9-12 shows a chart of the Ryland Group stock (RYL) that illustrates the cup and handle formation.

The entry strategy for this pattern is similar to that used for the trading range breakout. The trigger occurs when the stock price breaks above the handle on high volume. In the Ryland example, it occurs in early April, and is accompanied by a small breakout gap and a bullish single-bar pattern.

Notice that the stock traded back down during the next couple of days, retesting the former area of resistance. As often is the case, that former resistance level actually provided support after it was crossed. You'll see this phenomenon occur frequently.

The cup and handle is a reliable trading pattern, but that doesn't mean the pattern never fails. It does, and you need an exit strategy for when it does, just like every other trade. Exit strategies are discussed in Chapter 12.

Figure 9-12:
Ryland Group's stock prices show a cup and handle pattern.

Deciding what to do with a double bottom

Another transition pattern that often leads to profitable trading opportunities is the double bottom. Visually, a *double bottom* looks like a "W" on the chart, so it is very easy to see. However, a double bottom doesn't need to form a perfect "W" to be valid. In fact, we actually prefer the right-hand trough to be a little lower than the left-hand trough. When a minor new low forms, it tends to shake out the weakest owners of the stock and makes it much easier for bulls to drive the price higher.

Figure 9-13 shows a perfectly formed double bottom on the Hewlett Packard stock (HPQ) chart. The left-hand trough occurred in July 2002; the right-hand trough in October 2002.

The entry criteria for this pattern are similar to that of the trading-range breakout. In this case, the trigger point occurs when the stock breaks above the mid-point peak between the two troughs. This peak is sometimes called the *pivot point*. Ideally, higher-than-average volume confirms the trigger.

The trigger price on the HPQ chart is just above $15.25, which corresponds to the $15.30 close in August. The stock gapped above the trigger point in October with a volume of more than 20 million shares. That's more than double the average daily trading volume.

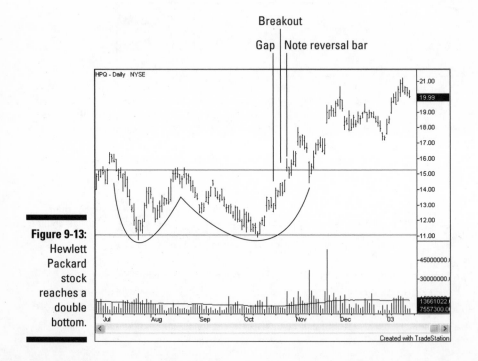

Figure 9-13: Hewlett Packard stock reaches a double bottom.

You'd need stronger constitutions than we have to actually enter a position based on the way this stock reacted after the trigger. The stock traded down the next day, almost completely filling the gap between the trigger price and mid-point peak. It's an example of how patience is sometimes rewarded when trading stocks. You don't have to trade every breakout.

When HPQ rallied and gapped higher several days later, taking a position might have been enticing for some, but we'd already gotten cold feet. Besides the fact the stock was trading erratically, Hewlett Packard's earnings had been disappointing for several quarters, and it had shown a loss in 2002. And at the time, if you'll recall, Hewlett Packard was trying to integrate Compaq into its operations. The story was not attractive enough for us to ignore the stock's erratic behavior.

Still, this trade could have been a profitable one. The trick would've been finding an entry point that made sense after all the gyrations HPQ went through after triggering a buy signal. Ah, but many fish are in the sea, and many trading opportunities are in the markets. If you don't like what you see, look elsewhere for something that you do like. That's what we did with the HPQ situation.

An alternative double-bottom strategy

One scenario where aggressive traders may want to anticipate the formation of a double-bottom pattern is when the "W" is particularly deep and the pivot is many points away from the trough. When that happens, taking a position as the stock is forming the right-hand trough sometimes makes sense.

If the price holds near or just below the left-hand trough, and volume confirms the reversal, then aggressive traders can enter a position. You may also want to enter a position if signals from other single-day patterns confirm the reversal. The risk is relatively small, and the potential reward is relatively large. If the stock falls below the lowest low, you'll know your trade has failed and you must exit. Otherwise, hold the position until the stock tests the pivot point (see previous section).

The HPQ scenario we showed you back in Figure 9-13 may not qualify for this strategy, because the trough isn't far enough from the pivot price. But you still can use the chart as an example to show this aggressive alternative strategy.

The buy trigger occurred on October 10 when HPQ rallied from $11.16 to $11.83, near the high. Notice the bullish single-day bar. If HPQ subsequently traded below $11.00, you'd presume the trade had failed and exit the position.

Looking at other patterns

Many other reversal patterns are published in technical analysis books and magazines, but the ones in the preceding few sections, we believe, are the most reliable.

Inexperienced traders always want to find the Holy Grail, that pattern or indicator that enables them to profitably trade the turn-on-a-dime "V" pattern. In truth, however, "V" bottoms don't happen all that often. And when they do, many reasons express why it's probably not the best trading opportunity available to you.

If you talk shop with other traders, you're certain to hear them discuss many esoteric patterns. We know them, but we rarely trade them. The simple techniques we've shown you in this chapter will enable you to trade profitably. There's no need to look for the esoteric when the simple does the job just as well.

Chapter 10

Following Trends for Fun and Profit

*T*echnical analysis helps you identify new price trends and look for endings to existing trends. Being able to identify those two extreme end points means you can develop a powerful, profitable trend-following trading system. Technical analysis can also help you evaluate the persistence of a trend, which is useful for finding secondary entry points and generating short-term trading signals.

In this chapter, we discuss trading strategies for several trend-following techniques. In addition, methods for identifying continuation patterns, retracement patterns, and reversal patterns are discussed, together with strategies for dealing with the inevitable failed trading signal.

Identifying Trends

Identifying a trend is relatively straightforward. Instinctively, you know it when you see it. Visual techniques and calculated indicators both can be used to identify trend signals. Indicators are discussed in Chapter 11. Visual identification techniques are discussed in this section.

A steadily rising or falling stock is a *trending stock.* But if you watch stocks for any period of time, you know that they rarely go straight up or down. Instead, you see a stair-step effect in which a stock rises several steps and then falls back. Talking about a trend as a series of intermittent highs interrupted by intermittent lows makes good sense. So an *uptrend,* then, is a series of higher intermittent highs and higher intermittent lows. Conversely, a *downtrend* is a series of lower intermittent highs followed by lower intermittent lows.

Figure 10-1 shows a price chart of Electronic Arts stock (ERTS) exhibiting a series of higher intermittent highs and higher intermittent lows. (From here on out, for simplicity's sake, we're calling these higher highs and higher lows.)

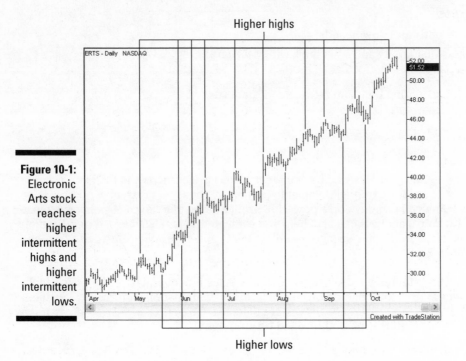

Figure 10-1:
Electronic Arts stock reaches higher intermittent highs and higher intermittent lows.

Higher highs

Higher lows

The ERTS example shows the type of trends that you hope follow the break-out patterns we discuss in Chapter 9. As long as the pattern of higher highs and higher lows continues, you can participate in a profitable trade.

Figure 10-2 shows a downtrending price chart of Kohl's Corporation stock (KSS) that identifies its series of lower highs and lower lows.

Lower highs

Retracement

Lower lows

Figure 10-2:
Kohl's
stock falls
to lower
intermittent
highs and
lower
intermittent
lows.

Supporting and Resisting Trends

You may have noticed in Figure 10-2 that a higher intermittent high formed in the midst of the downtrend exhibited by the chart. That anomaly is identified as a retracement on the chart (see the "Withstanding Retracements" section, later in the chapter). Although the series of lower highs and lower lows appeared to have been broken, Kohl's downtrend remained intact and continued its fall for the remainder of 2003.

In an uptrend, as long as the pattern of higher highs and higher lows continues, you can say that the trend persists. The converse (lower highs and lower lows) is true in a downtrend. Unfortunately, you cannot say that breaks in these patterns signal the end of any trends.

Sometimes you see an uptrend pattern broken when the stock fails to reach a new high or when it makes a lower intermittent low. You may actually see several of these disconcerting lower lows, only to witness the resumption of a strong uptrend. As such, you need to anticipate these eventual hiccups as you plan your trading strategy, and you need tools to help you determine whether a stock still is trending or the trend has reached its end.

Drawing trend lines to show support

Trend lines are drawn underneath a trend, much like support lines are drawn underneath a trading range as described in Chapter 9. And just like the support line, trend lines show areas of trading-range support that can be used to trigger short-term trading signals as you monitor the progress of a trend.

If you remember your days in geometry class, you'll recall that only two points are needed to define any line. Knowing which point to choose is the trick when drawing a trend line. You may, for example, choose to have the trend line touching two or more of the intermittent lows as is the case in Figure 10-3. Or you may choose to draw the trend line based on the lowest closing prices between those intermittent lows.

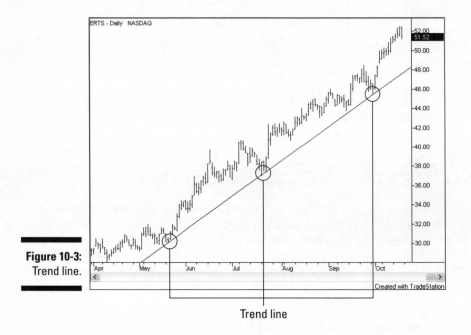

Figure 10-3: Trend line.

Trend line

Unfortunately, drawing trend lines is not a precise discipline, and no universal consensus exists for where and how to draw them. In fact, any two traders drawing trend lines in exactly the same place for the same stock is not something you're likely to find. Furthermore, you'll drive yourself crazy trying to touch all the important lows with your trend line.

Trend lines are drawn to fit historical data. That the trend rides atop the trend line is not surprising, given that you drew it that way. However, whether that trend line represents the actual trend or is able to generate reliable trading signals is constantly in doubt.

There are so many variables. You might, for example, draw the trend line on a traditional price scale, but that trend line will look very different from one drawn on a log or semi-log scale that shows percentage price changes. It's hard to know which is the better choice. Also, trend lines are often drawn using the oldest historical data, but newer data may be more relevant for generating trading signals. As such, constantly questioning your information and continually updating your trend line is a good habit to follow.

Watching the price bar cross below the trend line can be disturbing, because doing so can signal the end of the trend, or it may mean that you need to redraw the trend lines. Unfortunately, when the stock price closes below the trend line, you can't know whether the penetration represents the end of the trend or just another opportunity to redraw the trend line to conform to the newest price data.

An alternative technique for drawing the trend line reduces the ambiguity just a bit. Instead of drawing the trend line from left to right, they way most people instinctively do, draw the trend line backward, or from right to left. Using the two most recent intermittent lows in the trend, draw the trend line backwards as long as it is meaningful, then project the trend line toward the right. This approach has a couple of benefits:

- ✔ The slope of the trend line is more closely aligned with the most recent trading data, which usually is more relevant to your trading decisions.

- ✔ You'll resign yourself to the necessity of continually redrawing your trend lines based on the newest data.

Surfing channels

A *channel* is used by traders to identify potential entry and exit points during a trend. Channel lines are formed when a line is drawn parallel with the trend line across a trend's intermittent highs. This *top channel line* is analogous to the resistance line in a trading range, which we discuss in Chapter 9. After the top channel line is drawn, most traders start calling the trend line the *bottom channel line*. Figure 10-4 shows an example of a channel.

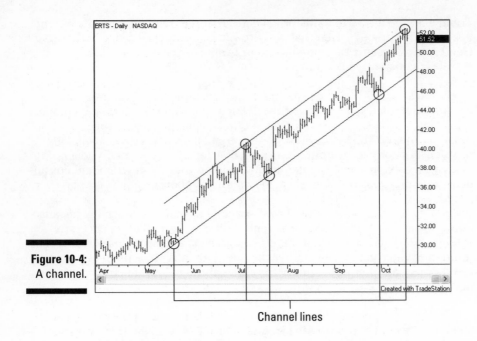

Figure 10-4:
A channel.

Channel lines

Trending and channeling strategies

The strategies for using trend lines and channels are similar. When an uptrending stock approaches the trend line or the bottom channel line, short-term traders often see an opportunity to take a position in the direction of the dominant trend. As long as the stock's price does not fall through this support level, they will hold the position. Position traders, on the other hand, may use these same conditions to validate their existing positions as still viable. If, however, the stock closes below the trend line and remains below it for longer than a day or two, position traders *and* short-term traders must consider the possibility that the trend has reached its end.

Trend lines and channels work better across longer periods of time. A stock price that violates a long-running, persistent trend or channel line on a weekly chart provides more meaningful guidance than when it breeches a support line on a daily chart or an intraday chart. In our experience, short-term trend lines add little information that isn't already present in the steady march of higher highs and higher lows.

When a stock breaks a short-term trend line, we believe it's best to step back one time increment to evaluate the situation. For example, if you're trading based primarily on daily chart data, display a weekly chart and examine the trend line and the series of intermittent highs and lows. If the march of higher highs and higher lows remains intact on the weekly chart, you may want to give your position a little room to work itself out. However, if a longer time frame shows a break in the pattern of higher highs and higher lows, you need to consider exiting your position right away.

We use trend lines for guidance while trading, but rarely do we make decisions solely on the basis of a trend-line penetration. Although initiating short-term positions in the direction of the dominant trend is possible by using channels to enter and exit the position, doing so is very difficult, and few traders are able to engage in that practice profitably. Some traders take this concept even one step further by trying to take positions in opposition to the dominant trend as the stock price approaches the upper channel line. We believe trading in the direction opposite that of a dominant trend and a stock's fundamental picture is foolhardy and an excellent way to lose a substantial portion of your trading capital.

Bottom line: Trend lines and channels are additional tools that you can use to monitor the progress of a stock price trend. They can be used to help identify trading opportunities, but we recommend they not be your primary method of determining entry and exit points.

Seeing Gaps

A *price gap* forms on a bar chart when the opening price of the current bar is above or below the closing price of the previous bar. Gaps occur mostly on daily charts, sometimes on weekly charts, and rarely on intraday charts. Depending on the circumstances, gaps can show continuation and reversal patterns, and they can signal an opportunity to enter or exit a position.

Some gaps are obvious and some are subtle. For example, if the opening price is above the previous close, but the low of the current bar is below the previous high, then those bars overlap and the gap is hard to spot. Many traders simply ignore that type of gap. If, however, the low of the current bar is obviously higher than the high of the previous bar, that will draw the attention of most traders. Examples of obvious gaps are shown in the following sections.

Gaps are divided into several broad categories based on where the gap occurs. These categories determine your trading strategy and are discussed in the sections that follow.

Common gap

Gaps that occur within a trading range, as described in Chapter 9, can be either a *common gap* or a *breakout gap*. If the gap occurs within a middle of the trading range, far from either the support or resistance level, it is a common gap.

Common gaps occur frequently and are, well, rather common. They rarely provide meaningful trading opportunities. Ignoring them usually is the best policy.

Breakout or breakaway gap

When a stock price exceeds a high of a price range during a specific time frame or falls below the low during that same period and simultaneously forms a gap, traders describe that situation as a *breakout* or *breakaway gap*. A breakout gap often provides excellent trading signals to enter a new position, in the direction of the gap. Figure 10-5 shows an example of a breakout gap from a long-standing trading range. Trading strategies for trading range breakouts are discussed in Chapter 9.

Figure 10-5: Breakout gap.

Breakout gap

Continuation gap

A *continuation gap* is also known as a runaway gap or an acceleration gap. This type of gap occurs within an uptrend when the open price of the current bar is higher than the close price of the previous bar. If the low of the current bar is also obviously above the high of the previous bar, this gap usually indicates that the trend is very strong. Continuation gaps may also occur in downtrends. The defining characteristics are opposite those of the uptrend.

Figure 10-6 shows an example of a continuation gap in an uptrend. Some short-term traders may use a continuation gap as a signal to enter a position in the direction of the gap. Position traders may use this same signal to confirm that a current trade remains viable. You sometimes see a series of runaway gaps occur in close proximity to each other, and these gaps usually are a strong confirmation of the prevailing trend. However, continuation gaps also warrant caution, because they can turn into an exhaustion gap.

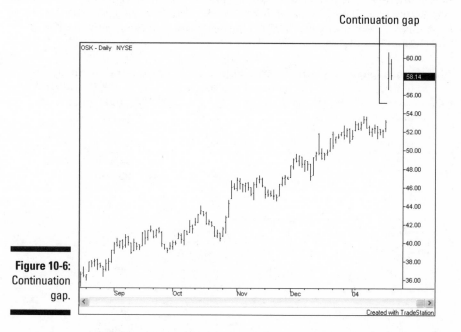

Figure 10-6:
Continuation
gap.

Exhaustion gap

Exhaustion gaps occur at or near the ends of strong trends. Unfortunately, the defining characteristics for an exhaustion gap are virtually identical to those for a continuation gap. Distinguishing an exhaustion gap from a continuation gap is impossible, until the stock price changes direction. By that time, it is usually obvious that something is wrong with the trade and you should exit your position.

In Figure 10-6, we actually assume this gap is a continuation gap, because if the stock price continues its trend, it will become one. If, however, the stock price retreats, or falls back, the gap may be classified as an exhaustion gap. Sometimes, an exhaustion gap turns into an island gap.

Island gap

An *island gap,* or an island reversal, forms when a trend changes direction. The pattern is actually two gaps that isolate either a single bar or a short series of bars from the dominant trend and the new trend. An island gap usually is a good indicator that the prior trend has been extinguished and can be used to signal an exit from an existing position. You may also use an island gap to initiate a new position, but only if the direction of the new trend aligns with the stock's underlying fundamental condition. Be sure to review the "Dealing with Failed Signals" section, later in this chapter, before initiating any positions based on an island gap.

Notice the single-day reversal bar in Figure 10-7. Single-bar patterns are discussed in Chapter 9. Not only is the single bar isolated from the two surrounding bars that form the island gap, but it also lends additional weight and emphasis to the reversal pattern.

Figure 10-7:
Island gap.

Island gap with single-day reversal bar

Waving Flags and Pennants

Flag and pennant patterns represent areas of consolidation on a trend chart. You've already encountered these patterns, just not by name. In a series of higher highs and higher lows, these patterns form the basis for the higher lows. In other words, the higher lows are made of flag and pennant patterns.

A *pennant pattern* looks like, well, a pennant. Support and resistance lines converge into a point forming what looks like a small pennant shape. A *flag pattern,* on the other hand, is bounded by parallel lines. Each of these patterns almost always fly counter to the prevailing trend, but the direction in which they're flying is not actually a requirement.

Figure 10-8 shows examples of flags and pennants on the chart of a trending stock.

The key for each of these patterns is the breakout. If the breakout from the formation is in the direction of the established trend, then the trend continues. If not, it's possible that the trend is over.

Flags and pennants typically are associated with a trend, but you may also see these patterns within the confines of a trading range. In fact, an example of a small flag can be seen back in Figure 10-5, just before the breakout gap. A flag or pennant forming near the top of a trading range hints of an eventual breakout. The flag or pennant pattern shows the stock consolidating near the top of the trading range, and that suggests that selling pressure is diminishing and the stock is preparing to test the zone of resistance.

Figure 10-8:
Flags and
pennants.

Withstanding Retracements

A *retracement* occurs when a trending stock revisits recent prices. You've already seen many examples. When a stock makes a higher intermediate high and then a higher intermediate low, that is a retracement. A trading range as discussed in Chapter 9 can also be considered a retracement. You may hear a retracement called a price consolidation or a pullback, but the concept is the same.

Flags and pennants are relatively simple forms of retracement patterns. More complex retracements can occur within the confines of a trend, and like their simpler counterparts, they don't actually signal the end of the trend. Unfortunately, complex retracements cause confusion and consternation for traders when they occur. Besides being difficult to anticipate, they send out conflicting signals to traders trying to make sense of which trading-plan adjustments are needed.

Three-step and five-step retracements

In an uptrend, you sometimes see breaks in the pattern of higher highs and higher lows when the stock price fails to reach a new high or makes a lower intermittent low. You may see several occurrences of these worrisome lower lows and lower highs happen one right after the other followed by a resumption of a strong uptrend.

You will see a couple of these benign multistep patterns frequently occur in the midst of a strong trend, so it is useful to watch for them. A *three-step retracement* makes at least one lower intermittent high and one lower intermittent low. A *five-step retracement* makes two lower highs and two lower lows. Multistep retracements also occur when a downtrending stock makes higher highs and higher lows.

Figure 10-9 shows an example of a five-step retracement that ultimately resolves in the direction of the prevailing trend. The five steps are identified, along with the corresponding intermittent highs and lows.

Trust us when we tell you that situations like these are disconcerting whenever you're holding a position. They're not, however, absolute signals that a trend has reached its end. Knowing when a trend has ended, however, is nearly impossible, so you need a plan for dealing with it when it happens.

Figure 10-9:
Five-step
retracement
pattern.

Where, within a trend, the multistep retracement occurs has some bearing on what plan you choose. If the stock price has just broken out of a long trading range and then falters, you may want to wait for a subsequent attempt to break out of the trading range, but closing the position is probably best. Look for trading opportunities elsewhere.

If a stock price starts what may be a three-step or a five-step retracement after a long period of trending, and your position is profitable, you may want to see how the retracement plays out. Absent any obvious sell signals, such as an island reversal or a downside breakout from a flag, pennant, or trading range formation, you can wait to see how the retracement resolves itself.

Checking out a chart that reflects a longer time frame can be helpful. For example, you can examine a weekly chart when the retracement occurs on the daily chart. If the trend shows no signs of faltering on the weekly chart, hold your position. If the stock recovers and heads higher, so much the better, but if it establishes another lower high and trades below its next lower low, it's time to exit.

Finally, considering fundamental factors before making your decision makes good sense. If a company's deteriorating financial situation is an underlying cause of the retracement, then exiting your position makes sense. You also need to be aware of the cycle the economy is in when making your decision. If the economy is approaching a turning point as your stock's technical situation deteriorates, getting out of the position usually is a good idea.

Dealing with subsequent trading ranges

A trading range or a cup and handle formation, like the ones described in Chapter 9, also are complex consolidation patterns. A trend that's interrupted by a period of range-bound trading may indicate either a pause before the trend resumes or the end of the trend. The only way of knowing which way the trend will go is to watch for the breakout. Unfortunately, you may be in for a long wait.

In the retracement pattern shown in Figure 10-9, you can make a valid argument interpreting the five-step retracement as a cup and handle formation. Technical analysis is an imprecise discipline, so you may encounter ambiguous situations like this. The results in this case were the same regardless of your interpretation. The stock broke out of its eight-week complex consolidation pattern and resumed its trend.

Breakouts that occur in the direction of the prevailing trend may indicate that the trend has further to run, but they may also be a prelude to a failed breakout signal. Trading-range breakouts are considered strong signals when they result in a change of direction from the previous trend.

The trading range breakouts that are described in Chapter 9 are just this type of reversal, and so is the example depicted in Figure 10-5, where the stock price was in a downtrend prior to the period of consolidation within the trading range shown on the chart. The breakout in the direction opposite that of the previous downtrend indicates a strong reversal that signals a buying opportunity.

Dealing with Failed Signals

All trading signals are subject to failure. Sometimes, things just don't work out as planned. However, even a failed signal provides additional information that you can use to revise your trading plans. In fact, sometimes the best trading signals are the direct result of a failed signal.

Trapping bulls and bears

Breakouts from trading ranges and cup and handle patterns sometimes fail. These failures happen to bullish and bearish signals, and when they fail, it is called a *trap*. The two kinds of traps are

- ✔ *Bull traps,* which occur after an upside breakout. The stock breaks out of its trading range to the upside but then reverses back into the trading range and ultimately breaks out to the down side.

- ✔ *Bear traps,* which occur after a downside breakout. This opposite scenario to the bull trap often is very bullish. The stock reverses course and reenters the trading range. If a bear trap occurs within a trading range that's preceded by a long period of declining prices, it often represents an excellent buying opportunity, because it's a sign that selling pressure has evaporated in the stock, which thus is likely to attempt an upside breakout.

Whenever you see a potential bear trap taking place and the stock meets all of your fundamental criteria, you may want to enter a long position as soon as the stock price reenters the trading range.

Filling the gaps

A gap that's forming usually is interpreted as a signal that the prevailing trend will continue. If a stock reverses and retraces prices within the gap, we say that the gap has been filled. A gap that's filled negates the trading signal that it generated.

When dealing with a breakout gap, a stock price that falls back through the trading range resistance zone and fills the gap is likely to be a bearish development. Similarly, when a continuation gap is filled, you need to consider it a failed signal and exit your position. The same is true for an island gap. If prices trade back into the area of the isolated island, the trading signal has failed and you need to exit your position.

Deciding whether to reverse directions

A bear trap shows an example of where taking a position based on a failed signal makes sense. If, however, you already have a position, and the signal fails, exiting your position is a wise choice, because you're letting the market sort out its psychosis without risking your money.

You also need to consider economic and fundamental factors when deciding how to handle a failed signal. Acting on a contrary signal makes sense only if economic and fundamental conditions support the decision.

For example, if a bullish signal fails and becomes a bearish signal, selling a stock short makes sense only if it's fundamentally weak and the stock's sector is in decline. Conversely, if a bear trap occurs and generates a buy signal, taking a position in the stock makes sense only if its earnings are strong and growing, its sector is performing well, and the economy is on an upswing.

Chapter 11

Indicators and Oscillators

● ●

In This Chapter

▶ Identifying trends using moving averages

▶ Using oscillators and indicators to generate trading signals

▶ Deciphering relative strength

● ●

*T*he personal computer ushered in a new era for technical analysts. Today's Internet-connected computers offer data access and analytic capabilities at speeds that were impossible only a decade or two ago. That's not to say that calculated indicators and oscillators weren't used before the PC, but rather that these indicators were so difficult to calculate and maintain that few technicians performed these calculations for themselves. Even fewer had access to real-time analysis tools that traders now take for granted.

However, the ease of calculating, modifying, testing, and using computer-generated trading tools is as much a curse as it is a blessing. New traders often shun visual pattern analysis, instead preferring computer-generated indicators and oscillators. Doing so is a mistake. Although the perceived precision of these calculations seems to add to their allure, you nevertheless need to be aware that computer-generated analysis tools are not necessarily more accurate, and neither are computers able to generate higher-quality trading signals than visual pattern analysis.

Indicators and oscillators that we describe in this chapter provide you with additional insight into the technical condition of a stock or the market; however, they can't provide faultless trading signals. No indicator works in every situation, finds every opportunity, and generates only accurate trading signals.

As a new trader, you risk paralysis by analysis by trying to follow too many indicators. You have too many choices. This chapter describes how to create and use a tiny subset of the tools that are available in today's charting packages. We recommend that you become familiar with a small set of tools that can help you trade profitably, rather than learning how every available tool works. Find out how to trade profitably using this subset of tools before deciding that you need to add to your toolbox.

The computer-generated tools that we use every day are described in this chapter. Two types of moving averages are discussed, along with the MACD indicator and the stochastic oscillator. In addition, the powerful concept of relative strength is described.

These tools are but a tiny subset of the technical analysis tools that are available online or in software charting packages. And yet this subset is more than enough to get you started as a profitable trader. Become familiar with these tools. Play around with them, using historical data to see when they work and when they fail, and try to understand why. That way, you can know when the tools can help you and when they can't.

The Ins and Outs of Moving Averages

A *moving average* is a trading indicator that shows the direction and magnitude of a trend over a fixed period of time. Some traders call it a price overlay, because it's superimposed over the price data in a bar chart. Moving averages visually smooth out the data on a price chart to help make trend identification less subjective. All moving averages follow a stock's price trend but can't predict changes. They report only what has happened.

As its name implies, a *moving average* shows the average of a stock's up-and-down price movements during a specific period of time. A stock's daily closing price usually is the value being averaged, but any value on a price chart can be displayed as a moving average. Some traders, for example, prefer using the midpoint between daily high and low prices for the moving average calculation, but you can also use the opening, high, or low prices or any coincident value on a price chart, including volume.

You'll find that moving averages are used as indicators by themselves or in conjunction with other indicators, and are the building blocks for other indicators and oscillators such as the moving average convergence/divergence (MACD) invented by Gerald Appel sometime in the 1960s. Before discussing how the MACD is used (see the section on "Discovering MACD," later in the chapter), we must explain moving averages and how they are calculated. Two of the many types of moving averages are described in this section.

Simple moving average

A simple moving average (SMA) is simple to calculate and simple to use. To calculate it, you add a number of prices together and then divide by the number of prices you added. However, an SMA is a little more complicated that just that.

An example makes the SMA clearer. In this example, a nine-day moving average of Intel's (INTC) closing price is calculated throughout May 2003 and then is plotted on a price chart. To start the SMA calculation, use the closing prices shown in Table 11-1. Add the first nine closing prices together, from May 1 through May 13, and divide by 9. The resulting value is placed alongside the ninth trading day and each day of the month after May 13.

Table 11-1	Simple Moving Average of Intel [INTC] Closing Price	
Date	*Close*	*SMA*
5/1/2003	18.55	
5/2/2003	19.05	
5/5/2003	19.02	
5/6/2003	19.54	
5/7/2003	19.16	
5/8/2003	18.87	
5/9/2003	19.58	
5/12/2003	19.99	
5/13/2003	19.82	19.29
5/14/2003	19.66	19.41
5/15/2003	20.00	19.52
5/16/2003	19.50	19.57
5/19/2003	18.67	19.47
5/20/2003	18.66	19.42
5/21/2003	18.84	19.41
5/22/2003	18.77	19.32
5/23/2003	18.81	19.19
5/27/2003	19.78	19.19
5/28/2003	19.74	19.20
5/29/2003	20.83	19.29
5/30/2003	20.82	19.44

Figure 11-1 shows a bar chart associated with the price data in Table 11-1. The SMA data is superimposed on the bar chart's price data. Notice that you need nine prices before you can plot the first SMA point. In other words, the first SMA point appears on the ninth price bar, and the first eight price bars do not display an SMA value.

To calculate the second SMA point, add the prices from May 2 through May 14 together, divide by 9, and place the result as the next SMA data point next to May 14. Another way to think of calculating SMAs is that you drop the oldest price in the calculation and add the closing price from the next price bar. Continue this series by dropping the oldest price, adding the newest price, and dividing by 9 for the remainder of the month.

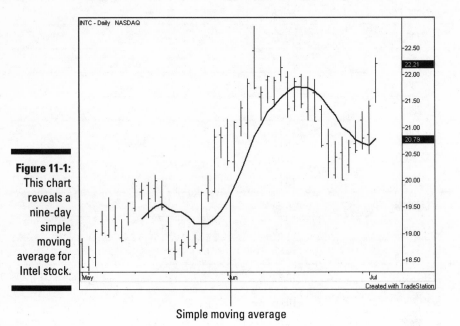

Figure 11-1:
This chart reveals a nine-day simple moving average for Intel stock.

Simple moving average

If you're mathematically inclined, here's what the series looks like as an equation:

$$SMA = (P_1 + P_2 + P_3 + \ldots P_N) \div N$$

Where:　N is the number of periods in the SMA

　　　　P_N is the price being averaged (usually the closing price)

Traders used to calculate SMAs by hand, but fortunately, computers now relieve them from this rather mundane chore. The way you use a moving average in your trading is discussed in the next section.

Exponential moving average

Another commonly used moving average is the exponential moving average (EMA), which can be superimposed on a bar chart in the same manner as an SMA. The EMA, however, also is used as the basis for other indicators, such as the MACD (Moving Average Convergence Divergence) indicator, which is discussed later in this chapter.

Although the calculation for an EMA looks a bit daunting, in practice it's simple. In fact, it's easier to calculate than an SMA, and besides, your charting package will do it for you. Here are the calculations:

$$EMA_{today} = (Price_{today} \times K) + (EMA_{yesterday} \times (1 - K))$$

Where: N = the length of the EMA

$$K = 2 \div (N + 1)$$

$Price_{[today]}$ = the current closing price

$EMA_{[yesterday]}$ = the previous EMA value

$EMA_{[today]}$ = the now current EMA value

The start of the calculation is handled in one of two ways. You can either begin by creating a simple average of the first fixed number (N) of periods and use that value to seed the EMA calculation, or you can use the first data point (typically the closing price) as the seed and then calculate the EMA from that point forward. You'll see other traders handling it both ways, but the latter method makes more sense to us. It's the method used in calculating the EMA amounts in Table 11-2, which shows a nine-day EMA calculation for Intel throughout May 2003. The EMA value for May 1 is seeded with that day's closing price of $18.55. The actual EMA calculation begins with the May 2 closing price. For comparison, we include the results of the earlier SMA calculation to illustrate the difference between an EMA and an SMA.

Table 11-2	Exponential Moving Average of Intel [INTC]		
Date	*Close*	*EMA*	*SMA*
5/1/2003	18.55	18.55	
5/2/2003	19.05	18.65	
5/5/2003	19.02	18.72	
5/6/2003	19.54	18.89	
5/7/2003	19.16	18.94	

(continued)

Table 11-2 *(continued)*			
Date	*Close*	*EMA*	*SMA*
5/8/2003	18.87	18.93	
5/9/2003	19.58	19.06	
5/12/2003	19.99	19.24	
5/13/2003	19.82	19.36	19.29
5/14/2003	19.66	19.42	19.41
5/15/2003	20.00	19.54	19.52
5/16/2003	19.50	19.53	19.57
5/19/2003	18.67	19.36	19.47
5/20/2003	18.66	19.22	19.42
5/21/2003	18.84	19.14	19.41
5/22/2003	18.77	19.07	19.32
5/23/2003	18.81	19.02	19.19
5/27/2003	19.78	19.17	19.19
5/28/2003	19.74	19.28	19.20
5/29/2003	20.83	19.59	19.29
5/30/2003	20.82	19.84	19.44

In this example, the EMA doesn't show the same nine-day lag at the beginning of the chart as the SMA. Notice that the results of the moving average calculations also differ. Figure 11-2 shows the data from Table 11-2 plotted on a bar chart. The EMA data is shown as a solid dark line on the bar chart. For comparison, the SMA data is also plotted using a lighter dashed line.

Comparing SMA and EMA

The SMA and EMA are used regularly by position and short-term traders alike. Each moving average has its strengths and weaknesses. Which one you choose is somewhat a matter of personal preference, but one probably is better suited than the other in several situations. As position traders, we use both. We use a relatively long-term SMA to help signal exit points, and we use EMAs whenever we rely on the MACD indicator (see the "Discovering MACD" section, later in the chapter).

Figure 11-2:
This chart reveals a nine-day exponential moving average for Intel stock.

Consistency

An SMA has the benefit of being consistently calculated from one charting package to the next. If you ask for a nine-period SMA, you can be certain that the result will be identical to every other nine-period SMA for the same stock during the same time period (as long as there are no errors in the price data — it's rare, but it happens).

Unfortunately, EMAs are not always consistent, because of the way the EMA is calculated — the starting point matters. You actually need more data when calculating an EMA than was used in the example in Table 11-2. In theory, you need to use all the price data available for any individual stock. In practice, however, that rarely is done. Some charting software packages enable you to specify how much data is used when calculating an EMA, but most Internet charting sites do not. The result: One charting vendor may calculate EMA values that are significantly different than the ones provided by another.

Discovering that you're basing your trading decisions on an inaccurate moving average is more than a bit disconcerting. This problem occurs with short-period calculations such as the nine-day EMA example in Table 11-2, but it is especially problematic for longer-term EMA calculations. Unfortunately, the only thing you can do is ask your chart supplier how much data it uses when calculating an EMA and then verify the resulting EMA by hand. Otherwise, you risk making trading decisions on faulty data.

Reaction time

In general, short-term traders are more likely to employ EMA, but position traders are more inclined to use SMA. The EMA usually is closer to the current closing price, which tends to make it change direction faster than the SMA. As a result, an EMA is likely to be quicker in signaling short-term trend changes.

The SMA probably is the better indicator for identifying long-term changes in a trend. Unfortunately, those signals are likely to take more time to appear than the ones generated by a comparable EMA. The method used to calculate the SMA causes it to react to price changes a bit slower, and that's the trade-off for getting a signal that is potentially more reliable.

Sensitivity

An unfortunate result of the method of calculating an SMA is that every time you add a price, another price falls off the back end of the equation. In other words, each new SMA data point is affected by two prices, the most recent closing price and the oldest closing price in the calculation. Ideally, you want the most recent data having a greater influence on your indicators than the impact of older data. But in an SMA, the oldest price affects the newest SMA point with the same weight as the newest price.

EMA calculations eliminate that problem. Each data point affects the EMA only once. You never have to drop the oldest price as a new price is added. For that reason, the EMA has a much longer memory than the SMA. Every price ever used in calculating EMA has some small effect. As an added benefit, EMA calculations place additional weight on the most recent price.

To understand how this works, examine the role played by the *coefficient K* in an EMA calculation. In the earlier example showing a nine-period EMA, the value of K (the newest price) is 0.20, or 20 percent.

$$\text{For } N = 9;\ K = 2 / (N + 1) \rightarrow K = 2 / (9 + 1) = 2 / 10 = .20 = 20 \text{ percent}$$

This means every new price added to the calculation represents 20 percent of the value of the EMA, while all the previous data represents 80 percent of it. The implication: The oldest data always has an impact, but slowly fades away, and newer data has a greater influence on the EMA value and the placement of the EMA data point.

Notice also that as the EMA period, represented by N, grows larger, the value of K becomes smaller, which means that each new data point has less influence on the EMA as the period grows larger.

Interpreting and using moving averages

Traders use moving averages to trigger buy and sell signals. In general, when a moving average slopes upward, you can infer that the trend is up, and when the moving average slopes downward, the trend is down.

One simple mechanical strategy that some traders employ works like this:

- ✔ Buy when the moving average slopes upward *and* the closing price crosses above the moving average.

- ✔ Close the position when the price closes below the moving average.

- ✔ Sell short when the moving average slopes downward *and* the closing price crosses below the moving average.

- ✔ Close the short position when the price closes above the moving average.

Although simple crossover strategies like this are remarkably effective in some trending situations, they're equally as ineffective in others. Many variables must be in alignment for this approach to work. For example, the stock must be trending (see Chapter 10), and the period for the moving average must be chosen carefully for the indicator to be effective. These trend-following systems fail miserably when a stock is range bound (see Chapter 9).

Figure 11-3 shows an example of this simple mechanical strategy on a 2003 calendar-year chart of Intel stock (INTC) with a 50-day SMA. Intel bottomed out in October in 2002 (not shown on this chart) and bounced around in a consolidation phase (see Chapter 10) through early March 2003. Using the trading rules of the mechanical strategy listed earlier in this section, the first buy signal occurred on March 13, when the stock closed above the SMA as the SMA turned higher. If you missed that signal in Figure 11-3 — easy to do because the upward movement in the SMA was barely perceptible — you had a second buy signal on April 2. Intel didn't close below the SMA and generate a sell signal until December 8.

On that date, the stock not only closed below its SMA, it also showed other signs of weakness. Intel failed to reach a higher high early in December and established a lower low at the same time that it closed below the SMA. On the chart, INTC's price looks like it may have entered a trading range by the end of 2003 with the stock fluctuating above and below the SMA.

This points out the difficulty you face when a stock is in a trading range and your trading strategy is based on a moving-average or any trend-following system. When a stock is range bound, determining whether the buy and sell signals the moving average crossover strategy generates are good, respective, entry, or exit signals is difficult. Keeping an eye on these complex retracement patterns (discussed at length in Chapter 10) helps you recognize that INTC may have entered a period of consolidation — another way of saying the stock is trading within a range — at the end of 2003. You can't know for sure whether INTC will break out of its consolidation to the upside or the downside until after the breakout actually occurs.

Figure 11-3: Chart of Intel stock with a 50-day SMA.

From our perspective, waiting for the breakout causes you little, if any, harm. When Intel entered a trading range late in 2003, the economic cycle appeared to be ascending and not about to peak and the company's fundamentals appeared strong. Other traders, however, argue that you risk missed opportunities elsewhere when you're waiting on position in a range-bound stock to break out. And although that argument is valid, and favors action on the SMA sell signal, we're still inclined to wait for the breakout before deciding.

We normally want some sort of confirmation signal before entering or exiting any position in a stock. For example, we might temper the buy signal in the simple mechanical strategy described earlier with a requirement that the stock price remains above its SMA for several days after the initial signal before entering a position. The same is true for the sell, or close, signal. You want the stock to close below the SMA for several days, or you'd like to see another coincident sell signal — perhaps one of the visual patterns discussed in Chapter 10 — before exiting your position. We use a long-period SMA to provide one of several signals to exit from existing positions. For example, if the price closes below a relatively long-term moving average and remains below it for a couple of days, we use that signal to exit our position.

Support and resistance factors

In addition to their trend-following abilities, moving averages also tend to provide support and resistance in stock prices that are trending up or down. When a price is trending higher, you often see the stock trade down toward the moving average only to reverse course and head higher. The same is true in reverse for stock prices that are trending lower. You often see a downtrending stock move up toward its moving average before heading lower. The moving average acts as an area of resistance.

Back in Figure 11-3, uptrending Intel approached its 50-day moving average in mid-April, late May, June, and again in August, and after each lull, headed higher. Short-term traders use these opportunities to enter positions in the direction of the dominant trend. When moving averages show a stock is trending higher by sloping upward, for example, short-term traders buy into a position when the stock price closes near or just below the moving average so they can ride the trend to sell at a higher price later on. Position traders also can use these signals as second-chance entry points, whenever they miss the first breakout. This strategy is called *buying on a pullback.*

Deciding the moving average time frame

Perhaps the most difficult decision you have to make when creating a moving average is determining the length or period that best fits the situation. Regardless of whether you select an EMA or an SMA, shorter periods yield more signals, but a greater percentage of those signals are false, and longer moving-average periods yield fewer signals, but a greater percentage of those signals are true. One hitch: Signals occur later in longer-term moving averages than they do in shorter-term ones.

In general, the shorter your trading horizon, the shorter the moving average you want to select. For us, a nine-period moving average is nearly useless. It generates too many signals that we have no intention of following. More isn't always better. We want our technical analysis tools to provide better signals, not more, because although getting good signals is important, avoiding bad signals is even more so.

To reiterate, we rarely use short-term moving averages to generate buy signals. Instead, we use a long-period SMA to monitor the health of a trend. Typically, we select either a 30-day or 50-day SMA, depending on the duration of the existing trend and prevailing economic conditions. If a trend has existed for a relatively long period of time, we choose the 50-day SMA as an exit indicator. However, if the economy appears to be nearing a peak, as described in Chapter 5, then we tend to tighten our exit procedures and shorten the SMA. See Chapter 13 for more on trading strategies and exit procedures.

Traders can fall into a trap when trying to fine-tune the moving average — or any indicator, for that matter — for a specific stock or situation. Logically, testing many different moving average periods using historical data to find the one that generates the most profitable trades and the fewest losing trades seems right, and charting software packages enable you to do just that to your heart's content.

However, you'll soon discover that what worked when using historical data often fails miserably when trading real money in real time. This problem is well known to statisticians and economists who build mathematic models to forecast future events. It is called *curve fitting*, because you are molding your model to fit the historical data. We talk about this problem more in Chapter 15. For now, know that fine-tuning an indicator for a specific stock or index rarely has any predictive value and you must avoid it. You simply can't trade using historical data. You're better off settling on a moving average period that satisfies the requirements for a great many situations, rather than trying to fine-tune the time frame of a moving average to fit each stock.

Understanding Stochastic Oscillators

The *stochastic oscillator* indicates momentum and attempts to show buying and selling pressure. This indicator compares current closing prices with the recent range of high to low prices and displays the results on a chart. Stochastic oscillator values cycle, or oscillate, between zero and 100 percent.

Calculating stochastic oscillators

The typical stochastic oscillator is measured across a 14-day period, but a different time frame can be specified. Here's the calculation:

%K = 100 × (closing price – lowest low (N)) ÷ (highest high (N) – lowest low (N))

% D = 3-period moving average of %K

Where: N is the number of periods used in the calculation (usually 14)

This calculation describes a fast stochastic. The names %K and %D, respectively, identify the stochastic oscillator and the signal line. We typically use a variation of this indicator that's called a slow stochastic. The slow stochastic oscillator calculation is

%K = 3-period moving average of (100 × (closing price – lowest low (N)) ÷ (highest high (N) – lowest low (N)))

% D = 3-period moving average of %K

Where: N is the number of periods used in the calculation (usually 14)

In effect, the slow stochastic uses the %D value from the fast stochastic calculation as its starting point. While the fast and slow stochastics look similar when plotted on a chart, the slow stochastic is smoother and less jumpy. It generates fewer and more reliable trading signals, but the signals appear more slowly than with the fast stochastic. *Note:* You will find that some charting packages permit you to specify different values for the moving average period, and some even permit you to change from an SMA to an EMA.

Interpreting stochastic oscillators

As mentioned earlier, the stochastic oscillator cycles between zero and 100 percent. Readings of more than 80 percent imply an overbought condition. Readings of less than 20 percent are interpreted as an oversold condition. An overbought condition can be resolved if a stock trades lower or enters a period of consolidation. Similarly, an oversold condition can be resolved if a stock trades higher or enters a period of consolidation.

Overbought and oversold conditions can persist for long periods of time; therefore, readings that stay above 80 percent or below 20 percent are not enough to generate trading signals. Instead, stochastic oscillator signals are generated

- ✔ When the stochastic oscillator moves from below to above 20 percent, triggering a buy signal.
- ✔ When the stochastic oscillator moves from above to below 80 percent, triggering a sell signal.

Figure 11-4 shows a slow stochastic oscillator on a price chart for Intel. Note the transitions from below to above 20 percent that occurred in late June, mid-August, and late September. All three represented good entry opportunities for this uptrend. Also note that the stochastic buy signals occurred coincidentally as Intel's price approached its 50-day moving average. And finally, note that few of the indicator's sell signals, where the stochastic oscillator crosses below 80 percent, represented good selling or shorting opportunities while Intel was trending higher.

Figure 11-4:
Chart of
Intel stock
prices
includes a
slow
stochastic
oscillator.

Some traders use a *stochastic oscillator crossover strategy* where buy signals are triggered when %K crosses above %D and sell signals are triggered when %K crosses below %D. For our style of trading, that generates too many signals, a very high percentage of which are false, as you can see in Figure 11-4.

Divergent patterns also provide good trading signals for the stochastic oscillator. A divergent pattern is shown in Figure 11-4 when Intel made a higher high early in October and another later in the month, but the corresponding stochastic oscillator showed a pattern of a high followed by a lower high for the same time period. This bearish divergence ushered in the trading range at the end of the chart.

The bullish counterpart occurs when the stock price establishes two lower lows but the stochastic oscillator makes two higher lows. Divergences that occur in the same direction as the dominant trend are useful for entering positions; however, as this example shows, a bearish divergence in a dominant uptrend is not likely to be a good signal to enter a short position. It may have been useful to exit the Intel position as it entered its trading range, had you been so inclined. But again, we're more likely to favor the signals from pattern analysis as describe in Chapters 9 and 10, so we will wait for the trading range breakout before deciding what to do with a position like Intel.

The stochastic oscillator is most useful when it's used in conjunction with other indicators. When a stock is trending, the stochastic oscillator is useful in finding entry points within a dominant trend. In an uptrend, for example, a buy signal that's generated when the stochastic oscillator moves from below to above 20 percent is likely to be a good one. The stochastic oscillator signals many overbought conditions within an uptrend and rarely generates useful sell signals. It works well in trading-range situations, and you'll find short-term traders who use it to trigger trading range signals.

Discovering MACD

The *moving average convergence divergence indicator* (MACD) is a trend-following momentum indicator. MACD is designed to generate trend-following trading signals based on moving average crossovers while overcoming problems associated with many other trend-following indicators. MACD also acts as a momentum oscillator, showing when a trend is gaining strength or losing momentum as it cycles above and below a center zero line. MACD is an excellent indicator and an integral part of our trading toolset.

Calculating MACD

Charting packages routinely calculate MACD for you, but knowing how this indicator is created is important for gaining a better understanding of how it works. The MACD calculation isn't complex; it's just three exponential moving averages. Here are the steps:

1. **Calculate a 12-period EMA (see the earlier section on "Exponential moving average").**

2. **Calculate a 26-period EMA.**

3. **Subtract the 26-period EMA from the 12-period EMA to create the MACD line.**

4. **Use the resulting MACD line to calculate a 9-period EMA to create the signal line.**

5. **Plot the MACD as a solid line; plot the signal line as a dashed line.**

Figure 11-5 shows a weekly chart of The Ryland Group stock (RYL) along with an MACD indicator. When using MACD, we prefer weekly charts. That's how the indicator was originally designed to be used, and for our style of trading, a weekly MACD indicator provides more useful information about the strength and direction of a trend and potential trend reversals.

RYL was one of the stocks discussed in Chapter 9, where we showed the cup-and-handle formation on the daily chart (see Figure 9-12). You may want to see whether you can identify the corresponding cup-and-handle formation on the weekly chart in Figure 11-5. It occurred from late October 2002 through March 2003, with the breakout in early April 2003.

Figure 11-5:
A weekly
chart of
The Ryland
Group stock
with MACD.

Now notice the corresponding period on the MACD. As the stock breaks out in early April, the MACD line (the solid line) crosses over the zero center line and actually anticipates the breakout by a week. In addition, notice the period in early January where the MACD line crosses the dashed signal line. This crossover signal is another early indication suggesting a possible new uptrend. See Chapter 13 for more about how we use this signal.

Using MACD

MACD provides a remarkable amount of information in a concise format. As you can see in Figure 11-5, MACD oscillates above and below a center zero line and is a good indicator for showing the direction of the dominant trend, signaling

✔ An uptrend when the MACD line crosses above the center line

✔ A downtrend when the MACD line crosses below the center

Some short-term traders use the signal line to trigger

✔ Buy signals when the MACD line crosses above the signal line

✔ Sell signals when the MACD line crosses below the signal line

We don't, however, find that technique to be very reliable, because it generates too many false signals. Instead, we prefer using the position of the MACD line relative to the zero line as an early indication that a stock's momentum is slowing and may be about to change direction.

Figure 11-6 shows a multiyear chart of weekly prices for the NASDAQ Composite Index. Notice the places where the MACD line crosses above the signal line, and how that corresponds with the NASDAQ Composite bar chart. Although these crossovers occur as the NASDAQ turns higher, making profitable trades based on these signals would've been difficult.

Figure 11-6: Chart of the NASDAQ Composite Index shows a divergent MACD pattern.

Now notice how the NASDAQ Composite establishes a series of lower highs and lower lows, but the MACD line establishes a series of higher lows during the period from April 2001 through October 2002, creating what's known as a divergent pattern. This particular example of a divergent pattern is a bullish divergence. In a bearish divergence, the stock establishes a series of higher highs and higher lows, while the MACD establishes a series of lower highs.

This bullish divergence on the NASDAQ Composite Index needs to be interpreted as a signal showing that the momentum of the multiyear NASDAQ decline was slowing and a buying opportunity likely would soon present itself. Each time the MACD line crosses above the signal line suggests a potential change in the direction of the dominant trend. While this is not an outright buy signal, it does suggest a change is in the wind. The best way to exploit that information is to begin monitoring the strongest stocks in the strongest sectors for breakouts. In Chapter 13, we provide additional ideas to help integrate the information generated by the MACD indicator into a useful trading strategy.

Most charting packages enable you to fine-tune the MACD calculation. Many traders vary the 12-, 26- and 9-week values. Although nothing is inherently wrong with this approach, you nevertheless risk the curve-fitting problem whenever you try to find parameters that give you better results for a specific stock. That said, Gerald Appel, the man who developed MACD, uses values different than the original 12, 26, and 9. He also uses different values to generate buy signals than he does to generate sell signals. So feel free to experiment and have fun after you gain some experience with the default parameters.

Revealing Relative Strength

Relative strength measures the performance of one stock against another, or more commonly, against the performance of an index such as the S&P 500. The idea is to determine how the stock is performing compared with the broad market.

Unfortunately, you may run across another indicator with a similar name when working with your charting software. The other indicator is called the *relative strength index* (RSI) and it is something completely different than the relative strength discussed here. RSI is an oscillator that is used in a similar way as the stochastic oscillator described earlier. To keep the two separate, I suggest you call the RSI by its initials and use the phrase "relative strength" when you mean to compare the performance of a stock against a broad-based index or another stock.

Calculating relative strength

Among the many ways that you calculate relative strength is simply dividing the stock price by the index value and plotting the result, like this:

Relative strength No. 1 = stock price ÷ index value

Another technique compares the price of the stock during a given period of time against the index during the same period. Our preference is comparing percentage changes during the same period. The calculation looks like this:

Relative strength No. 2 = percentage change in stock price ÷ percentage change in index value

Either of these approaches, or any other that you may invent, can be plotted on a stock chart. Some Internet sites provide a relative strength capability. See www.stockcharts.com/charts/performance for an example. Unfortunately, if you're using a charting software package, you'll probably have to program it into your system by using its formula-editing capabilities.

Or, you can look it up. *Investor's Business Daily* has a proprietary calculation for relative strength that ranks stocks based on their six-month performance. It is a handy tool.

Putting relative strength to work

The goal when examining a stock's relative strength is not necessarily to find the best performing stocks in the universe of all stocks, but rather to subtly try to find stocks that are performing better than the average stock as each stock signals a buy.

Relative strength is one of the final pieces to the technical analysis puzzle. You've found a trading candidate when you find a stock that:

- Exhibits fundamentals as a strong company
- Has earnings that are growing faster than average
- Functions well in a strong sector
- Operates in a growing economy
- Is approaching a technical buy signal on its bar chart
- Performs better than the average stock

These characteristics favor a long position, of course. For short position candidates, reverse each criteria.

Part IV
Developing Strategies for When to Buy and Sell Stocks

The 5th Wave   By Rich Tennant

"SELL".

In this part . . .

All of the pieces come together in this part as we show you how to get started as a trader and use fundamental analysis and technical analysis to develop a profitable strategy. In addition, we show you how to create a trading system of your own that matches your trading goals and your personality, and we explain how you can effectively implement that strategy and work with your broker to enter trading positions and exit them under the right circumstances. But most important of all, in this part, we show you how to manage your money to achieve profitable results.

Chapter 12

Money Management Techniques: Know When to Hold 'Em; Know When to Fold 'Em

*Y*ou may find this hard to believe, but some successful traders have a greater number of losing trades than winning trades. How? Their profits from winning trades overwhelm the losses from losing trades. The key to this success is knowing when to hold 'em and when to fold 'em.

The key to long-term trading success is disciplined money management. You must develop a discipline that keeps your losses under control by quickly closing losing positions. The trick is following the rules you set. Good money management minimizes your trading losses when they occur and helps you realize a profit when it hits you right in the old kisser. Ouch. Recognizing the differences between winners and losers — and setting your target prices before ever entering a position — is crucial to your money management strategy. In this chapter, we provide you with a set of rules to follow to get you started.

Identifying Important Characteristics of a Successful Trader

Successful traders share a common trait. You'll find that they all successfully manage their money. The critical points of successful money management may be difficult to implement, but they're easy to identify. They include

- ✔ Planning your trades carefully by identifying entry and exit points
- ✔ Minimizing losses by ruthlessly adhering to your stop-loss points
- ✔ Protecting your profits with trailing stops
- ✔ Exiting your position when the trend ends

When using technical analysis to make your trades, you won't get the lowest entry price or the highest exit price. You will, however, always leave something on the table. The idea is identifying when a trend has begun, entering the position, and riding the trend until it ends.

Opening the Door to Successful Trading

Because your way to successful trading is disciplined money management, the key to opening that door to success is developing a plan for your trades and sticking to that plan, even if it goes against what your gut tells you. Sometimes you think you've picked what seems like the perfect stock, but then it just doesn't perform the way you expected.

Before entering that trade, you need to set an entry point, the price at which you'll enter a trade, and an exit point where you will exit the trade if it goes poorly. Don't deviate from your plan, even if it means accepting the fact that you made a mistake. We discuss setting entry and exit points in the section "Protecting Your Principal." For more info about entering and exiting positions, check out Chapters 10 and 11.

Although it may be cliché, it's nevertheless true: You need to cut your losses short and let your profits run. In other words, fold (sell) when your losses first appear and hold as your profits continue to build.

Your most important money-management goal is to get out of losing positions as quickly as possible. After taking normal up and down price fluctuations (as discussed in Chapters 9 and 10) into consideration, you must develop a method of recognizing when a stock is not behaving the way you expected, and as a result, be prepared to close a losing position before it consumes too much of your trading capital. Try to keep losses below 5 or 6 percent for any position. Or you could think in terms of your total trading capital and try to keep the loss from any single position below 1 or 2 percent.

Unfortunately, achieving a balance between recognizing your losers and dumping them before you lose too much (knowing when to fold 'em) is more difficult than it sounds.

Managing Your Inventory

To be successful, you need to treat trading as a business and your stocks as your business inventory. And just like any other business, you must carefully manage your inventory to succeed.

Factors that are paramount to successful trading are

- ✔ **Viewing trading as a business.** You trade to make money. Sometimes you pick the wrong stock and have to accept a loss. Losses are a part of any business. The key to good business planning is minimizing losses.

- ✔ **Overcoming the most common trader's dilemma.** Many traders get caught up in the moment, trying to defend their position even as it moves in the wrong direction. When your choices no longer make good business sense, you must quickly make cold, hard decisions and decisively act to cut losses short.

- ✔ **Approaching the solution to your trading dilemma as if it's a business problem to solve.** Sell when you stand the chance of making a healthy profit or when you must accept that you've made a mistake and it's time to move on. Select your entry and exit target points before you buy the first share of any stock.

Thinking of trading as a business

So, how do you start thinking of trading as a business? Conceptually, it's simple. Like any other business, traders have fixed costs; variable costs; finite amounts of working capital, assets, and liabilities; fickle customers (or fickle market conditions); and inventory. Managing these business factors results either in profits or losses, and you, of course, want to maximize the profits and minimize the losses. The most important step you can take in treating trading as a business is thinking of the contents of your portfolio as your inventory.

Traders need to manage their businesses with the same clear-eyed, cold-hearted detachment as any successful business owner. Unfortunately, many traders, even the experienced ones, find thinking about trading as a business a difficult task. They make a decision, take a position, and then stick with it regardless of how far prices go down — even when their stock flushes farther down the toilet.

Recognizing the trader's dilemma

Selling is hard. For some reason it's emotionally more difficult to close a position, especially a losing position, than it is to open it. Traders rationalize holding a losing position by saying to themselves, "I'll give it some room to work out, it's only a paper loss." But that rationalization is foolhardy. You never hear traders describe a winning trade as a paper gain, and you shouldn't rationalize losing positions that way, either.

Falling in love

Traders fall in love with their stocks. Understanding how falling in love with a stock can happen is easy. You spend many a late night finding the right stock. You evaluate the economy, find a strong sector, research the financial condition of the top companies in the sector, and check the charts.

You didn't mean for it to happen, but you try to justify your actions as nothing more than a fling . . . really. You find a stock that looks promising, and then something clicks. You hardly notice at first, but now you're in love.

So you enter your trade, and . . . your stock's price goes the wrong way. Which way is the wrong way depends on your position. If you own the stock and its price falls, obviously that's the wrong way. But if you sell the stock short, the wrong way is if its price rises. We discuss the mechanics of selling short in Chapter 14. Either way, you're losing money.

Breaking up is hard to do

After all the late nights, the hard work, and the brilliant analysis, you may end up asking yourself, "How could I have been so wrong?" You're not alone. We just kept thinking: "How can everyone else be so wrong? This is a great stock. It has to go up. We'll wait for everyone else to come to their senses, to realize the error of their ways, and then this trade will turn out just fine." Nope. Didn't happen.

The idea that the market may not love your stock, too, sometimes is hard to swallow. After you've taken a position, a psychological quirk (everyone has it) makes you want to be right. Somehow, you need to overcome this quirk. Otherwise, it can lead to many losses and possibly to financial ruin.

Finding a better plan

Approaching the trader's dilemma as though it were a business problem for you to solve can be helpful. The business of women's fashions provides an analogy that will do so nicely. The fashion industry works in obvious cycles. For example, you see long-term cycles at work as hemlines rise and fall and even longer cycles as you witness periodic mysteries that cause Capri pants and bell-bottom trousers to appear and just as easily disappear. You also see shorter cycles as clothing for the current season is discounted to make way for the next season's fashions. These shorter seasonal cycles illustrate the day-to-day issues that traders face.

Picking stock for the seasons

As spring approaches, retailers stock up on colorful, lightweight merchandise. You may even see swimsuits before then for those lucky souls who head to the tropics to escape the frosty chill. Fall clothes start showing up in stores as summer heats up. Before summer is over, heavier-weight clothes, including a selection of winter coats, begin appearing on clothing racks.

Ideally, retailers try to sell all their winter coats — and all their bathing suits and spring outfits — before the next season arrives, but that rarely happens. For whatever reason, retailers often have unsold inventory as the end of the season approaches.

Cleaning out the stock

You can use a couple of alternatives for handling unsold seasonal inventory, but neither is pleasant. The retailer can store the merchandise until next year, but storage costs carry charges that eat into capital. The greatest cost of storing merchandise is the lost opportunity. The retailer's capital gets locked up in unsold merchandise and thus can't be used to buy current-season inventory that's more in demand. Making matters worse is the fact that fashions offer no guarantee that they'll remain fashionable, so selling this year's inventory next year may be impossible.

Another alternative is marking down the price of your merchandise beginning relatively early in the season and continuing to do so until all the merchandise is sold. This approach quickly:

- Frees up capital that the retailer then can use to buy newer inventory
- Stops the accrual of carrying charges
- Clears out storage and display space
- Avoids the risk that the merchandise will become worthless in the future

This solution is better, even though it often means selling the merchandise below cost.

Clothiers buy inventory to sell it at a profit. They know their costs, and they determine the profits they want to earn from the sale of each item. Retailers try to earn as much profit as possible, but start cutting prices whenever sales don't happen quickly enough.

Retailers cannot afford to fall in love with their winter coats. They need the space and the capital for spring merchandise. They won't be choked up when it's time to sell.

Keeping your inventory current

Managing your trading business as if you were a retail merchant is a good idea. The cycle of economic expansion, peak, recession, and trough, as described in Chapter 5, is somewhat akin to the four seasons. Your stocks are your inventory. Their prices rise and are discounted in anticipation of the changing economic cycles, as described in Chapter 13. And your trading account is your working capital. Just like the retail merchant, your goal is to protect your principal, your working capital, so you can stay in business.

However, you may find that some factors differ. The stock market is, of course, a much more efficient pricing mechanism than the retail clothing industry. You cannot set the price of your merchandise; the market does it for you.

You have several approaches you can take to keep your trading inventory current. Many traders use trend analysis and relative strength analysis, as described in Chapters 10 and 11, to try to take positions in the best performing stocks and sectors. Some traders also track general market conditions, quarterly and annual SEC filings, company announcements, and key analysts' reports, as described in Chapters 5, 6, and 7.

We tend to combine both approaches in the ways we trade. We want to own strong stocks in strong sectors, and we want to know how well the companies manage their business. Although any changes in these elements are worth a look-see, we don't have immediate hair-trigger reactions. We do sometimes replace positions that begin to underperform, relative to the market, with emerging leaders, and yet we show a little extra patience with positions that are profitable but are beginning to slightly underperform. If, however, a stock position starts losing money, then we close the position without a second thought. The goal is to protect your trading capital, and we show you some techniques and examples to accomplish this in the next section.

Protecting Your Principal

In the same way that retail merchants face the possibility of holding on to their stock of winter coats that may fall out of style, you can avoid the risk of owning a stock that falls out of favor with other investors and loses its value. By acting quickly when you see changes in the market, you can avoid losing a large chunk of your trading capital (or *principal*). As long as you get out of your position quickly, your trading capital won't be tied up in a losing stock position any longer, and you'll escape the losing trade with most of your cash intact. More important, you'll be able to trade another day.

It makes sense, of course, to hold onto a stock as long as its price is appreciating. However, being mindful of when your stock price begins to fall is important. You must have a plan for dealing with losing trades or deteriorating profits. Time to fold up the stock and get out!

If your goal is to keep trading for a long time, the only way to do that is to not lose too much money. This might seem patently obvious, but you would be surprised how few investors, and even some traders, make capital preservation their highest priority. To keep from making that mistake, it helps if you keep these important goals in mind as you trade:

- ✓ Protecting your principal comes first
- ✓ Not letting a large profit turn into a small profit
- ✓ Not letting a small profit turn into a loss
- ✓ Not letting a small loss turn into a large loss

Recovering from a large loss: It ain't easy

When thinking about protecting your principal, you need to accept that taking a small loss is better than risking a larger one. You need to understand how badly (and quickly) things can go wrong, and how that can result in a loss of a huge chunk of your principal with little chance of recovering it. To illustrate this concept, check out an example of the impact that large losses can have on your money.

Perhaps you bought XYZ stock for $10 per share. The stock falls to $9, representing a $1 loss. You've lost 10 percent of the original price of the stock.

To recover from that loss, the stock price must rise from $9 to $10, but notice that 10 percent of $9 is only 90 cents. In other words, your stock must gain more than 10 percent to recover from a 10 percent loss. Here's how to review the math using percentages.

To find the percentage loss, push or click on the respective percent buttons on your calculator, use a computer spreadsheet, or simply divide $1 by $10.

$$\$10 - \$9 = \$1 \rightarrow \$1 \div \$10 = 0.10 \rightarrow 0.10 \times 100 = 10\%$$

To find the percentage gain required to recover that $1 loss — again notice that your stock is now a $9 stock and that 10 percent of $9 is only 90 cents, not $1 — divide $1 by $9.

$$\$1 \div \$9 = 0.1111 \rightarrow 0.1111 \times 100 = 11.11\%$$

In other words, your $9 stock needs to gain a little more than 11 percent to get back to even.

For losses of less than 10 percent, the required gain isn't significantly greater than the loss you've just experienced. But for larger losses, the problem grows unmanageably. Look at Table 12-1 to see what we mean.

Table 12-1	Percentage Gain Required to Recover Loss
Loss of	*Percentage Gain Required to Recover Loss*
5%	5.2%
10%	11.1%
25%	33.3%
50%	100%
75%	300%
100%	Game Over

Getting a stock to go up 5 percent or even 10 percent is a hard enough task. It seems irrational to hope for a stock that's fallen by 50 percent to recover 100 percent, or a stock that's fallen by 75 percent to recover 300 percent.

Selling quickly and avoiding large losses is a much better course to take. Otherwise, you'll be out of trading capital, and out of business, in a mighty quick hurry.

Why traders use percentages to describe results

Why do traders use percentages to describe their results? The use of percentages is a simple way of accurately comparing the results of one trade with the results of another — as a percentage, a $1 gain on $10 stock is identical to a $10 gain on a $100 stock. The price per share is not as important as the percentage gain (or loss) or the total gain (or loss).

Look at it like this: If you have a total of $1,000 in your trading account, you can buy 100 shares of a $10 stock, or you can buy 10 shares of a $100 stock. If the price of either stock rises by 10 percent, your account total is the same in either case — $1,100. A 10 percent rise in a $10 stock is $1. A 10 percent rise in a $100 stock is $10. But the total amount of money earned is the same in either scenario.

If you think in terms of percentage gains or losses, you can correctly compare the results of one trade with that of another. The actual price of a stock, and the actual number of points gained or lost, isn't as important as the size of the move in percentage terms. Although you can buy many more shares of the lower priced stock, it's equally difficult for either stock to move 10 percent. If you think about it like this, you will see that there is no reason to favor the lower priced stock, even if you can buy more shares, over the higher priced stock.

Setting a target price for handling losses

The most important concept of protecting your principal is accepting the fact that you made a mistake and moving on. Sell that loser. Don't let a small loss turn into a large one. Before entering a trade, make sure you set a target price that you're willing to initially pay for a stock, and set a target price for selling it if the trade results in a loss.

Setting a stop-loss price (or, as traders say, "setting your stop") is more akin to an art than a science. You can employ several techniques for determining your stop-loss price. One that others often advocate, but we don't recommend, is choosing a predetermined percentage loss as your stop-loss price. We think using technical analysis (see Chapters 9 and 10) to identify when a trade has failed is a better approach. Here's an example.

Figure 12-1 is a daily price chart of Time Warner (TWX) stock that shows support and resistance lines, respectively, drawn on the chart at approximately $14.75 and $16.85 and indicates the stock has just broken out of a long trading range on high-volume. Support, resistance, and breakouts are discussed in Chapter 9. The breakout is identified on the chart.

Figure 12-1 represents a picture-perfect setup for entering a trade. As discussed in Chapter 9, your entry point for this trade occurs at $17, when the stock breaks through the resistance line. But how do you handle the trade if it doesn't work out? Or, perhaps a better question to ask is, how do you know when the trade has failed?

One of several approaches suggests that if the breakout fails (the stock price declines back below the resistance level), you need to exit your position immediately. Using the Time Warner example in Figure 12-1, if the stock were to fall below the resistance line ($16.85) after it traded above $17, then you need to exit the position.

Figure 12-1:
Daily chart
of Time
Warner
(TWX)
stock.

Another approach suggests that if the stock falls below the mid-point of the trading range, in this case somewhere around $15.88, then the breakout buy signal has failed. In that case, you can use any price below $15.88 as the stop-loss price to exit from this position.

In the first scenario, the financial risk is small. As long as you get good fill prices (fills) on both your entry and exit orders, your risk should be no more than 25 to 50 cents per share, which reflects a loss of only 1.5 percent to 3 percent on the trade. Fills are discussed further in Chapter 15.

In the second approach, the risk is greater. The difference between the $17 breakout price and the $15.88 stop-loss price is $1.12, or about 6.5 percent of the purchase price. Poor fills on either entry or exit orders increase that amount.

The trade-off between the two approaches is clear. The first one risks a smaller amount before triggering the exit trade, but is prone to whipsaws, which means that you may be bumped out of a potentially winning trade. The second risks a greater amount but is less prone to whipsaws. In general, shorter-term swing traders and day traders (see Chapters 16 and 17) are more likely to choose the first, and position traders who expect to hold a trade for several weeks or months are more likely to choose the second.

Either approach is rational, so you need to choose the one that makes you feel comfortable. If you start second-guessing your stop-loss points, they're no longer useful, so be sure to use an approach that you'll honor. Using the first approach may make more sense for new position traders, so tight stops can serve as educational tools. You'll risk less on each trade but you'll be subject to a few whipsaws, and you'll get into the habit of selling when you have small losses. And that's a good habit to learn.

Determining good trading candidates

Whether the stock in this example (Figure 12-1) is a good trading candidate is open to discussion. From a technical perspective (see Chapter 9), it is. But Time Warner (TWX) had very poor financial results in fiscal 2002, losing more than $10 per share before extraordinary items, and more than $22 per share afterward. The company also lost money in fiscal 2001 and had poor but positive earnings for the prior three years.

The TWX breakout on high volume was probably driven by news that AOL, which is owned by Time Warner, announced significant cost-cutting efforts in a bid to return to profitability. Traders who remember AOL's heyday were encouraged by the news and drove the stock price higher.

This trade has the potential to be profitable. However, because of the firm's recent financial history, we'd probably pass on this trade and save our capital for another stock with a better financial profile.

In general, this example is applicable to any *new* trading positions. To find good trading candidates, you need to decide whether the trade makes sense from a financial and technical perspective. Then you'll be better able to identify a trading pattern that clearly shows when the original trading signal has failed and to place a stop-loss order nearby, thus reducing your risk of losing too much of your precious trading capital. Only under those circumstances should you enter the trade.

Strategies for handling profitable trades

Profitable trades are somewhat easier to handle than losses, but they're not without complications. You must decide whether you want to leave your stop-loss point where it is or try to lock in a small profit by moving it up.

You obviously want to try to keep any profit from turning into a loss. For example, say that you enter the TWX trade in our Figure 12-1 example, and a few days after entering the order it remains in positive territory with a small profit. For this discussion, assume that your original stop price is $15.88, the mid-point of the trading range. Your choice is to leave the stop where it is or move it above the resistance line, to $17. If you choose the former, and the stock trades below $15.88, your formerly profitable trade will be closed for a loss. If you choose the latter, you will be stopped out if TWX trades below $17. You must now decide whether to move your stop-loss order to protect the small profit, or leave the stop where it is to keep from jeopardizing the stock's chances of gaining more.

This kind of balancing act is a delicate one. You're trying to catch a bigger trend higher and ride it, which argues for leaving the stop where it is for a little while longer. But sooner, rather than later, you'll want to move your stop-loss above your entry price. This decision becomes easier as the position progresses. As your profit grows, you'll want to continue adjusting your exit points upward. This is called a *trailing stop,* and is discussed in the section "Using trailing stops."

Breaking the pattern of higher highs and higher lows

Trends are easy to see on charts. Examine Figure 12-2, and you can easily identify the trend that carried the price of this stock from less than $34 to more than $50 per share. In this case, the stock bounces around a bit, moves higher and lower over time, and creates a series of higher highs followed by higher lows. See Chapter 10 for more on trends and higher highs and higher lows.

Although this pattern sometimes is difficult to define rigorously, you can easily identify it on a chart. We point out some of the significant interim highs and interim lows on the chart. Take note that the stock price appears to ride the moving average line (see Chapter 11) as it progresses. As a trader, this kind of trend is the type you want and like to ride for as long as you can, because it'll make you some money.

Figure 12-2 also provides a couple of clues that this trend came to an end in October. Notice the price gap (see Chapter 10) that occurs in mid October, and the accompanying high trading volume. That gap was your first hint that your stock may be in trouble. Another hint is shown at the point where the line indicating the stock's actual price closes significantly below the line indicating its moving average. And a third hint occurs when the stock fails to reach a higher price after the gap occurs.

Figure 12-2:
Broken
pattern of
higher highs
and higher
lows.

Any one of these events may carry enough weight for you to close your position. Taken together, they clearly signal that the upward trend probably is over, and you need to exit your position.

Using trailing stops

After you've entered a position and it becomes profitable, you want to move your stop to protect your profits. This is known as a trailing stop, because you keep moving the stop higher as your profits grow. In an uptrend, a stock makes intermittent higher highs and intermittent higher lows (see Chapter 10). Use the higher lows to define your stop points. After the stock has made a higher high, reset the stop to either the most recent higher low, or the one just before it. Using Figure 12-2 again, after the stock reaches its August low around $41, and is heading for the September high, reset the stop using the July low around $37.50.

Tracking market indexes

Individual stocks and entire sectors of similar stocks regularly fall in and out of fashion. Sometimes these changes happen in a grand way, such as when the Internet sector fell out of favor, along with the NASDAQ Composite Index, in 2000.

Look at the chart of the NASDAQ Composite in Figure 12-3. Although the NASDAQ index peaked in March 2000, by early April it formed a lower high that violated (fell below) its recent intermittent lows and crossed below its 50-day moving average.

By the time April rolled around, the vast majority of Internet stocks were in worse shape than the NASDAQ. This bursting bubble was a prime example of a dramatic shift in market conditions. If you were trading at the time, you had two choices:

- ✔ Sell your positions when you began to realize that prices, market fundamentals, and technical indicators were simultaneously deteriorating.

- ✔ Wait out the market, hoping things would get better.

If you held Internet stocks during that time and chose the second option, you took a much greater loss by selling later. Unfortunately, many buy-and-hold investors unwisely believed that the downturn was a temporary blip and that Internet investments would remain viable. In fact, a number of stocks never recovered and some no longer are trading.

Figure 12-3:
Chart of the NASDAQ Composite Index, 1999–2000.

The right choice then, as usual, was to close your positions. By following these simple strategies in April 2000, you'd have had more than enough information to know that things were not going according to plan. Although you wouldn't have sold your stocks at the highest prices, neither would you have ridden them to their ultimate lows. By selling, you protect your profits and your trading capital, so you can trade another day.

Knowing when a trend is complete is just as difficult as knowing when it began. You can't trade with perfect knowledge, and you can't predict the future — neither can we. But you can use these tools to identify when a trend is likely to begin, and when it's likely to end. And if you use excellent money management, you're likely to trade profitably.

Understanding Your Risks

You need to look at the risks that traders face. The three general categories are market risks, investment risks, and trading risks.

Market risks

Market risks are pretty much out of your control. Of course you understand the risk that the markets are bound to rise and fall, but understanding the risks you face when they do helps you manage your money better. Three key risks that you can manage as a trader are

- **Inflation risk:** Although inflation is a risk that traders rarely face, it nevertheless impacts people who are afraid to take risks. You definitely can't be a trader if you're afraid of taking risks. Basically, the risk that this factor poses is that your money won't grow fast enough to exceed the increases in costs that inflation causes. As you know, the basics — housing, clothing, medical expenses, and food — increase in price each year. By investing in monetary vehicles that don't keep pace with inflation, you actually end up losing money.

- **Marketability risk:** This factor relates to how liquid your investment is. If you're restricted from selling your investment when you want to do so, your target selling point won't mean much. For most stock traders, this factor isn't an issue, but if, for example, you choose to invest in a small company whose stock isn't traded on one of the major stock markets, then you risk not being able to close your stock position when the time is right.

- **Currency translation risk:** Currency translation refers to disparities in trading stocks of companies in foreign countries. It's only a factor when you trade foreign stocks, because you then must be concerned with fluctuations between the values of the U.S. dollar and the currency in the country where the company is located. Even if the stock increases in price, you can still lose money based on the currency exchange rate. If the value of the dollar falls against the other country's currency, your investment can be worth less when you convert it back to dollars.

Investment risks

Investment risks relate directly to how you invest your money and manage your entry and exit trades. Two critical risks that you must understand and manage are

- ✔ **Opportunity risk:** This kind of risk involves balancing your trade-offs. When you trade, you establish a position that ties up money that otherwise can be used elsewhere. After you choose a stock and buy it, you lose the opportunity to buy something else that may strike your fancy, until you trade out of the first position. Essentially, you can miss other opportunities while your money's tied up in another position.

- ✔ **Concentration risk:** This kind of risk happens when you put too many eggs in one basket. You may think you've found that hot stock that's going to make you a millionaire, so you decide to invest a huge portion of your principal into that stock. By concentrating so much of your money on one investment, you also concentrate the risks associated with that investment and with the possibility of losing it all.

Trading risks

Risks that are unique to trading increase simultaneously with increases in trading volume. Day traders and swing traders often see a greater impact caused by these risks than do position traders, but everyone needs to be aware of these issues. See Chapters 16 and 17 for more information about swing trading and day trading, respectively. Risks associated with trading are

- ✔ **Slippage risk:** Hidden costs associated with every transaction are the focus of this risk factor. Every time you enter or exit a position, your account balance dwindles by a small amount. Every time you execute a trade, you subject yourself to the problem of buying at the ask price but selling at the bid price. The ask price is the lowest price available for the stock that you want. The bid price is the highest price someone is willing to pay for shares you own. Unfortunately, the bid price is always less than the ask price. Although you can mitigate bid/ask problems by using limit orders, doing so subjects you to the risk that your order won't get filled. Find out more about the spread between bid and ask prices in Chapter 14. The amounts for each trade may at first seem small, but as your trading volume increases, so do the amounts you lose to slippage.

- ✔ **Poor execution risk:** This problem occurs whenever your broker has a difficult time filling your order, which can result from any number of factors, including fast market conditions, poor availability of stock, or the absence of other buyers and sellers. The result is always the same: The price you expect is somewhat different than the price you actually receive. Although you can mitigate this problem to a degree by using limit orders, you still risk having the stock trade through your limit price and not getting your order filled at all.

✔ **Gap risk:** This kind of risk comes into play whenever a break in trading occurs. Sometimes a stock opens at a price significantly higher or lower than its previous close, and sometimes a stock trades right through your exit price. For example, a stock may close at $25 a share today and open tomorrow morning at $20. If your planned exit price is $24, and you have a stop order in place, your order is likely to be filled at the opening price or worse. Price gaps created in this way occur most often at the open. And although relatively rare, a gap also can occur during the trading day whenever surprising news is reported or trading halts.

Chapter 13

Using Fundamental and Technical Analysis for Optimum Strategy

Knowing the current state of the economy can help you improve your trading results. However, knowing the current state of the market is crucial, because you obviously want to buy stocks in a bull market and sell them, or short them, in a bear market. Besides the obvious, you also want a strategy for trading stocks during market transitions and consolidation phases.

As a result, you need a method for identifying and categorizing the differing phases of bull and bear markets. We recommend using the six phases in the list that follows. Doing so enables you to adjust your trading strategies for each phase of the market, regardless of whether you're trading stocks, bonds, indexes, futures, or options. The six phases of the market are

- ✔ **Bullish transition** — the market is transitioning from a bear market to a bull market

- ✔ **Bull market** — a persistent rising trend in the market

- ✔ **Bullish pullback** — a bull market in the midst of a pullback

- ✔ **Bearish transition** — the market is transitioning from a bull market to a bear market

- ✔ **Bear market** — a persistent downtrend

- ✔ **Bearish pullback** — a bear market in the midst of a consolidation

This chapter shows you how to identify these phases of the market using the techniques of fundamental and technical analyses that we describe throughout this book. Although no single detail or event can enable you to out-and-out declare a bull market or bear market, we address many small details that, when taken together, enable you to make informed conclusions. Likewise, distinguishing a transition phase from a pullback phase can be difficult. This chapter helps you methodically analyze the economy, the market, leading and lagging sectors, and individual stocks, so you can identify the particular phase a market is in. Furthermore, this chapter describes unified trading strategies that are built around these market phases.

Seeing the Big Picture

Identifying the current economic climate is the first step toward identifying the current phase of the markets. Only a tiny fraction of available economic data is required to develop a snapshot of the economy from which you can infer the current state of the markets. The conditions that you need to know (and questions you need to ask) to be able to evaluate and determine the cycle that the economy currently is in are

- Where interest rates are headed. Are they rising, falling, or staying the same?

- What officials of the Federal Reserve System (the Fed) are doing now. What is the Fed likely to do in the future?

- How business is performing, in general. Is industrial production rising or falling?

- Which sectors are leading and which are lagging. Are economically sensitive stocks appreciating or declining in value, or are traders currently favoring defensive stocks?

This information is crucial for determining the cycle in which the economy currently is functioning. (For more about economic cycles, see Chapter 5.) Fortunately, the economic picture doesn't change quickly, so taking the temperature of the economy, if you will, can be a weekly or monthly exercise. Ultimately, maintaining a background knowledge of the cycles through which the economy is passing helps you identify current phases of the markets, which, in turn, can help you make better trading decisions.

Knowing when the Fed is your friend

Current interest rates and current interest-rate trends help determine the current position of the economy within the business cycle. Low interest rates are associated with economic troughs and high rates with economic peaks. In a nutshell, the Fed lowers rates to stimulate economic activity and raises rates to slow it. But the time lag between the Fed's activity and any reaction by the economy often is a long one, making the Fed's monetary policy an imprecise indicator. Nevertheless, you can use interest rates to get a rough idea about the current economic landscape.

Interest rate reductions that the Fed okays generally are good news for the stock market. The opposite also is true. When the Fed tightens its monetary policy by raising interest rates, stocks normally react poorly. Either way, stock markets may not react immediately, and unfortunately, many months can pass before either the stock market or economy responds in either direction to the Fed's action. Although the old stock market saying, "three steps and a stumble," doesn't always hold true, markets do often head lower after the Fed raises rates for the third time.

In short, falling interest rates typically lead to a rising economy and to a market that's changing from a bear market to a bull market — in other words, a bullish transition. Ultimately, a bullish transition leads to a new bull market. Conversely, however, rising interest rates sooner or later lead to a market that's changing from a bull market to a bear market — a bearish transition, and ultimately a bear market. The problem: No consistent timetable exists that enables you to anticipate when these changes will occur, so you should use interest rate changes only as a hint that a transition may be coming and wait for an additional confirmation before you act on a trading strategy.

Keeping an eye on industrial production

In addition to interest rates, industrial production is another indicator that provides insight into the health of the economy. You can monitor industrial production by keeping track of the Federal Reserve's monthly report, "Industrial Production and Capacity Utilization," at www.federalreserve.gov/releases/G17/Current/default.htm. New economic growth is suggested when industrial production statistics start inching higher, a sign that usually indicates the market either is entering a bullish transition or will soon do so. Similarly, robust growth numbers often accompany a bull market phase. Conversely, leveling off or falling industrial production data shows that a bearish transition can be expected. And finally, a bear market phase often accompanies falling production data.

Watching sector rotation

Monitoring leading and lagging economic sectors (see Chapter 5) provides direct insight into the current state of the stock market, because some industries tend to perform well at the beginning of an economic expansion and others tend to perform relatively well as the economy cools. Traders often try to anticipate changes in the economy by watching specific sectors that they know have tendencies to rise or fall in specific patterns that coincide with one economic or market cycle. These patterned tendencies are called *sector rotation.* Although you won't see picture-perfect sector rotation every cycle, you will see enough similarities from cycle to cycle to enable you to gain additional insight into the current phase of the economy and the stock market.

Sectors that perform well during specific economic cycles and market phases are described in the following sections.

Anticipating a new bull market

Economic conditions that foster a new bull market include low interest rates and hints that industrial production is beginning to rise. Traders who monitor these economic conditions often respond to them by buying the stocks of cyclical and technology-based companies. Bullish transition phases usually begin in this manner.

The stocks of companies whose business is sensitive to the economic cycle have traditionally been called cyclical stocks. Within the past few decades, technology-based companies have joined these so-called cyclical companies as bell-weather economic indicators. The stocks of cyclical and technology-based companies, and the companies themselves, perform best when interest rates are low. Increased sales of their products drive industrial production numbers higher. These companies usually lead the market and often rally before an economic trough, or recession, completely bottoms out. Unfortunately, traders jump the gun as often as they get it right, so whenever you see cyclical and tech stocks begin to rally, it pays to be skeptical. Rather than jump to the conclusion that a sector rally means a bull market is just around the corner, you need to instead consider that it indicates only a bullish transition.

Industries known for making up cyclical sectors include

- ✔ Automobile and automotive component manufacturers
- ✔ Consumer durable manufacturers that produce products such as appliances and consumer electronics
- ✔ Retailing, such as department stores, big-box discounters, and specialty retailers (excluding food, beverage, pharmaceutical, and other non-durable retailers)
- ✔ Media companies, such as movie studios, radio and television companies, and book publishers
- ✔ Hotels, restaurants, and entertainment and other leisure companies

Technology-sector industries include

- ✔ Semiconductor (computer chip) manufacturers and manufacturers of equipment to produce semiconductors
- ✔ Computers and computer peripheral device manufacturers
- ✔ Software and service companies
- ✔ Telecommunication and Internet service companies
- ✔ Information technology service companies

Watching the economy rebound

Strength in the industrial sectors is a condition that usually indicates the markets may be entering a bull market phase. As the economy begins showing signs of growth, you often see a rally in industrial sectors. Large industrial companies often need to borrow money to increase production, a factor that makes them sensitive to interest rate changes. These companies tend to perform best in a low interest rate environment. Rising industrial production that drives industrial-sector earnings and stock prices higher is no coincidence.

Companies in the industrial sectors include

- ✔ Building products manufacturers
- ✔ Construction and engineering firms
- ✔ Aerospace and defense companies
- ✔ Electrical equipment manufacturers
- ✔ Airlines and air freight, transportation, and infrastructure companies
- ✔ Major manufacturing conglomerates (which are widely diversified companies such as GE, Rockwell, and Tyco)

Approaching a market top

When the economy is firing on all cylinders, industrial production is robust, and interest rates are beginning to rise. However, the stock market is trying to anticipate what happens next and it's probably nearing its peak. Basic material stocks, energy stocks, and consumer staple company stocks tend to do well under these conditions. When you begin seeing strength in the consumer staples sector, you need to begin searching for confirmation of a bearish transitional phase.

Companies in the basic industry and materials sectors include

- ✔ Metals and mining companies
- ✔ Chemical companies

✔ Construction material companies

✔ Forest-product companies, including paper, packaging, and container companies

The energy sectors include

✔ Oil and natural gas exploration and drilling services

✔ Refineries

Companies in the consumer staple sectors include

✔ Food and beverage companies

✔ Household product companies and other consumer staples, such as personal-care companies

✔ Tobacco companies

✔ Retailers, specifically food, beverage, drug, and other non-durable retailers

Weathering a bear market

Healthcare and other service-sector stocks often perform better than the average stock as the economy peaks and bullish market tendencies fade to bearish outlooks. The stocks of utility and financial companies also tend to perform better than average during bear markets, because they're considered safe havens from the accompanying tide of rising interest rates and flattening industrial production. As these stocks begin showing higher relative strength, you need to move your indicator from bearish transition to a bear market phase.

Consumer service sectors include

✔ Healthcare equipment and supplies companies

✔ Healthcare providers

✔ Pharmaceutical and biotechnology companies

The utility sector includes

✔ Electric power generation and distribution companies

✔ Natural gas distribution companies

✔ Water utilities companies

Companies in the financial sectors include

- ✔ Diversified financial service companies, including banks and brokerage firms
- ✔ Commercial and investment banks
- ✔ Insurance companies

Taking a relatively long point of view as you monitor the markets for sector rotation is a good idea. By that we mean you're not interested in the day-by-day ups and downs, but rather, you're trying to evaluate sector performance during periods of many weeks and even months. Remembering that bull markets tend to lift prices for all stocks is also important. So when you monitor sector performance, you try to find the sectors that are performing better than others. In bear markets, stocks that hold their values, for example, will outperform all stocks that have falling prices.

Finding the dominant trend

You need to own stocks during bull markets, and sell them, or short them (see Chapter 14), during bear markets. In other words, you want to trade with the *dominant trend.* The stock market tends to lead the economy, so using the market's performance as your primary reference to find the dominant trend makes sense. Combining your analysis of the dominant market trend with the background knowledge you gained from analyzing interest rates, industrial production data, and sector rotation helps you refine the way you categorize the current phase of the market. That kind of refinement means your trading performance will improve when you can make trades with the dominant trend or market phase on your side.

Looking at weekly index charts

You need only a handful of tools to determine the dominant trend or phase of the market. We use two, the weekly charts of broad market indexes and the bullish percent index, which is discussed in the next section. Significant changes in the markets happen slowly, and thus show up better in weekly charts than they do in daily charts, because insignificant changes get filtered out.

We typically monitor charts of the major indexes such as the S&P 500 (SPX) or the NASDAQ Composite Index (COMPX). Doing so makes visually identifying bull markets and bear markets easy. They appear as trends, exactly like the ones shown on the stock charts in Chapter 10. A bull market appears as a series of higher highs and higher lows on weekly index charts. A bear market appears as a series of lower highs and lower lows. These are the dominant trends.

Pullback patterns, such as the flag and pennant patterns discussed in Chapter 10, correspond to the bullish pullback and bearish pullback conditions. And bullish transition and bearish transition phases may signal a trend reversal, in much the same way that reversal patterns and trading ranges often lead to a change in direction.

Figure 13-1 shows the phases of a bull market using a weekly chart of the NASDAQ Composite Index. Figure 13-2 shows the phases of a bear market using an earlier weekly chart of the NASDAQ Composite Index.

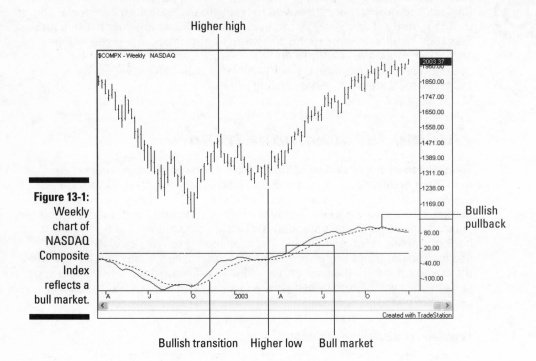

Figure 13-1:
Weekly
chart of
NASDAQ
Composite
Index
reflects a
bull market.

Higher high

Bullish
pullback

Bullish transition   Higher low   Bull market

Trend identification tools that we discuss in Chapters 9, 10, and 11 all apply to these weekly charts. For example, you can easily spot the higher high and higher low in Figure 13-1 that occurred at the end of 2002 and the beginning of 2003. These higher highs and higher lows correspond to a bull market. You also can easily see the lower highs and lower lows in Figure 13-2; they accompanied the long-running bear market.

You also need to be able to identify the Moving Average Convergence Divergence (MACD) crossover points and divergent patterns on these charts. We describe MACD in detail in Chapter 11. MACD signals provide you with additional information to augment the way you categorize current phases of the market.

Lower highs

Bullish transition

Bear market   Lower lows

Bearish transition

Figure 13-2:
Weekly chart of NASDAQ Composite Index reflects a bear market.

Using MACD to indicate bull and bear markets is straightforward:

- ✔ A bull market is indicated when the MACD line is greater than the zero line and the MACD line is greater than the trigger line.

- ✔ A bear market is indicated when the MACD line is less than the zero line and the MACD line is less than the trigger line.

However, pullback and transition phases are not as clearly defined:

- ✔ Either a bullish transition — or a bearish pullback — is indicated when the MACD line is less than the zero line, and the MACD line crosses above the trigger line.

- ✔ Either a bearish transition — or a bullish pullback — is indicated when the MACD is greater than the zero line and the MACD line crosses below the trigger line.

Use the bullish percent index (BPI), described in the next section, in conjunction with pattern analysis, as described in Chapter 10, to help distinguish between the transition and pullback phases.

Using Figure 13-2, you can see where the MACD indicator on the weekly chart is less than zero and crosses above its trigger line. Because of the length and depth of the bear market, traders were looking for a transition phase instead of a pullback phrase. Therefore, when the MACD crossed above its trigger line, it suggested the market may have been trying to turn from a bear market to a bull market in a bullish transition phase. You can see three instances in Figure 13-2 where the MACD signaled three of these bullish transitions in 2002. Two of them failed, but the third resulted in a bull market, which, as you can see in Figure 13-1, lasted at least through the end of 2003.

Using the bullish percent index

You can use the *bullish percent index* (BPI) to fine-tune and confirm trading signals you see on the weekly index charts. The BPI is a powerful indicator that shows the percentage of stocks that have generated buy signals compared with the total number of stocks in a given index. This indicator originally was used to track all the stocks on the NYSE, but it also can be applied to any broad market index, including the S&P 500, the NASDAQ Composite, or even the more narrowly defined NASDAQ 100 and sector indexes. BPI, however, is most useful when evaluating larger groups of stocks.

The BPI is based on point-and-figure charts — probably the oldest and simplest stock charting technique — and helps you evaluate the strength of the market as a whole. Calculating the BPI is a bit daunting, but fortunately, it's published online. For example, you can find BPIs at Stockcharts.com, where the current states of this indicator for the major indexes and several sector indexes are displayed and interpreted. See stockcharts.com/education/glossary/bullishPercent.html for details.

As an indicator, BPI works a bit like an oscillator (see Chapter 11). It displays values ranging from zero to 100 percent to identify overbought and oversold market conditions. For example, when fewer than 30 percent of all stocks are on a buy signal, the BPI shows that the market is oversold and ripe for correction. When more than 70 percent of all stocks signal a buy, the BPI shows the market is overbought and ripe for a downturn.

However, like individual stocks, broad market indexes can remain overbought or oversold for extended periods of time, so by themselves, BPI readings below 30 percent or above 70 percent don't necessarily represent respective buy or sell signals. BPI can and does provide readings well above 70 percent and well below 30 percent for extended periods of time.

Changes in BPI levels are triggered by reversal patterns. A 6 percent change in the stocks of a given index is required to trigger any changes (up or down) in the BPI. These reversal patterns are interpreted to describe the state of the market using six unique conditions that roughly correspond with the six phases of the market described in the introduction to this chapter. The six states of the BPI are

- ✔ **Bull alert** — Corresponds with the bullish transition phase. It's triggered when the BPI is less than 30 percent and reverses direction when 6 percent (or more) of all stocks change to buy signals.

- ✔ **Bull confirmed** — Corresponds with the bull market phase. When the BPI indicator forms a higher high, a *bull market is confirmed.*

- ✔ **Bull correction** — Corresponds with the bullish pullback phase. This condition occurs only after the BPI confirms a bull market and a minimum of 6 percent of all stocks change from buy to sell signals. If the BPI is greater than 70 percent, this change may lead to a bear alert (that's up next).

- ✔ **Bear alert** — Corresponds with the bearish transition phase. It's triggered when the BPI is greater than 70 percent and reverses direction after 6 percent of all stocks change to sell signals.

- ✔ **Bear confirmed** — Corresponds with the bear market phase. When the BPI indicator forms a lower low, a bear market is confirmed.

- ✔ **Bear correction** — Corresponds with the bearish pullback phase. This condition occurs only after the BPI confirms a bear market and at least 6 percent of all stocks change from sell to buy signals. If BPI is less than 30 percent, this change may lead to a bull alert.

Although BPI is not a leading indicator, it gives you a good feel for the overall health of the market. When used with broad-based indexes, the BPI doesn't speak often. After all, more than 2,000 stocks are traded on the NYSE. For the BPI to register a reversal, at least 6 percent (or approximately 125) of those stocks must change from a buy signal to a sell signal (or vice versa). Actually, the distinction's a bit more subtle than that. A total of 125 more stocks must change to sell signals than are changing to buy signals for the index to change from bull confirmed to bull correction conditions.

The BPI for smaller stock indexes generates considerably more signals. A 6 percent change on the NASDAQ 100 requires only a balance of six stocks to change from buy to sell signals. Although the BPI provides information about the condition of these smaller indexes, you must use the signals with care. We believe this indicator is best used with broader-based indexes such as the NASDAQ Composite, the NYSE, or the S&P 500.

Selecting Your Trading Stock

After you've identified the dominant trend, the leading and lagging sectors, and the current state of the business climate, it's time to select stocks to trade. Beyond general market conditions, two factors drive a stock's price higher or lower:

- ✔ The fundamental condition of a company's business
- ✔ The technical condition of a company's stock

These topics are covered in great detail in Parts II and III of this book, so in this section, we highlight only a few important factors for you to consider when selecting your trading stock. On the fundamental side, earnings matter more than any other fundamental data. Traders pay particular attention to the rate of earnings growth as characterized by the earnings per share (EPS) growth rate. In general, the bigger the EPS growth rate, the better the stock price, and vice versa. Stocks without earnings often make very dangerous trading candidates. Although some special situations may merit your consideration, stocks without earnings carry a special risk. Any hint of unfavorable press sends the stock's price reeling. Besides, the downside risk is simply too great for our taste.

TRADER'S SECRET $

Exchange traded funds

Up to this point in the chapter, we've talked about trading individual stocks, but at times, you may want to consider trading a basket of stocks. For example, say your indicators all suggest a new bullish transition or bull market phase, but few, if any, stocks are showing reliable trading patterns. You want to enter the market with a small position to take advantage of these relatively early signals, but you can't quite identify a good trading stock.

If that's the case, you may want to try an exchange-traded index fund, known as an *exchange traded fund* (ETF). An ETF is similar to an index mutual fund but is traded on the stock exchanges, just like shares of stock. However, an ETF differs from a traditional mutual fund in several important ways. For example, an ETF order is filled at the price when the trade is executed, not at the end of the trading day like most mutual funds. Also, you can place your ETF order just like any other stock order. You may use market orders, limit orders, stop orders, and stop-limit orders. And, unlike a traditional mutual fund, you may short shares of an ETF. See Chapter 14 for the mechanics of selling short.

ETFs are available for indexes such as the NASDAQ 100 (stock symbol QQQ), the S&P 500 (stock symbol SPY), the Dow Jones Industrial Index (stock symbol DIA), and even many narrowly focused stock sectors. Many brands of ETFs are on the market, and they go by names such as Select Sector SPDR (pronounced "spider"), HOLDRS, iShares, and so on. You need to stick with ETFs that trade in high volume. See www.spdrindex.com or www.morningstar.com/Cover/ETF.html for additional information on ETF trading volumes and on which stocks are included in each ETF.

After you identify a new bullish transition, for example, you may want to consider the NASDAQ 100 or the S&P 500, or perhaps other ETFs for cyclical and tech stocks. Doing so enables you to take a position in the market while continuing to search for stocks that meet your fundamental and technical criteria.

You also need to consider the company's size when selecting a trading candidate. Although small companies can and sometimes do return outsized trading profits, they also present problems for traders. Stocks of small companies usually are lightly traded, which makes them difficult to buy and even more difficult to sell. You can afford to be patient when entering a trade but not when exiting a position, especially when the stock hits your stop-loss price. Lightly traded shares make exiting a position difficult, because the price is likely to fall quickly and dramatically when many traders are trying to exit simultaneously. You're bound to lose more of your precious trading capital (when selling) or spend more of it (when buying) than you intended.

On the technical side, you want to trade the strongest stocks in the strongest sectors. You want to enter positions in these high relative strength stocks as they break out of trading ranges or reversal patterns. And you want to hold them as long as they remain relatively strong compared with other stocks.

Trading Strategies

Categorizing the phases of the market enables you to adjust your trading strategies based on current market conditions. The idea: Trade aggressively when you're confident in your market assessment, but protect your capital when you're uncertain. In this section, we present strategies for dealing with various market phases.

Trading the bullish transition

When you first decide the market may be entering a bullish transition phase, you need to use extreme caution when trading, because at this phase of the market your primary goal is preserving your capital. Your secondary goal is getting in on the bull market, if it materializes.

You may take new positions during a bullish transition, but the situation is not urgent, so you can be selective. You need to take small, partial positions rather than full positions (an example is shown in the upcoming section "A hypothetical trading example") by

✔ Identifying the strongest stocks in the strongest sectors

✔ Looking for trading-range breakouts and other reversal signals

Keep your stops very tight and honor them rigorously. Consider an ETF if you have difficulty finding individual stocks that meet your fundamental and technical criteria.

Trading in a bull market

In a bull market, your primary goal is to become fully invested. Your secondary goal is capital preservation. Emphasize establishing long positions in your trading. You shouldn't take on new short positions. Buy breakouts and take full positions, because your goal is to be 100 percent, or fully, invested. If you have a margin account for leverage, now is the time to use it. (The mechanics of using a margin when trading are discussed in Chapter 14.) You may loosen your stops a bit, because doing so allows for more ebb and flow of higher highs and higher lows.

The most reliable bull market signals occur during the early part of a bull market — after a bullish transition rather than following a bullish pullback. You may want to adjust your strategy to be a bit less aggressive following later-stage bull market signals. For example, you may want to tighten your stops a bit, especially when you're using margin for leverage.

Trading the bullish pullback

A bullish pullback is a consolidation phase within a bull market in which your trading strategy needs to continue looking for high quality stocks that are breaking out of new or subsequent trading range bases. When you decide the market has entered a bullish pullback phase, you may want to tighten your stops and seriously consider hedging your positions by using options, especially when you're using margin for leverage. Hedging is like buying insurance. In this case, put options can be purchased to protect most of your trading capital in case the market moves dramatically against you. The cost of hedging depends on the amount of protection you buy. Options are discussed in Chapter 18.

A bullish pullback still is a bull market, so you can continue taking full positions on breakouts, but you need to be selective. Make sure that your new *and* existing positions are the best performing stocks in the best performing sectors. You need to become a bit more cautious when the particular bullish pullback isn't the first to occur during the current bull market.

Trading the bearish transition

A bearish transition indicates the market may be transitioning from a bull market to a bear market. You react to a bearish transition by

> ✔ Tightening stops on all your open positions
>
> ✔ Monitoring your positions closely
>
> ✔ Honoring your stops rigorously
>
> ✔ Exiting any long position at the first sign of trouble

You also need to consider hedging long positions by using options, as discussed in Chapter 18. If you're using margin for leverage, exiting failing positions quickly is even more important.

If you are so inclined, you can begin looking for short sale candidates, but only nibble at these trades. If you plan to short, take small positions and keep your stops very tight. The mechanics of selling short are discussed in Chapter 14.

Trading in a bear market

When you're certain a bear market has begun, don't enter new long positions. Your open positions are likely to hit their stops and be closed, but for the ones that remain, tighten your stops and exit any existing long positions at the first sign of trouble. Hedge any remaining long positions with put options.

If you're inclined to short stocks, a confirmed bear market is the time to do it. The mechanics of shorting stocks are discussed in Chapter 14. You may want to take full-sized short positions and become fully invested on the short side. (See the upcoming section "A hypothetical trading example," for an example of position sizing.) *Note:* A margin account is required for selling short. We rarely use margin for leverage when trading short, but if you're going to do it, now is the time.

Trading the bearish pullback

A bearish pullback is a consolidation phase within a market that nevertheless remains a bear market. As such, a bearish pullback is not a good opportunity for taking new long positions. You need to tighten stops on existing short positions, and consider hedging these positions using call options, especially when you're using margin for leverage. A bearish pullback is an opportunity to take short-side profits and enter additional short positions when you see new or subsequent downside breakout patterns (see Chapter 9). Confirm that new and existing short positions are the worst performing stocks in the worst performing sectors.

A hypothetical trading example

Here's a hypothetical scenario. The market is trying to begin a new bull market by entering a bullish transition phase. At this time, your $100,000 example portfolio is 100 percent in cash. Your goal: Establish 10 positions by the height of the bull market, which means that you plan to allocate $10,000 of your initial capital for each position.

When you begin seeing signs of a bullish transition, you're likely to be chomping at the bit to start taking positions, but you haven't found stocks that fit your trading criteria. Still, you'd like to participate in the new bull market, and you're willing to risk a small loss if the bull market doesn't appear.

In this case, you may want to start by taking a small position, perhaps a half-sized $5,000 position, using exchange traded funds (ETFs) for the broad market indexes and perhaps for a sector fund or two as they break out. For example, you can take a $5,000 half-sized position in the NASDAQ 100 index fund (QQQ), with a similar commitment to the S&P 500 index fund (SPY), and similarly sized positions in the cyclical and technical sector ETF. In all, you'd have positions totaling $20,000, which is 20 percent of your capital, committed to the market. That kind of commitment is appropriate for a relatively risky bullish transition phase.

As stocks break out of their trading-range patterns, you may add positions, but you need to continue taking small positions until you're certain the market has changed to a bull market. You also need to set an upper limit to the amount of capital that you're willing to commit during a bullish transition phase, perhaps no more than 40 percent or 50 percent of your total trading capital.

If market conditions turn to a bull market, you then can start taking full positions and become fully invested. You may also want to reallocate your positions from the ETFs into high relative strength leading stocks. If you plan to use margin as leverage, a bull market is the time to do it. In this case, you could leverage your $100,000 of trading capital into a portfolio of stocks and ETFs worth up to $200,000 (see Chapter 14 for more about trading on margin). You can either add to existing positions or add new positions in leading stocks as they break out of trading-range patterns. Whatever you decide, keep the number of positions small.

When the market consolidates into a bullish pullback phase, you need to tighten your stops and consider hedging your positions. Doing so enables you to use your stops to get out of underperforming stocks. If you're stopped out of a position, forget about it. If it's a profitable trade, pay your taxes and be pleased with your profits. If you're leveraged, you want to get out of your margined positions quickly whenever they move against you, so you don't give up your profits.

During a bullish pullback, you first must decide whether to hedge the portfolio and then whether you want to hedge each individual position or the portfolio as a whole. In general, you're probably concerned more about a marketwide downdraft than you are about a major stumble in any single position. If that's the case, then hedging the whole portfolio with index options makes sense. However, the larger the portfolio, the more hedging your individual positions makes sense.

As a bullish pullback reverts back to a bull market, reallocate your capital into the new leaders as they break out. After each bullish pullback, becoming a bit more conservative is prudent. For example, you may tighten your stops, use less leverage, or continue providing a hedge against a significant downdraft.

When the bull market transitions to a bear market, you need to exit your long positions when your stops are hit. You may continue to hold your positions as long as they're not losing money, but don't lose your bull market profits. If you want to sell short, the bear market is the time to do so.

Making profitable trades is significantly easier if you buy during bull markets and sell or sell short during bear markets. Subtleties, of course, may exist. You may, for example, take long positions in defensive stocks, such as utilities and financial companies, during bear markets. Some traders find it profitable to hold a two-sided portfolio, where the best performing stocks are purchased and poorly performing stocks are simultaneously shorted, even during a raging bull market, but our advice is to keep it simple. Become proficient by trading with the dominant trend before trying to fine-tune your strategy.

Chapter 14

Executing Your Trades

- -

In This Chapter

▶ Identifying the mechanics of a trade: Entering and exiting a position

▶ Grasping the nuances of selling short

▶ Staying on the right side of the regulators

▶ Understanding margin and leverage

▶ Remembering the tax man and avoiding the wash-sale rule

- -

You've picked your stock and you're ready to enter a position. As long as you're entering the position while the market is open, you have some flexibility in the way your order is entered and executed. However, if you cannot monitor the market during business hours, or if you're entering your order after the market is closed, you need to be much more precise when placing your order and indicating the type of fill (or terms of the order) you're willing to accept. Otherwise, you're likely to run into a nasty surprise when you review your broker's fill report.

This chapter reviews available alternatives when you enter an order to buy, sell, or sell short, and how the choices you make can affect the trade. We also review margin requirements, discuss how trading affects your tax return, and identify situations in which you can run afoul of stock trading regulations.

Entering and Exiting Your Trade

When it's time to enter or exit a trade, you have to tell your broker what you want to do. To do that, you enter an *order* with your broker. This order tells the broker the number of shares and the symbol for the stock or security you're planning to trade. Your order also specifies the type of transaction you'd like to execute and how you'd like the broker to handle your transaction. See Chapter 2 for more about the types of orders available. We discuss your choices for instructing your broker how to handle your order in this section.

Before entering your trade order, you'll probably want to check for a stock quote. Ideally, your quote system provides information similar to that shown in Figure 14-1.

Figure 14-1:
Quote
screen for
AT&T stock.

Description	Exch	Last	Net Chg	Net %Chg	Trade Dir
AT&T Corp	NYSE	16.87	0.25	1.50%	+–+=+
Bid	Bid Size	Ask	Ask Size	Open	Bid-Ask
16.86	1000	16.88	1900	16.81	0.02
High	Low	Close	Volume	Trade Time	Trade Date
16.97	16.77	16.87	1,359,500	11:15:18 am	05/18/2004

The fields depicted in Figure 14-1 are as follows:

- Description — the name of the stock, or its symbol.

- Exchange — the exchange on which the stock is traded.

- Last — the price recorded for the most recently executed trade when the markets are open. It will be the same as the close price when the markets are closed.

- Net Change — the change in price (+ or –) from the previous day's close.

- Net Percentage Change — the change in price expressed (+ or –) as a percentage difference between the previous day's close and the current closing price.

- Trade Direction — a series of plus signs, minus signs, and equal signs that shows the direction of the last few trades in the stock during the day, or at the end of the day for which the quote is effective. A plus sign indicates a trade that was higher than the previous trade, or an *uptick*. A minus sign indicates a trade that was for less than the previous trade, or a *downtick*. And an equal sign indicates a trade at the same price as the previous trade.

- Bid — the highest price someone is willing to pay to buy the stock.

- Bid Size — the number of shares being bid at the bid price.

- Ask (or offer) — the lowest price someone has offered to accept to sell the stock.

- Ask Size — the number of shares being offered at the ask price.

- Bid-Ask — the difference between the bid and ask prices.

- Open — the price obtained for the first trade of the day.

- High — the highest trade price of the day.

    ✔ Low — the lowest trade price of the day.

    ✔ Close — the last trade price for the day.

    ✔ Volume — the daily trading volume.

Understanding bid and ask

Most of the information displayed on the quote system is straight fact, but a few items need additional explanation. For example, many new traders are confused by the *bid* and *ask* prices through which stocks are auctioned. Although it seems backward, if you look at it from the point of view of the *specialist* or the *market maker* (the people who either manage trading activity or actually execute the trades, see Chapter 2 for more detail), it starts making more sense. These professional traders make money in several ways. One is by buying stocks from a *retail investor* (that's what specialists and market makers call you and me) at one price and turning around and selling those shares to another retail investor at a higher price. They buy at the *bid* price, and then sell at the *ask* price. Their goal is to sell for a price higher than they buy.

A *market order* tells your broker to buy or sell at the current market price. This means that if you use a market order when buying, your order is likely to be filled at the ask price. When selling, your market order is likely to be filled at the bid price. Occasionally, your broker may be able to fill your order between the bid and ask prices, but you never should count on it, because it doesn't happen very often. Your order can, however, become the highest bid or the lowest ask, if you use a *limit order*. A limit order specifies the highest price you're willing to pay when buying or the lowest price you're willing to accept when selling. If you place your limit order between the current bid and ask price, your order becomes either the best bid price if you're buying or the best asking price if you're selling. **Note:** You run the risk of having your order not execute at all when using a limit order if the current market price moves away from your limit price. Also, the NYSE and NASDAQ each handle this a little differently. Your broker can help you sort through the details if you encounter problems.

Understanding the spread

The *spread* is the difference between the bid and ask prices. It sometimes is referred to as the *inside spread,* which is the difference between the highest bid and the lowest ask. Back when stock prices were quoted in increments of eighths (12.5 cents) and quarters (25 cents), the minimum spread was either an eighth or a quarter. Today, with decimal pricing, the spreads tend to be a little tighter, and can be as low as a penny per share on actively traded stocks. While the major exchanges do not support spreads less than one cent, some ECNs (electronic communications networks, see Chapter 2) permit tighter spreads for a small number of securities.

When you place a limit order within the spread, so that your limit price is between the current bid and ask prices, your order will usually become either the best bid if you're buying or the best ask if you're selling. This approach makes sense whenever the spread is particularly wide and the price isn't moving very fast. When the spread is narrow, the way it is in Figure 14-1, using a market order is probably best, that is, as long as the market is open and the stock is widely traded.

The biggest problem with trying to squeeze a profit out of the inside spread is that prices move. Remember that stock quotes are only snapshots of current bid and ask prices. By the time your order reaches the market, these quotes can (and do) change. Even the fastest real-time quote systems lag a bit behind the market, so it's possible that the limit order you just entered between the spread is now outside the spread, and won't be filled — and believe us when we say that can be disappointing.

Devising an effective order entry strategy

During trading hours, you can be reasonably confident that a market order will be filled at or near current market prices. But if you're like most people, you won't spend all your time watching the market. As such, you need another strategy for entering and exiting positions. You can use one or more of several alternative approaches to better control the terms and prices that you're willing to accept when your orders are filled.

Using limit orders

If you're buying a stock, choose the maximum price that you're willing to pay, and then pay no more. That means you can't use market orders to enter your positions. Instead, you can use limit orders, which enable you to set the highest price that you're willing to pay for a stock, making that your *limit price*. If you're selling short, choose the lowest price at which you're willing to sell, and set that as your limit price.

Limit orders are effective for opening a position, but are problematic for exiting a position. For example, if you need to exit your position because the breakout has failed (see Chapter 9), you simply need to exit the position without trying to finesse the price. Failed trades rarely recover, and they often get worse. You have no reason to be patient when things are going against you.

Level I and Level II data

The quote screen shown in Figure 14-1 is called a Level I quote. The bid and ask prices, and their associated numbers of shares, give you a little insight into the current state of the market. However, a Level I quote won't show you the full depth of the market or the number of traders and market makers currently participating in the market for any one stock. For that information, you need a Level II quote or display.

A Level II display shows all the outstanding bid and ask prices for a specific stock, the number of shares associated with each price, and the identification of key market makers participating in the stock. Some Level II systems offer a display that consolidates onto a single quote screen all the outstanding bid and ask quotes from all the exchanges, along with all the bid and ask quotes from the ECNs (electronic communications networks, see Chapter 2 for details) where a stock trades. The following figure shows an example Level II display for INTC.

Although interesting, most of the information available on Level II displays is unnecessary for a typical position trader. Unless you're swing trading (see Chapter 16), day trading (see Chapter 17), or trading low-volume stocks, you're not likely to need a Level II data feed.

Similarly, whenever you have a profitable trade and you're trying to protect your profits, a limit order rarely is your best choice for exiting the position. You're better off exiting the position by using either a market order or a stop order after you've identified a reversal pattern.

Using stop orders and stop-limit orders to enter a trade

Traders normally talk about using stops for exiting or trading out of a position, but stops are also effective for opening a position. If you identify the stock that you want prior to an actual breakout, you can enter a buy stop at a price above the breakout point. These orders can be entered on a *GTC* (good until cancelled) basis, so that even if the trading range lasts a while, your order is poised to trigger a transaction whenever the breakout occurs.

Most brokers limit the length of time that orders can remain open, so make sure you know your broker's GTC policies and remember that NASDAQ doesn't have any provisions for handling stop orders. If you're trying to use stops when trading NASDAQ stocks, your broker has to provide the mechanism for triggering these trades when your stop price is hit. Make sure that your broker can handle the stop orders that you want to use.

The downside to this approach is obvious, because you're unable to confirm the breakout. If the breakout fails, and you've triggered a buy order on the breakout, you now hold a position that's losing money.

Although we generally recommend waiting a few days to confirm the breakout, using this strategy at times may be more appropriate than others. For example, if you're convinced that the market is in a bull market phase (as described in Chapter 13), the stock's trading range is long and tight, and you can identify an obvious breakout, then entering a GTC buy stop order at a price that's a bit higher than the breakout price is probably okay. However, you need to be much more tentative when the market is only in a bullish transition or pullback phase, or when you're monitoring second and subsequent breakouts. When that's the case, make sure the breakout is confirmed within a few days before entering your order. If you have any doubt, wait for confirmation.

Another problem with this approach is that after the stop price is reached, your order is triggered and it becomes a market order to buy or sell. You're in the exact situation you'd be in if you'd entered a market order while the market was closed. You have no control over the fill price after your stop is triggered.

For example, say the stock price gaps higher (Chapter 10) as it breaks out of its trading range and surpasses your stop price by two or three dollars. Your order is triggered and will likely be filled at a price that's much higher than your stop price, and much higher than you had anticipated. If the stock price falls below your fill price, you're now holding a losing position. The only way to avoid this problem is by using a stop-limit order, which means when your stop price triggers the release of your order, the order becomes a limit order rather than a market order and is filled only if the stock price pulls back below your limit price (see Chapter 2 for more on limit and market orders). Again, remember to confirm that your broker permits stop-limit orders on NASDAQ stocks.

You can also use a stop order or a stop-limit order to open a short position. You specify a sell stop or a sell stop-limit order, while designating your trade as a short sale. Again, you must confirm that your broker supports these types of orders for NASDAQ stocks.

Using stop orders to exit positions

After your buy or sell order is filled, you need to enter your stop-loss instructions. You need to protect your open positions and simultaneously stay clear of short-term traders trying to *run the stops*. Running the stops is a little game played by short-term traders where they try to find and execute open stop orders before driving the stock price in the other direction. It can be very lucrative for them and infuriating, not to mention expensive, for you. You can try to avoid being run over when they're running the stops by keeping your stop prices away from the most obvious location. For example, if a breakout occurs at $35.75, don't put your stop loss one cent below at $35.74. Move down a few cents, to $35.69, or even $35.63, to stay away from the obvious stop-loss spots. Stop-loss measures, and the reasons for them, are discussed more fully in Chapter 12.

Entering orders after the market closes: Be careful

As long as you're entering your trades during market hours, using a market order is fine; however, if you're planning to check your charts each evening and then enter your trades before heading to work in the morning, you must use a different approach. Otherwise you risk having your orders filled at prices that can differ significantly from the previous closing prices. To make matters worse, you may discover that your position is losing money soon after being filled.

Don't be surprised to discover that many traders trade this way. Because of their daily schedules, they analyze stock charts in the evening and enter orders before the markets open. Unfortunately, common breakout and reversal patterns (see Chapter 9) cause many traders to react in a predicable fashion. After many traders enter buy orders for the same stock, a scarcity of that stock is likely to occur just after the market opens. Scarcity causes prices of individual stocks to rise, sometimes even dramatically, so that all those after-market orders are filled at prices significantly higher than the previous closing price. Making matters worse, after the flurry of buy orders are filled and buying pressure disappears, the stock price tumbles back toward the previous closing price.

Professional traders — including floor traders, market makers, day traders, and swing traders — exacerbate the problem even further. These short-term traders see the same technical analysis signals that you see, and their goal is to profit from your enthusiasm, and perhaps your inexperience, as you try to open your position.

As a result, you need to think about the tactics these short-term traders employ before you enter any positions. When they see breakout or reversal patterns, short-term traders anticipate a flurry of buying activity in that stock, and they know that few people are going to be eager sellers when a stock breaks out of a trading range. Under those circumstances, the only way buyers can get an order filled is if they bid the price higher or accept whatever price is being asked for the stock. When that happens, the best asking price is going to be relatively high.

Someone will sell the stock to position traders but only at a relatively high asking price. Short-term swing traders and day traders, who rarely ever own the stock, offer those asking prices, agreeing to provide the stock to the position traders as long as the buying pressure pushes the price of the stock upward. If the short-term traders don't own the stock, they must sell the shares short, in other words, they must borrow the stock before selling (see the section "Selling Stocks Short"). After the short sellers absorb all that buying pressure, the rally fades, the stock's price falls back toward the break-out price, and that's when short-term traders buy the stock (at prices lower than they sold it) so they can cover their short positions, or, in other words, return the shares that they borrowed to sell at higher prices to the position traders. How's that for taking a quick profit.

This scenario is at the heart of why being patient usually makes sense. By steering clear of these moments of buying pressure, you're more likely to get a much better fill, and you find out whether enough buying interest is present to keep the stock price above the breakout price. Being patient doesn't always work, of course. Sometimes buying pressure drives the price higher, forcing short sellers to cover at a loss, which, in turn, drives the price even higher, resulting in a *runaway stock*. When that does happen, you'll probably be left standing on the platform, watching the runaway stock as it leaves you behind. Fortunately, runaway stocks don't happen all that often. Thus, banking on runaway stocks is a poor tactic.

Our advice remains the same. Don't chase these breakout and runaway stocks. When the cycle exhausts itself, as it ultimately must, the stock returns to a more rational price, and you can reevaluate whether your position continues to make sense. As a position trader, you can afford to be patient.

Reviewing a week in the life of a trader

To help you get a feel for this, we'd like you to look at a couple of sample trades made by a hypothetical position trader. The idea is to help you understand the rationale and the timing of each trade. As a position trader, your week begins during the weekend. You have a couple of things to accomplish:

- ✔ Evaluate the current state of the market.
- ✔ Evaluate the current state of your existing positions.
- ✔ Find potential replacement candidates for any failing positions.

We will use the first full week of April 2004 as the example week. At this time, the market appears weak. It has been in a steady decline for almost eight weeks, but it has rallied a bit over the most recent two weeks.

The technical analysis indicators and fundamental economic conditions show a mixed picture:

- ✔ Economic growth is strong.
- ✔ The Fed is hinting that interest rates may rise some time in the future, but rates currently remain at multiyear lows.
- ✔ The energy and consumer staple sectors are the best performing sectors in the market. The sector rotation model (see Chapters 5 and 13) suggests that strength in these sectors often occurs near bull market peaks.
- ✔ The weekly MACD indicator (Chapter 13) for both the Standard & Poor's 500 Index and the NASDAQ Composite Index is above its zero line but below its trigger line, signaling either a bullish pullback or a bearish transition phase.
- ✔ The NYSE bullish percent index (BPI, see Chapter 13) is signaling a bullish correction. However, the NASDAQ Composite Index is signaling a bear confirmed condition.

Given the above factors, you conclude that the market is most likely in a bullish pullback, but considering the NASDAQ's especially poor performance, extra caution is warranted.

Next, you analyze your current positions. D. R. Horton (DHI), one of the profitable positions in your portfolio, is acting poorly. This is a position you have held for over one year, and it is fully margined. DHI actually broke out of a one-month consolidation last week, but immediately fell back into the trading range, creating a bull trap (Chapter 10). Due to recent market weakness and this stock's recent performance, you decide to tighten the stop, to $33.68, a level just below the current one-month trading range, and a little below the obvious stop-loss location. The stock will hit its stop if the price falls further.

WARNING!

Using GTC orders cautiously

You, and you alone, are responsible for monitoring your open orders. It is not uncommon for many stocks to break out almost simultaneously, so you need to be careful not to overcommit. If, by some fluke, all your open orders trigger simultaneously, or within a short period of time, you must maintain enough purchasing power to adequately fund all your trades. Otherwise, your broker will call and demand that you pay for all those trades that you inadvertently executed. Expect repercussions from your broker, including restrictions on your account, if you don't send the money immediately.

Given the current market condition, the sale of this fully margined stock is probably for the best. If it does hit its stop price, you decide to replace the position — after all, you've decided it is a pullback phase, but still a bull market. However, you plan to reduce your risk level and not margin the replacement position.

To find a replacement candidate, you first look at the strongest sectors, the energy and consumer-staples sectors, but find no fundamentally attractive stocks (Chapters 5, 6, and 7) in a long-lasting trading range (Chapter 9). So you look in the healthcare sector for trading candidates — it's the sector expected to rally next, based on the sector rotation model (Chapters 5 and 13) — and find a couple of viable trading candidates.

Your final step is to determine the breakout points and your entry prices for each of the healthcare-sector candidates (Chapter 9).

During the trading week, your daily activities are comparatively easy. At the end of each trading day, you must:

✔ Evaluate the current condition of your existing positions.

✔ Evaluate the current condition of any trading candidates you identified during your weekend analysis.

On Monday, DHI falls below its stop price and your position is automatically closed. This has been a profitable trade, so put one big check mark in the win column.

Coincidentally on the same day, one of your healthcare trading candidates, Coventry Health Care (CVH), gaps higher (Chapter 10) and breaks out of its trading range on very high volume (Chapter 9). Given that the market is in a bullish pullback, you decide to wait a couple of days to confirm the breakout before entering your trade. After trading closes on Wednesday, CVH is still trading above the trading-range breakout price, so you enter a limit order to buy CVH on Thursday. You enter your buy order with a limit price of $44.75, which was the high reached on the day of the breakout. For the sake of our example, say you received a fill price of $46.65, the opening price for the day. Immediately after receiving confirmation of your trade, you enter a stop-loss order at $43.75, just below the trading-range breakout price.

Because we are omniscient (or maybe it's because we are writing this after the fact), we can tell you that this trade did not work out. During the following week, CVH fell back into the trading range and hit your stop price, giving you a 6 percent loss on this trade. The market continued to deteriorate throughout April and early May. Due to this continued weakness, you are unable to find viable candidates to replace this failed position. In this circumstance, the best thing for you to do is wait patiently for the next opportunity. It may take more than a few weeks before the market is ready to revert to bull market status. And, of course, the possibility exists that the market could slide into bear market territory.

Selling Stocks Short

When you sell a stock short, you sell something you don't have first and buy it later with a goal of profiting from a falling stock price. To sell a stock short, you, in essence, borrow shares of a stock from your broker so that you can sell them in the open market. Your broker gets those shares either from its own inventory, or more likely, from other clients. The proceeds of that sale go into your account. To close that position, you must buy the shares on the open market and return them to the broker. If the price you pay for the stock, or the *buy-to-cover price,* is less than your selling price, you've earned a profit on the short sale. Conversely, if the buy-to-cover price is higher, you've suffered a loss.

Let's say you borrow 100 shares of Company X and sell them for $100 per share. When the price drops to $80 per share, you buy the shares back and return them to your broker. You sold the stock for $100 per share, and bought them back for $80, netting a profit of $20 per share. It's exactly the same profit as if you had purchased the stock for $80 first and sold it for $100 later. Conversely, say you borrow 100 shares of Company Y and sell them for $100 per share. The stock price rises to $120 per share, and you decide to cover your loss. You buy back the shares and pay $120 per share, but you sold them for $100 per share. You have lost $20 per share on this trade.

Some of the quirks that are unique to selling stocks short include

> ✔ **Paying dividends to the lender.** If the stocks pay a dividend during the time a short seller holds a position, short sellers pay the dividends on the ex-dividend date to the people who loaned them the stocks.

✔ **Being forced to close a position.** Whenever the original owner sells the stocks you borrowed, your broker can *call away* the shorted shares, which means your broker can force you to return the borrowed shares by buying them on the open market at the current price. This happens rarely, and occurs only when no shares are available for shorting.

✔ **Mandating the execution of short sales from only a margin account.** Short sales must be executed in a margin account, because your broker loans you the stock to sell short, and charges you interest on any margin balance in the account.

✔ **Paying margin maintenance requirements.** Your broker can force you to close a short position if you're unable to satisfy maintenance margin requirements.

✔ **Having no or only minimal access to selling some stocks short.** Lightly traded stocks may be unavailable for selling short, and when they can be sold short, they may be more likely to be called away (which happens when the original owner sells the stock you borrowed and your broker is unable to borrow additional shares).

✔ **Restricting short sales on certain stocks.** You can't short a stock that's less than $5 per share, and you can't short initial public offerings (IPOs).

✔ **Limiting short selling to only stocks on an uptick.** This *uptick rule* often trips up new short sellers. The essence of the rule says that you can't sell a stock short in a falling market. Although implemented a bit differently on various exchanges, the result is the same. Short sellers cannot easily pile into a falling stock. Exchange traded funds (ETFs) offer an exception to the uptick rule. You can sell an ETF short during a market rout.

One unusual aspect of shorting is that it creates future buying pressure. Every shorted sale must eventually be covered, and that means that every share of stock that's been shorted has to be repurchased. Future buying pressure can cause the price of a heavily shorted stock to jump dramatically if all the short sellers simultaneously clamor to get out of their positions as the price rises, a situation called a *short squeeze.* You can find out how many others are shorting the stock by looking at statistics published in *Barron's* and *Investor's Business Daily* near the end of each month. From those statistics, you get some idea whether your short position is likely to be squeezed.

Avoiding Regulatory Pitfalls

Several regulatory pitfalls may cause you problems as you trade. You want to avoid running afoul of these regulations. Otherwise, you risk having severe restrictions placed on your account.

Understanding trade settlement dates

In the United States, the Securities and Exchange Commission (SEC) regulates when traders must settle their securities transactions. Stock trades, for example, settle three business days after a trade is executed, meaning the buyer must pay for stock trades and the seller must deliver the stock within three business days after the trade is executed. For example, if your trade date is Monday, the trade settles Thursday, three business days after the trade date. Short sellers are subject to the same settlement regulations as everybody else. That means the short seller must deliver the borrowed shares to the buyer three business days following the trade.

Most securities, including broker-traded mutual funds and bonds, settle in this three-day cycle. The shorthand for this settlement period is known as *T+3*, which means *trade date plus three days*. Stock options and government securities, on the other hand, settle the day following the trade date, or *T+1*.

Your broker may even insist that the money for all trades be available in your account before allowing you to execute any trades. Brokers can exercise this restriction because they're permitted to set more stringent restrictions than regulations require. They can't, however, set more lenient terms. Just ask Martha! Regardless of your broker's restrictions, the trade settles during the period specified by SEC regulations. One consequence of this settlement cycle is that your broker is unlikely to allow you to withdraw funds that are part of the trade until the trade settles. However, brokers typically do allow you to trade with those funds as if they are available, as long as other trading regulations are not violated.

Avoiding free riding

Whenever you choose to trade in a cash account, you must take care to avoid free riding. Free riding occurs whenever you buy and sell a stock without depositing sufficient funds before settlement to pay for the transaction. For example, if you have $5,000 in your cash account and you buy $1,000 shares of a $10 stock, for a total transaction cost of $10,000, you receive a money call to deposit $5,000 to settle the trade. Of course, we ignored commission costs in this example.

One way that a trader may mistakenly violate the free-riding rules is trying to use the same capital on two transactions in a single day. Here's the scenario. Say you have $10,000 of equity in your account, and you buy 1,000 shares of a $10 stock. Later that same day, you're stopped out of the position. So far there is no problem. But if you try to reenter the position on the same day, then you receive a money call for the full price of the second trade. The bottom line: You can't use the same capital to open two positions on the same day in a cash account. That's *free riding.* Note, however, that these trades are permitted in a margin account. Trading in a margin account means you're not at risk of violating free-riding regulations.

If you fail to satisfy the money call within the specified time, your broker either issues a warning or places your account on restricted status. When you're restricted, you have to have enough funds in your account to cover your trade before the broker executes your order. Restrictions usually are imposed for 90 days.

Avoiding margin calls and forced sales

Although trading on margin is very powerful, it also is potentially very risky. You may recall from our discussion about differing types of accounts in Chapter 2 that a margin account enables you to borrow money from your broker, which, in turn, permits you to leverage your trading capital. This leverage can improve your total return when things go well, but it can also amplify any losses when a trade goes against you. A margin account is required if you plan to sell stock short.

Before using your margin, you must become familiar with the rules governing its use. The Federal Reserve determines the maximum amount that your broker can loan to you. Currently, the Fed permits your broker to loan you up to 50 percent of the value of each trade. The Fed hasn't changed the margin requirement values since 1974. Prior to 1974, however, the Fed had adjusted margin requirements 22 times to limit stock market speculation and inflationary pressures.

Understanding margin fees

Your broker charges interest on the average daily margin balance, regardless of whether it's cash or stocks. The margin balance is an adjustable rate loan for which the interest rate is based on the current *broker call rate,* which sometimes is known as the *money call rate.* Brokers usually quote their respective margin rates as the broker call rate plus a percentage, where the added amount is dependent upon the size of your loan. You can find the current broker call rate in the Tuesday edition of *The Wall Street Journal.*

Understanding margin collateral

Your trading positions represent the collateral used to secure your margin loan. Brokers require the value of your collateral to be more than sufficient to cover any outstanding loan. The amount required by your broker, called the *minimum maintenance margin,* can range from 25 percent upward. In other words, your broker requires the equity in your account to be at least 25 percent of the market value of your margined stocks.

If the equity value of your account falls below the minimum maintenance margin, you receive a *margin call,* a demand from your broker to deposit more money in your account. If you fail to satisfy your broker's demand for additional funds, your broker liquidates some or all of your trading positions. In fact, your broker may even liquidate your positions before you satisfy the margin call, if the value of the equity in your account continues to fall. Falling stock prices mean falling equity values.

As an example, say that you buy 1,000 shares of a $20 stock, which is $20,000 worth of stock. Current margin regulations require you maintain a deposit of at least 50 percent of the value of that trade in your account to open that trade, and 25 percent of the total value of the position to maintain it. After purchasing the stock, your account has $10,000 of equity and $10,000 in a margin loan. A margin call occurs in our example when the price of the stock falls dramatically the next day from $20 to $12, representing a loss of 40 percent. At this point, you still owe the $10,000 margin loan to your broker, but the total equity in your account now is only $2,000. The 25 percent minimum maintenance requirement is $3,000 (that's 25 percent of $12,000, or 1,000 shares at $12 each), so you'd receive a maintenance margin call to deposit $1,000 to bring your account up to the $3,000 minimum equity amount.

Notice in the example that you're also dangerously close to owing more to your broker than the stock is worth. If the stock's price falls much further, the broker likely will liquidate your position to satisfy your outstanding loan. Brokers are allowed to liquidate your position at any time, without your explicit approval. In fact, they're allowed to liquidate any position in your account to satisfy your loan.

This example illustrates the risks of using margin. The value of the stock fell 40 percent in the example, but you lost 80 percent of your equity. Leverage cuts both ways. Earning double profits may be nice, but doubling your losses is very painful. Our recommendation is to never satisfy a margin call — close the offending position instead. In our example, you should have set stops so you'd be able to get out of the losing position long before you got the margin call. But after that margin call is generated, you need to liquidate the losing position(s) immediately to pay off the margin loan.

When you open a margin account, you must sign a *hypothecation agreement,* a binding agreement that explicitly entitles your broker to liquidate positions to satisfy outstanding margin loans. The hypothecation agreement also permits your broker to loan any stock in your margin account to another client to provide shares for that client to short the stock. When you short a stock, the shares of the stock that you sell must come from somewhere, and that somewhere is from other clients who own the stock. If you're the one shorting stock, one "gotcha" can accompany this scenario. If the stock you borrowed is sold to someone else, then your broker can call away your short position in a forced sale. Although forced sales like this don't happen very often, they nevertheless are a risk that you must assume if you short stock.

Avoiding pattern day trader restrictions

Another risk you run when using a margin account is being classified as a pattern day trader. A *day trade* is defined as entering and exiting a single position in the same day. You can buy a stock and sell it, or you can short a stock and cover the position. Either way, if both transactions occur on the same day, it is considered a day trade.

If you day trade four or more times within a five business–day period, you're classified as a *pattern day trader,* unless your day trades represent fewer than 6 percent of the total number of trades executed during the same period, which is a huge threshold. After you're classified as a pattern day trader, your account must have at least $25,000 of equity before you're permitted to execute additional day trades. Day trading margin rules are discussed in Chapter 17.

The Tax Man Cometh

Trading profits are taxable and are usually taxed as income at the trader's marginal income tax rate. Check out *Taxes For Dummies,* which Wiley also publishes, for more info than most of us ever will need on the subject of taxes. Traders rarely hold positions long enough to qualify for the special capital gains treatment that is available to long-term investors. Still, paying taxes is better than losing profits or principal.

One tax trap that snares traders is the wash sale rule. Normally, you can deduct trading losses from trading gains before calculating your income tax burden. However, if you sell a stock for a loss and then repurchase the stock within 30 days, the trading loss cannot be deducted. Fortunately, the loss isn't lost forever. You can use it to adjust the cost basis on the trade by the amount of the loss, which ultimately reduces the amount of tax owed when the position is finally closed. This adjustment effectively raises the cost of a stock purchase, for tax purposes, so you owe less tax. A similar adjustment is available when selling short.

Day traders receive special tax treatment, but you must be a bona fide day trader to qualify. The details are reviewed in Chapter 17.

Chapter 15

Developing Your Own Powerful Trading System

A *trading system* is a collection of technical and fundamental analyses tools woven together to generate buy and sell signals. Trading systems often are built using common indicators, oscillators, and moving averages (see Chapter 11 for additional information on indicators, oscillators, and moving averages). You can combine these various technical-analysis tools to create a virtually unlimited number of trading systems. For the new trader, the advantage to this approach is that you don't need to invent something new to create and personalize a workable system.

The downside, however, is equally obvious. Many traders use these common tools and end up with a system that offers little competitive advantage and only modest (if any) profits. In addition, these systems can be difficult to use, because the signals of one trading system mirror the signals of many others, which makes entering and exiting positions troublesome.

Ultimately, you want to develop or adapt a trading system that closely fits your personality and trading objectives. This chapter helps you methodically develop and add to an approach to trading that utilizes your own personalized repertoire of trading systems. It also helps you recognize and avoid destructive and costly habits that can sabotage your trading efforts. In addition, we discuss ways for you to evaluate some of the claims being made by trading systems that are for sale and whether buying someone else's trading system makes sense.

Understanding Trading Systems

Although individual trading systems differ in many ways, thinking about them on the basis of a couple of broad characteristics is helpful. The first characteristic has to do with the two ways a trader interacts with the system. In this case, trading systems are one or the other of the following:

- **Discretionary trading systems:** A system that presents trading candidates for your consideration, but leaves the final trade execution decision to you.

- **Mechanical trading systems:** A computer-based system that automatically generates buy and sell signals.

The other way to categorize a trading system is by how it treats trends in the markets. In this case, trading systems are one or other of the following:

- **Trend-following trading systems:** A system that tries to identify trade entry and exit points for new or existing trends.

- **Countertrend trading systems:** A system that tries to identify trade entry and exit points by finding tops and bottoms.

Although these categorizations are not mutually exclusive of each other — mechanical and discretionary systems, for example, can both be trend-following systems — each approach has adherents and detractors, so we discuss the strengths and weaknesses of each type of system in the sections that follow.

As you read through our descriptions of the trading systems, understand that *no* system generates profits without any losing trades. Put another way, no system works in every situation. Keep that firmly in mind when you're developing ideas for and designing your personal trading system. Your goal needs to be designing a trading system that is useful to you across a large number stocks and a large number of situations. Believe us when we say that you will run into trouble whenever you try to tailor a trading system to a specific stock. Additionally, try making your system work across long periods of time and across many different market conditions.

Discretionary systems

A *discretionary trading system* makes you an active participant in all phases of the trades you make and provides you with a great deal of leeway when making trading decisions. With this approach, evaluating the economic data, analyzing the broad market indexes, determining which sectors are showing strength, and identifying high relative-strength stocks that are breaking out of long trading ranges and hoping to catch a new trend all are up to you. You make decisions based on what you see in charts and in fundamental economic data, and you enter and exit (buy and sell) positions based on that information.

A discretionary system requires a great deal of discipline, which can be a source of problems for some traders. This type of system works well for traders who are capable of making good decisions quickly under pressure. But discretionary systems may prove troublesome if you allow your emotions to wreck havoc with your ability to think clearly, act rationally, and make thoughtful trading decisions.

When emotions cloud your trading decisions, you may end up:

- ✔ Overtrading
- ✔ Prematurely liquidating your positions
- ✔ Holding positions too long
- ✔ Anticipating trading signals in attempts to get better entry and exit prices

Another problem with discretionary systems is that they're difficult to test, which probably is their greatest drawback. System testing is useful, because it helps you understand situations in which an indicator works well and in which it fails. With a discretionary system, you can test the indicators, but you cannot reliably test your discretion.

Mechanical systems

A *mechanical system* addresses some of the problems that arise when using discretionary systems. Mechanical systems usually are computer-based programs that automatically generate buy and sell signals based on technical and/or fundamental data. You're expected to blindly follow the resulting trading signals. Some mechanical systems actually enter buy and sell orders directly with your broker without your intervention.

If your greedy impulses or your fear of losing routinely cause you to make poor trading decisions, a mechanical system may be a better choice for you. An automated approach tends to reduce the stress and anxiety that arise when you have to make difficult decisions quickly. As such, you can make and execute trading decisions in a consistent, methodical way. A mechanical trading system also enables you to automatically include rigorous money management in your trading methodology.

Another benefit of the mechanical approach is having the ability to thoroughly test the system. Through testing you can confirm whether your trading system performs the way you expect it to and explore ways to improve your system before actually committing your trading capital. You can adjust and fine-tune your system after seeing the test results. Unfortunately, fine-tuning your system may lead to other problems. We discuss ways to avoid them in the "Identifying system optimization pitfalls" section, later in this chapter.

Trend-following systems

Trend following is favored by many technicians for one simple reason: Trends offer excellent opportunities for profit. Unfortunately, the popularity of the trend-following approach is one of its weaknesses. Too many of these systems generate many similar buy and sell signals, which, in turn, makes outperforming the average trader difficult for any individual trend-following trader.

Even the best trend-following systems have a relatively large percentage of failed trades, primarily because they depend on several extremely profitable trades to make up for the large percentage of losing trades. If your trend-following system also is a discretionary system, your discretion (or lack of it) can cause you to miss a few of these profitable trades, and your overall results will suffer.

Trend-following systems typically are based on either moving averages or breakout patterns (see Chapters 9 and 11). Moving average–based trading systems are the most popular and can be quite profitable; however, they work only when a stock is trending. These trading systems depend on long-lasting trends to generate enough profit to outweigh a relatively large number of losing trades. When a stock is range bound (stuck in a specific price range), a moving-average system generates a large number of losing trades. Because of the large overall number of trades, this system often is accompanied by relatively high transaction and slippage costs (see the section "Accounting for slippage"). Money management is critical when using a trend-following trading system.

You can make some adjustments to a trend-following system that may improve its performance. For example, you can insist that its trading signals be confirmed by another condition before actually entering any positions. If your system triggers a buy signal, for example, you may want to see whether the signal remains in effect for at least a day or two before entering a position. We show some examples of moving-average and breakout systems, along with some ideas to improve the performance of these systems, in the section "Developing and Testing Trading Systems."

Countertrend systems

For many traders, the quest to find a profitable countertrend trading system is all consuming. *Countertrend systems* appear desirable because their goal is to buy low and sell high. These systems try to identify *inflection points,* or the moments when stocks change direction, so traders can take positions close to when they occur. This approach may work in a few narrowly defined situations, such as in a trading range (Chapter 9) or a trend channel (Chapter 10), but it is likely to fail in a spectacular and expensive way if attempted on a broader scale.

The vast majority of trading systems follow market trends. Trend-following systems tend to outperform countertrend systems, especially for position traders. Swing traders and some day traders sometimes use a countertrend approach, but even then, they usually do so in conjunction with a trend-following component.

Countertrend systems usually depend on oscillating indicators, reversal patterns, and channeling strategies to find turning points. Some countertrend systems also are based on cycle theory, and others are based on volatility, expansion, and contraction. We briefly review some of these techniques in Chapter 16.

We discourage you from spending too much time evaluating countertrend systems, at least until you're confident in your ability to use trend-following systems to successfully make your trades. Countertrend systems generate a large volume of trades, and the more you trade, the more you spend on transaction and slippage costs. These costs alone often swamp potentially profitable systems. Although a countertrend strategy can sometimes work profitably in a trading range or trend channel (Chapters 9 and 10), it is still risky, especially for a new trader.

Selecting System Development Tools

Conceptually, you can use the back of an envelope to develop your trading-system ideas. However, most traders want some way of confirming that their newly designed systems can perform profitably before they commit real trading capital. That means you need a way to test your system, which further means using computer software to precisely define the system and evaluate its performance. Typically, this requires simulating trades by using historical data.

Regardless of whether you decide on a mechanical or a discretionary approach to trading, your system will benefit from testing. Although thoroughly testing a discretionary system is difficult, you can still test the component indicators to learn when they do and don't provide effective trading signals. To begin, you need a computer, development and testing software, and historical data.

Choosing system development hardware

Doing the math that's required when testing your system can really slow down your computer, and it can generate a lot of data. Almost any computer will do the job when you're getting started, but if you end up testing many system ideas, you definitely need a large amount of disk storage and a fast computer. The computer equipment required to run a proprietary trading platform, including products such as TradeStation or MetaStock, is usually enough for system development and testing. (See Chapter 4 for more information about the hardware requirements for a typical proprietary trading platform.)

Selecting system-development software

Many trading system–development and testing products are on the market. Some proprietary trading platforms, such as TradeStation or MetaStock, include system-testing capabilities. Spreadsheet software, like Microsoft's Excel, also is useful for analyzing simple trading systems and for analyzing the results generated by specialized-development and testing software.

Trading system–development and testing software

You need to consider several of the following criteria when evaluating your system-development and testing software:

- ✔ All trading system–development and testing programs use some type of computer language to describe and test your system. Some are terse and difficult to use, others are much more intuitive. Traders with strong computer skills have little problem mastering any of these languages, but others with lesser skills may struggle. Pay careful attention to this language before selecting a system. Be certain that you're actually able to use the system you choose.

- ✔ You need to integrate your trading system with your stock charts. Some system-development software requires you to actually write computer code that enables you to display your trading system and stock charts simultaneously. Avoid these systems if you're uncomfortable writing computer code.

✔ The manner and effectiveness by which your system-development and testing software reports on how your trading system is performing is critical. Some systems provide extremely detailed statistics about the performance of your trading systems. Others, however, list little more than the buy or sell signals. In general, more information is better.

✔ Make sure your system-development and testing programs are capable of exporting the data they generate, historical price data included, into a spreadsheet program for further analysis.

TradeStation is the gold-plated system-development platform. It has many built-in tools that make your development and testing job relatively easy. For those of you on tight budgets, one of the less expensive alternatives you may want to consider is a charting and system-development program like AmiBroker (www.amibroker.com). Although flexible and powerful, AmiBroker isn't as feature-rich or polished as TradeStation, and it requires significantly more effort on your part. For example, AmiBroker includes well-known technical-analysis indicators like moving averages and MACD (see Chapter 11), but the number of indicators included is a tiny subset compared with what TradeStation offers. Similarly, you have to use AmiBroker's formula language to create and enter any other indicators that you may be using.

Spreadsheet software

A spreadsheet program is another invaluable testing and analysis tool. Although a spreadsheet program can't do everything that a specialized system-development and testing program can do, it can add quite a bit of analysis horsepower to your system-development tool kit. You can actually code and test simple trading systems directly into the spreadsheet. You can also evaluate the results of your trading-system tests more thoroughly using the spreadsheet's built-in statistical and analysis functions.

You can, for example, copy the price data for a stock into your spreadsheet, calculate moving averages and other indicators, and then configure buy, sell, or sell-short signals. You can also export trading signals from your system-development program and import the results into your spreadsheet for further analysis.

One of our favorite spreadsheet projects is calculating the maximum favorable and unfavorable moves after our system has triggered a buy or sell signal. Simple to do, it helps you understand the strengths and weaknesses of your trading system in great detail. You can see whether problems with your trading system might be solved by using different exit procedures or tighter (or looser) stop-loss points.

For example, although your entry signals may show promise, your exit signals are causing you to leave a lot of money on the table. These situations are hard to see when you're working only with charts; however, they sometimes jump out when you're working with raw data during your spreadsheet analysis. You can find an example using this testing technique in the "Working with break-out trading systems" section, later in this chapter.

Some system-development programs provide a great deal of statistical analysis, so choosing between spreadsheet tools and system-development tools is a trade-off between thoroughness and expediency. After you've been through the testing exercises a few times, you get a feel for the strength of each approach. So it's likely that you'll decide to use both a system-development program and a spreadsheet program when creating and testing your new trading systems.

Finding historical data for system testing

When you need to test your system, you can, of course, test it in real time, with real money, and in the real markets. But getting some idea of how your system will perform before risking your hard-earned capital is usually better. Typically, that means testing your system by evaluating how it performs when simulating trading using historical price data. Ten to 20 years of historical end-of-day data for the indexes and stocks in which you plan to trade is usually more than enough to properly simulate trades for testing your system.

Many sources can provide the data. You can download historical data from the Internet, and some online data is available free of charge. Some proprietary trading platforms likewise include access to historical data.

MSN MoneyCentral provides free historical data and permits you to download the data into a spreadsheet. To access the MSN data feed, bring up a chart of the stock and select "Show Table;" you will then see a button to download the data into a spreadsheet format. You can generally get five years of end-of-day price data from MSN.

Many online services offer data in a more convenient format, but for a price. Some sell historical data recorded on CDs. Sources for intraday price data also are available. Here are the URLs for a few of the many sites offering various forms of historical data:

- ✔ **Historical data:**
  - **MSN MoneyCentral:** moneycentral.msn.com
  - **Lycos/Quote.com:** www.quote.com
  - **Quotes Plus:** www.qp2.com
- ✔ **Intraday data:**
  - **eSignal:** www.esignal.com
  - **IQ Feed:** www.iqfeed.net

- **Price Data:** www.price-data.com
- **Quote Tracker:** www.quotetracker.com

✔ **Historical data on CD:**

- **Profit.net:** www.profit.net
- **CSI:** www.csidata.com

Developing and Testing Trading Systems

The ideas that you may want to include in your system development and testing are virtually limitless. Many new traders begin system testing by combining a few off-the-shelf indicators, trying to obtain better trading results. Doing so is as good a place as any to begin.

However, we want to caution you to keep your systems simple enough that you can understand not only the system but also the result. Simplicity usually is better when trading, especially when you're first becoming familiar with the processes of system development and testing. We describe the process by looking at a couple of examples in the sections that follow.

Working with trend-following systems

Many trend-following systems use a moving average for their starting points. In this trend-following example, the system is designed for position trading, which means we use a relatively long moving average. Short-selling won't be permitted with this simple system.

The first step is defining buy and sell rules for your initial testing. The actual code for defining these rules depends on your specific system-development package. Therefore, trading rules are described as generally as possible. The rules for an initial test may look like this:

✔ Buy at tomorrow's opening price when today's price crosses and closes above the 50-day exponential moving average (EMA).

✔ Sell at tomorrow's opening price when today's price crosses and closes below the 50-day EMA.

To test whether using a moving average as a starting point is a good idea in a trend-following system, apply these two rules to 10 years of historical data for the stock or stocks of your choice. After testing this idea, you find that this simple system works fairly well when stock prices are trending, but it's likely to trigger many losing trades when the prices of stocks are range bound. You can try to avoid these losing trades, and possibly improve your overall trading results, by filtering out trading-range situations. One way to accomplish that goal is changing the buy rule to read: Buy at tomorrow's open when the following conditions are true:

- ✔ Today's closing price is above the 50-day EMA.
- ✔ The stock crossed above the 50-day EMA sometime during the last five days.
- ✔ Today's 50-day EMA is greater than the 50-day EMA from five days ago.

These added conditions serve as signal confirmation. When you test these rules, you find they reduce the number of whipsaw trades for most stocks, but they're also likely to delay buy and sell signals on profitable trades, and thus usually result in smaller profits on those trades. Yet this adjustment makes the overall system more profitable, because the number of losses is reduced.

You can find out whether other changes that you can make in your simple system actually can improve profitability. You may, for example, test different types of moving averages. Try, for example, a simple moving average instead of an exponential moving average (see Chapter 11 for the types of moving averages). Or, you may want to try using different time frames for your moving average, such as 9-day, 25-day, or 100-day moving averages.

Identifying system optimization pitfalls

Most system-development and testing software comes equipped with a provision for system optimization, which allows you to fine-tune the technical analysis tools used in your trading system. You can, for example, tell the system to find the time frame of the moving average that produces the highest profit for one stock, and then ask it to do the same thing for a different stock. Some systems enable you to test this factor simultaneously for many stocks.

Although something is alluring about using this approach, doing so is likely to cause you trouble. If you find, for example, that a 22-day moving average works best for one stock, a 37-day moving average works best for the next stock, and another stock performs best using a 74-day moving average, you're going to run into problems. The set of circumstances leading to these optimized results won't likely repeat in precisely the same way again. We can almost guarantee that whatever optimized parameters you may find for these moving averages won't be the optimal choices when trading real capital.

This is a simple example of a problem that is well-known to scientists and economists who build mathematic models to forecast future events. It is called curve fitting, because you are molding your model to fit the historical data. You can expend quite a bit of effort fine-tuning a system to identify all the major trends and turning points in historical data for a particular stock, but that effort is not likely to result in future trading profits. In that case, your optimized system is more likely to cause a long string of losses rather than profits.

Testing a long moving average and comparing the results to a short moving average is fine, and so is testing a few points in between a long moving average and a short moving average. As long as you use this exercise to understand why short moving averages work best for short-term trades and longer moving averages work better for traders with longer trading horizons, you'll be fine. Otherwise, you're probably moving into the realm of curve fitting and becoming frustrated with your actual trading results.

Testing with blind simulation

Blind simulation is a method for setting aside enough historical data so that you can test your system optimization results and avoid the problem of curve fitting. For example, you may test data from 1990 through 1999, and thus exclude data from 2000 through the present. After you've developed a system that looks good enough for you to base your trades on it, you can then test your system against the data that was excluded. If the system performs as well with the excluded data as it did with the original test data, you may have a system worth trading. If it fails, you obviously need to rethink your system.

Another approach is choosing your historical data with extreme care. You can expect trend-following systems like a moving-average system to perform well during long, powerful trends. If your stock had a strong run-up during the long-lasting 1990s bull market, that kind of price data can skew your results, magically making any trend-following system appear profitable. Whether that success actually can be duplicated during a subsequent bull market, however, must first be thoroughly tested.

If the majority of your profits come from a single trade, or only a small number of trades, the system probably won't perform well when you begin trading real money. You may want to address this problem by excluding periods from your test data when your stock was doing exceptionally well or when the results of any trades were significantly more profitable than the average trade. This technique is a valid approach to eliminating the extraordinary results arising from extraordinary situations in your historical data. Using it should give you a better idea of your system's potential for generating real profits in the future.

Working with breakout trading systems

Similar to moving average–based systems, a breakout system can take many forms. You may already be familiar with the trading-range breakout system we describe in Chapter 10. To test a different approach, you can define a breakout system as follows:

- ✔ Buying at tomorrow's opening price when today's closing price is above the highest high price that occurred during the last 20 days.

- ✔ Selling at tomorrow's opening price when today's closing price is below the lowest low that occurred over the last 20 days.

These trading rules are loosely based on the rules for *Donchian Channels* (sometimes called *Price Channels*), which comprise a breakout system developed by Richard Donchian in the 1950s. Donchian was one of the early developers of trend-following trading systems.

A spreadsheet may be helpful for evaluating this system. You can, in fact, configure this system into a spreadsheet, include buy and sell signals, and perform analyses to determine how well the system performs. You also can use the spreadsheet to dig into the system's results to find out what works and what doesn't. Figure 15-1 shows an example.

Recreating the spreadsheet in Figure 15-1 is straightforward. After downloading the historical price data into a spreadsheet format, all you have to do is encode the formulas into the correct columns. The formulas are described in the nearby sidebar "Creating the Donchian Channel spreadsheet."

If you're like most traders, the first thing you'll do is calculate some statistics about the system. For example, you can use spreadsheet functions to calculate:

- ✔ Total gain or loss for the system
- ✔ Average gain (the numerical average)
- ✔ Median gain (the middle result)
- ✔ Maximum gain for any single trade
- ✔ Maximum loss for any single trade
- ✔ Standard deviation

Then you can look at aggregate results to find out whether the system actually made money. In the case of the Donchian Channel breakout system, initial results don't look promising. The system lost money during the entire test period.

Figure 15-1: Spreadsheet analysis for Donchian Channels.

#	Date	Open	High	Low	Close	Volume	Donchian High	Donchian Low	Change Flag	Buy/Sell	Buy Price	Gain Loss	MFE	MAE
1	Date	Open	High	Low	Close	Volume	Donchian High	Donchian Low	Change Flag	Buy/Sell	Buy Price	Gain Loss	MFE	MAE
532	4/18/2001	43.72	51.00	43.35	45.55	129,199,600	$43.83	$33.60	FALSE	-				
533	4/19/2001	46.10	48.75	45.58	48.30	110,467,600	$51.00	$33.60	TRUE	Buy	46.10	0.00%	5.75%	-1.13%
534	4/20/2001	48.18	49.44	47.00	48.40	80,598,096	$51.00	$33.60	TRUE		46.10	4.51%	7.25%	-2.62%
535	4/23/2001	46.99	47.72	44.89	45.15	79,317,600	$51.00	$33.60	TRUE		46.10	1.93%	3.51%	-5.10%
536	4/24/2001	45.10	46.42	43.75	45.10	88,888,304	$51.00	$33.60	TRUE		46.10	-2.17%	0.69%	-6.51%
537	4/25/2001	43.90	45.73	43.10	43.95	68,418,400	$51.00	$33.60	TRUE		46.10	-4.77%		-4.84%
538	4/26/2001	45.90	46.25	43.87	45.15	71,108,896	$51.00	$33.60	TRUE		46.10	-0.43%	0.33%	-4.03%
539	4/27/2001	45.15	45.70	44.24	45.70	56,469,800	$51.00	$33.60	TRUE		46.10	-2.06%		-1.41%
540	4/30/2001	46.25	47.59	45.45	46.15	73,859,104	$51.00	$33.60	TRUE		46.10	0.33%	3.23%	-1.95%
541	5/1/2001	46.20	48.08	45.20	48.05	54,498,300	$51.00	$33.60	TRUE		46.10	0.22%	4.30%	
542	5/2/2001	48.80	49.40	47.50	48.98	77,566,496	$51.00	$33.60	TRUE		46.10	5.86%	7.16%	
543	5/3/2001	47.90	48.50	45.17	46.80	67,124,896	$51.00	$33.60	TRUE		46.10	3.90%	5.21%	-2.02%
544	5/4/2001	45.30	48.20	45.17	48.20	72,673,600	$51.00	$35.50	TRUE		46.10	-1.74%	4.56%	
545	5/7/2001	48.00	48.60	47.10	47.20	45,562,200	$51.00	$35.85	TRUE		46.10	4.12%	5.42%	
546	5/8/2001	48.30	48.35	46.99	48.20	56,970,700	$51.00	$37.78	TRUE		46.10	4.77%	4.88%	
547	5/9/2001	47.05	47.95	45.09	45.77	61,130,300	$51.00	$39.90	TRUE		46.10	2.06%	4.01%	-2.19%
548	5/10/2001	47.92	48.05	45.00	45.55	60,984,600	$51.00	$39.90	TRUE		46.10	3.95%	4.23%	-2.39%
549	5/11/2001	45.84	46.42	43.35	44.82	48,760,400	$51.00	$39.90	TRUE		46.10	-0.56%	0.69%	-5.97%
550	5/14/2001	45.30	45.36	43.10	45.15	43,056,800	$51.00	$39.90	TRUE		46.10	-1.74%		-6.51%
551	5/15/2001	44.90	46.30	44.06	47.15	69,008,096	$51.00	$43.10	TRUE		46.10	-2.60%	0.43%	-4.43%
552	5/16/2001	44.31	47.52	44.06	47.90	80,110,496	$51.00	$43.10	TRUE		46.10	-3.88%	3.08%	
553	5/17/2001	47.45	48.79	47.00	48.04	73,810,704	$49.44	$43.10	TRUE		46.10	2.93%	5.84%	
554	5/18/2001	47.64	48.38	47.09	51.05	41,095,100	$49.44	$43.10	TRUE		46.10	3.34%	4.95%	
555	5/21/2001	48.17	51.15	47.65	50.90	85,426,896	$49.44	$43.10	TRUE		46.10	4.49%	10.95%	
556	5/22/2001	51.31	51.96	50.02	48.65	77,237,400	$49.40	$43.10	TRUE		46.10	11.30%	12.71%	
557	5/23/2001	50.44	51.01	48.64	49.90	65,618,000	$51.15	$43.10	TRUE		46.10	9.41%	10.65%	
558	5/24/2001	48.97	50.05	48.27	48.99	61,792,800	$51.96	$43.10	TRUE		46.10	6.23%	8.57%	
559	5/25/2001	49.96	50.02	46.10	48.50	36,191,100	$51.96	$43.10	TRUE		46.10	8.37%	8.50%	
560	5/29/2001	48.50	48.95	47.50	46.12	66,609,600	$51.96	$43.10	TRUE		46.10	5.21%	6.18%	
561	5/30/2001	45.43	45.85	44.08	44.43	81,397,400	$51.96	$43.10	TRUE		46.10	-1.45%		-4.38%
562	5/31/2001	44.54	45.85	44.30	44.73	68,018,304	$51.96	$43.10	TRUE		46.10	-3.38%		-3.90%
563	6/1/2001	45.54	46.23	44.44	46.05	61,874,300	$51.96	$43.10	TRUE		46.10	-1.21%	0.28%	-3.60%
564	6/4/2001	46.33	46.66	45.29	45.83	41,696,100	$51.96	$43.10	TRUE		46.10	0.50%	1.21%	-1.76%
565	6/5/2001	46.30	48.36	46.20	47.85	68,147,504	$51.96	$43.10	TRUE		46.10	0.43%	4.90%	
566	6/6/2001	48.08	48.75	46.82	47.48	61,170,400	$51.96	$43.10	TRUE		46.10	4.30%	5.75%	
567	6/7/2001	47.13	48.89	47.07	48.70	65,400,200	$51.96	$43.10	TRUE		46.10	2.23%	6.05%	
568	6/8/2001	48.72	48.90	46.95	47.35	56,391,400	$51.96	$43.10	TRUE		46.10	5.68%	6.07%	
569	6/11/2001	46.90	47.00	45.49	46.90	48,874,400	$51.96	$43.10	TRUE		46.10	1.74%	1.95%	-1.32%
570	6/12/2001	44.87	46.80	44.23	46.05	78,450,496	$51.96	$43.10	TRUE		46.10	-2.67%	1.52%	-4.06%
571	6/13/2001	46.27	46.75	44.52	44.55	68,535,400	$51.96	$43.10	TRUE		46.10	0.37%	1.41%	-3.43%
572	6/14/2001	44.02	44.40	42.00	42.25	91,050,304	$51.96	$44.06	FALSE		46.10	-4.51%		-8.89%
573	6/15/2001	41.80	43.10	41.28	42.60	84,589,400	$51.96	$42.00	FALSE	Sell	46.10	-9.33%		
574	6/18/2001	42.64	43.17	41.40	42.03	63,539,100	$51.96	$41.28		-				

If you're like most traders, your impulse is to discard the idea and move on to another. But with the Donchian Channel breakout system, you need to dig a little further before you do. During the five-year time frame of this test, the system triggered 15 trades, 10 of which were losing trades. However, six of those losing trades were profitable at some point during the process, and all the winning trades gave back a large part of the profits before the sell signal was triggered. In fact, three of them gave back more than half of the profits before the sell signal.

Creating the Donchian Channel spreadsheet

The opening, high, low, and closing prices and the volume data for the QQQ exchange-traded fund were copied into columns B through F of the spreadsheet found in Figure 15-1. The remaining columns are configured as follows:

✔ **Column G** is the *upper Donchian Channel.* Use the spreadsheet MAX function to find the highest price value for the previous 20 trading days. Looking at row 533, the calculation for this cell is: =MAX(C531:C532)

The formula doesn't include the current row. If it did, the current close never crosses above the channel line.

✔ **Column H** is the *lower Donchian Channel.* Use the MIN function to find the lowest low for the previous trading day. Looking at row 533, the calculation for this cell is: =MIN(D531:D532)

The formula does not include the current row.

✔ **Column I** is the *Change Flag* indicator. This flag is a simple way to avoid triggering more than one sequential buy or sell signal. It's also useful for calculating the remaining cells. Simply stated, the cell checks out as either TRUE for a buy signal or FALSE for a sell signal. If yesterday's close is greater than the Donchian high, turn on the TRUE condition. If yesterday's close is less than the Donchian low, turn on the FALSE condition. Otherwise, copy the TRUE or FALSE into this column from the previous day to today. The formula from row 533 is: =IF(E532>G532, TRUE(),IF(E532<H532,FALSE(),I532))

✔ **Column J** is the *Buy/Sell* indicator. This column shows when a buy or sell signal first is triggered. It compares the current Change Flag value with the previous value. If they're equal, a dash goes in the cell. Otherwise, the word "Buy" is shown when the Change Flag is TRUE and "Sell" when it's FALSE. The formula from row 533 is: =IF(I533=I532,"-",IF(I533,"Buy","Sell"))

✔ **Column K** is the *Buy Price.* This column shows the trade entry price. If the Buy/Sell flag indicates a buy, then put today's opening price in the cell. Remember the trading rule is to buy at the opening price on the day following the trade entry signal and sell at the opening price on the day following the trade exit signal. Therefore, the sell signal requires a special case. If the Change Flag indicator is TRUE for either today or the previous day (the special sell signal case), copy the trade price from the previous day to today. Otherwise, the Change Flag is FALSE, so leave the cell blank. The formula from row 533 is: =IF(J533="Buy",B533,IF(OR(I533,I532),K532,""))

✔ **Column L** is the *Gain/Loss* indicator. This column shows a running total of the gain or loss in the trade, assuming the trade closes at the current opening price. The first row after a buy signal always shows 0 percent. The last row following a sell signal is the actual gain or loss from the simulated trade. The formula from row 533 is: =IF(OR(I532, I533),(B533-K533)/K533,"")

✔ **Column M** is the *MFE,* which is short for *Most Favorable Excursion.* This column shows a running total of the best possible outcome for the trade as though it were closed at the high price of the day. This column is useful for what-if analyses but not for estimating your actual gains or losses. You rarely, if ever, sell at the high price for the day, or the MFE for a trade. The calculation is simple. If the Change Flag indicator is TRUE, and if today's high is greater than the purchase price, calculate the percentage gain. Otherwise, leave the cell blank. The formula from row 533 is: =IF(I533,IF(C533>K533,(C533-K533)/K533,""),"")

✔ **Column N** is the *MAE,* or *Most Adverse Excursion.* This column shows a running total of the worst possible outcome for the trade as though it were closed at the low for the day. This column is useful for what-if analyses but not for estimating actual gains or losses from the trade. You rarely, if ever, sell at the low price for the day, or at the MAE for a trade. The calculation is simple: If the Change Flag indicator is TRUE, and if today's low is less than the purchase price,

calculate the percentage loss. Otherwise, leave the cell blank. The formula from row 533 is: =IF(I533,IF(D533<K533,(D533-K533)/K533,""),"")

You need at least 20 rows worth of data before you can calculate the first Donchian price channels. Until the system generates the first buy or sell signal, the formula values for columns K through N will be undefined.

To evaluate the results, you can copy the trading signals, gain and loss values, and MFE and MAE values from your system to a new spreadsheet. Paste the values using the spreadsheet's Paste Special function. You then can sort and analyze the data in any way you choose.

Figure 15-1 shows how a single position from the spreadsheet progressed. The entry trade was triggered when the price of QQQ closed above the Donchian high that occurred April 18, 2001. In this simulated trade, the stock was purchased at the opening price for April 19 and then sold June 14, 2001, the day after the price of QQQ closed below the Donchian low that occurred June 13, 2001.

If you look down columns L through N, you'll notice that this simulated trade was profitable part of the time but ultimately closed at a loss. If that happens once during simulated trading, you may not need to worry much about it, but if it occurs frequently, you need to think of ways to remedy the problem.

In the Donchian Channels system, buy signals obviously work better than sell signals. Therefore, you need to consider different types of stops and sell signals. One simple idea that's worth testing is stopping out (selling at a predetermined price) of a position if the stock's low (instead of its close) falls below the Donchian low. Another is to shorten the time frame for the exit signal by using a 5-day or 10-day Donchian Channel. You can, for example, use a trailing stop or some completely different criteria to exit these positions.

In any case, this example gives you ideas about how you can use a spreadsheet to test and analyze any trading system. It also provides you with some suggestions about how you can use this kind of analysis to improve your system's results.

Accounting for slippage

Slippage is the term traders use to describe the costs of trading, which is made up of two components. The first is the actual transaction or commission cost for executing your trade, and the second is a bit more difficult to measure, because it's the sum of the cost of unfavorable fills. If, for example, you're planning to buy at tomorrow's opening price based on today's closing price, those two prices can be much different. An unfavorable fill is a cost of trading, and accounted for as slippage.

Most trading-system development packages have a provision for estimating slippage costs when testing your trading ideas using historical data. If you know your transaction costs, enter the exact amounts. Otherwise, estimate the transaction cost. You probably need to overestimate the cost of unfavorable fills, because it always seems to end up being worse in actual trading than most traders ever imagine. You may want to start with an estimate of 25 cents per share and adjust it as you gather data on your actual slippage costs.

Keeping a Trading Journal

Keep track of all your trading activities in a trading journal. Doing so eventually turns your trading journal into a reference manual that can become an invaluable tool for helping you recall what you've done to identify what works and what doesn't. A trading journal also can help you analyze your trades and trading systems to determine which aspects of trading you do well and which ones you need to work on.

When you develop a trading system, save ideas and test results in your journal. When you enter a position, record everything about the trade. Include your thoughts as you contemplate making the trade. When you have a what-was-I-thinking moment later on, you can find the answer in your journal.

Using a loose-leaf binder to hold your trading journal is probably best. Print before and after charts for each trade and include them in the journal. Keep detailed notes about each trade, and about the system you used to trigger the trade. At a minimum, your notes need to include

- Trade date
- Stock symbol
- Number of shares, and why you chose that number of shares
- Whether you bought long or sold short

✔ Which system triggered the entry signal

✔ Which system triggered the exit signal

✔ Where you placed your initial stops

✔ If and why you moved your stops

✔ What caused you to exit the position and why

✔ The percentage gain or loss from the trade

✔ Whether any economic reports or announcements were made around or during the time of the trade

✔ Your thoughts, hopes, and fears that you had before opening the position and while the position was open

You can also use your journal to save magazine articles that influenced your thinking. Cut out and save the new high and new low lists from the newspaper. Keep a record showing leading and lagging industries. Save sector charts along with your trade records. Whatever information you use to make trading decisions needs to be in your trading journal.

You can improve only the things that you measure. Record statistics about your trades. Include the duration of each trade, the MFE, and the MAE. After you close a trade, write down what you might have done differently. Find out whether you can identify signals that can help you recognize similar situations in future trades.

Although keeping the journal is important, it is useful only when you review it regularly. Spend a little time every week or month reviewing all your trades, so you can pinpoint consistent mistakes or missed opportunities.

Evaluating Trading Systems for Hire

You'll see advertisements on the Internet, in trade magazines, and in newspapers for foolproof systems that promise amazing returns. Sometimes you'll even see claims for systems that regularly return hundreds of percent with little or no risk.

Although some stocks do actually achieve astronomical returns of hundreds and sometimes thousands of percent, those cases are rare. Consider this: A system that offers profits of 100 percent per year supposedly grows $10,000 into $10 million dollars in only 10 years. ***Be skeptical.*** Experienced traders know that no system consistently returns 100 percent per year.

If you created such a system, would you sell it?

When evaluating these systems, the devil is in the details. Advertisements often are unclear about how a system actually works in real-world trading, and some vendors make claims based on nothing more than the results of system testing based only on simulated trades and historical data. In fact, the system's author may never have traded the system using real capital.

Constructing a system that shows great profits when simulating trades with historical data is easy. If you designed a trend-following system and tested it against data during the period 1997 through 2000, you can be fairly certain that the system is going to perform well in simulated testing. But you shouldn't use it to trade real money.

If a system sounds too good to be true, well, it probably is. So do your own homework. Find out what works and what doesn't, and save your hard-earned trading capital for trading.

Part V

Risk-Taker's Paradise

The 5th Wave — By Rich Tennant

"That's the Harrisons. Never have I seen an investment portfolio start so strong and go south so quickly."

In this part . . .

You discover several alternative approaches to trading, including some of the attractions and drawbacks of swing trading and day trading. We also introduce you to more advanced forms of trading like options trading, futures trading, and foreign currency trading, and we provide details about the licenses and certifications that are required if you plan to do any trading for others.

Chapter 16

The Basics of Swing Trading

In This Chapter

▶ Selecting stocks for swing trading

▶ Understanding the role of volatility in swing trading

▶ Substituting options for stocks

▶ Identifying tax issues and account restrictions for swing traders

*S*wing trading is a trading strategy that tries to take advantage of short-term opportunities in the market. It occupies the middle ground between position trading and day trading. Swing traders use trend-following and countertrend strategies to participate in trading-range and trending stocks. This turbo-charged trading style requires an exceptional understanding of the inner workings of the markets and excellent analysis capabilities.

In this chapter, we discuss a few of the basic techniques used by swing traders along with the risks that are unique to the discipline. We also talk about tax issues and account restrictions unique to swing trading.

Stock Selection Is Key

REMEMBER

Swing trading is a *technical discipline*. Although there is no hard and fast rule, swing traders often trade in 1,000 share increments and usually limit the number of simultaneous positions to ten or fewer. A swing trade can last for as little as a few hours to as long as a few weeks, but typical swing trades span no more than a few days. On this kind of time scale, fundamental analysis has little impact on a stock's price movement; therefore, stock selections are made using technical analysis tools. Careful trade management is crucial to swing trading success.

Stock selection is even more important for swing trading than it is for position trading. When you're looking for a stock to move right away, you base your decisions on selection criteria that are different from when you're positioning for a move that may last for several weeks to several months. A few of the important selection criteria that swing traders use are

- **Volume and liquidity:** Swing traders typically focus on actively traded and relatively large stocks. The goal is finding stocks that are easy to buy, sell, and sell short. When trading time frames are short, you need to be able to execute your orders quickly. Unfortunately, stocks with the greatest liquidity and trading volumes are closely followed by the largest number of professional traders, which usually constrains the number of profitable swing trading opportunities, so swing traders often scout opportunities outside of the 25 or so stocks that have the highest trading volume and greatest liquidity.

- **Trending:** Trending stocks provide the best opportunity for swing-trading profits. You may use either the methods described in Chapter 9 for identifying trending stocks or the *average directional index* (ADX) indicator. This indicator has three components, the ADX reading, and two *directional movement indicators* — the +DMI and the –DMI. An ADX reading of more than 30 or so indicates a trending stock. A comparison of the two DMIs shows you whether the AMX is trending up or down. If the value of +DMI is larger than the value of –DMI, then the stock is trending higher. If the value of –DMI is larger than the value of +DMI, the stock is trending lower. The ADX indicator is included in most charting applications.

- **Volatility:** Swing traders depend on larger, or more volatile, short-term moves for profits. As a result, they want to trade stocks that have histories of making large moves in short periods of time. One popular approach to finding them is keeping an eye on the *average daily ranges* (ADRs), which are simple moving averages that track the day-to-day differences between an individual stock's daily high and low prices. If you're swing trading, you want stocks that show high ADRs. Volatility also can be measured using historic volatility, which is discussed in the "Trading volatility" section.

- **Sector selection:** Just like position trading, swing traders try to trade stocks in the strongest sectors, and the weakest sectors are candidates for short sales. Use the techniques described in Chapter 13 to identify strong and weak sectors.

- **Tight spreads:** As a means of controlling slippage (see Chapter 15), you need to pay close attention to the difference between the bid and ask prices of the stocks you're considering as swing-trading prospects. Stocks with wide spreads make profitable swing trading difficult. Low-priced stocks rarely are good candidates for swing trading, because the spread, as a percentage of the stock price, is usually too wide.

Swing-Trading Strategies

Swing trading fluctuates between the use of trend-following and countertrend strategies:

- ✔ When a stock is trending strongly, swing traders primarily employ trend-following techniques, but may use countertrend techniques to fine-tune exit points.

- ✔ When a stock is range bound, swing traders use countertrend methods to identify entry and exit points.

Trading trending stocks

Technical analysis patterns that we cover in Chapters 9 through 13 are all applicable to swing trading. Patterns repeat in all time frames. The difference is in how swing traders use and interpret these common patterns. Trend-following strategies are more aggressive for swing trading than they are for position trading. Although swing traders use some of the same indicators and patterns used by position traders, they often use them in different ways. We explain a few examples in the sections that follow.

Trading pullbacks

A *pullback* is another name for a consolidation within a trend. Consolidation patterns include the flags and pennants discussed in Chapter 10. Swing traders use daily charts and intraday charts — ranging from 1-minute bars to 60-minute bar charts — to identify the dominant short-term trend and any pullback patterns within the trend. They try to enter a position when the price of a targeted stock stops declining or pulling back, so they can capture the next move higher in the trend. Conceptually, pullback trading is simple, but in practice, it's trickier than it sounds.

After you identify a trending stock and find a flag or pennant pullback pattern (Chapter 10) by visually examining the daily charts, you must try to enter a position just as the pullback is ending. The classic setup is finding an orderly pullback in which the high of each bar on a chart of the pullback is lower than the previous one. Figure 16-1 shows an idealized example of the type of pattern you're trying to find.

Entering a position is done by placing a buy-stop order with your broker. A buy-stop is like any stop order; when the price is hit, the order is executed. See Chapter 12 for details. Entering a position to trade pullbacks is an iterative process so it's best to use a day order instead of a GTC (good until cancelled, see Chapter 14) order. Here are the steps:

✔ Select your buy-stop price so it's just above the intraday high price shown in the last bar of the chart.

✔ If the stock price trades above your buy-stop price, your order is executed. Otherwise, the order is canceled at the end of the day.

✔ As long as you're still interested in this trade, adjust your buy-stop price to just above the intraday high of the most recent bar on the chart and reenter your order.

✔ After your order is filled, place a stop-loss order (Chapter 12) using a stop price just below the intraday low of the lowest bar in the pullback on the chart.

✔ As long as the trade is active, continue adjusting the stop price to be just below the intraday low of the most recent bar on the chart.

Figure 16-1:
Example of
an orderly
pullback.

Figure 16-2 is a price chart of the stock of Symantec Corporation (SYMC) that's showing a strong uptrend. Several opportunities for trading pullbacks are also shown on this chart. Keep on reading while we review them for you.

The first pullback occurred when Symantec traded to a new high of $42.30 on February 19, 2004. That new high is labeled Bar #1 on the chart. After identifying the pullback, you begin the iterative process of setting the buy-stop price just above the high of the last bar on the chart. At the end of each day, you reset the buy-stop price, again setting it just above the high of the last bar, and reenter the order.

In this example, the trade is triggered on Bar #2, which occurred February 26. You had set the buy price just above the February 25 high, which was $40.30. Symantec opened February 26 at $40.15, traded as high as $40.27 in the first few minutes of trading, but then fell back to $38.90 within the first hour. The trade was triggered, however, when the stock recovered, climbing above $40.30 early in the afternoon and rising to as high as $41.59 before backing off to close at $41.05. You could expect your order to fill very near your $40.30 stop price. For the sake of our example, we'll assume a fill price of $40.35.

Figure 16-2:
Chart of
Symantec
(SYMC)
showing
pullback
trading
examples.

Immediately following the trade execution, you set a stop-loss order. Normally, you would choose the low of the previous bar, $39.50 in this case. Because the low of Bar #2 is well below that price, you may select $38.90, today's low. Either approach makes sense, so it's your call. Each day the trade remains active, reset the stop order just below the low of the last bar on the chart.

The thrust of this trend lasted through March 8, 2004, a duration of seven days. This position hit the stop price on March 9, 2004, labeled Bar #3 on the chart in Figure 16-2, when the stock traded below the March 8, 2004, low of $43.55. Assuming a purchase price of $40.35 and a fill price of $43.50 to close the position, the profit for this trade is $3.15, which is a gain of 7.8 percent, excluding transaction costs.

The next opportunity to trade a pullback occurred during the pullback that began with Bar #3. The trade triggered on March 12, the bar before Bar #4, when Symantec traded above the March 11 high of $43.13. The position hit its stop price on March 16 when the stock traded below its Bar #4 low of $43.40. Given slippage and transaction costs, this trade was no better than a break-even trade.

Finally, the next opportunity came following the poorly formed pullback from March 16 through March 22, 2004. You entered the trade on Bar #5 when Symantec traded just barely above the March 22 intraday high of $42.49. This new mini trend continued for five days. The position is closed on Bar #6 when Symantec fell below $46.63, which was the low for the previous day. The trade netted about $4.14, or just under 10 percent, excluding transaction and slippage costs.

Swing trades don't all work out so nicely, of course. Complications and frequent losing trades always are possible. For example, you may have decided that the pullback from March 16 through March 22 didn't qualify as being orderly and skipped that last trade.

Surfing channels

Another trend-following approach to swing trading uses a channeling strategy to identify entry and exit points. Chapter 10 explains the channeling strategy and how to construct the channel lines. After a channel is identified on the daily charts, channel lines are treated as lines of support and resistance. Figure 16-3 shows an example.

Resistance channel line

Figure 16-3: Chart of Electronic Arts (ERTS) in a trend channel.

Support channel line

After identifying support and resistance levels for a channeling stock, you can monitor its chart for reversals near the channel lines. As the stock price approaches the lower or *support channel line,* you have an opportunity to take a position in the direction of the trend. After entering a position, your stop-loss order is entered just below the support channel line. As the stock price approaches the upper or *resistance channel line,* that signals when to exit your position.

You can use intraday charts to fine-tune this strategy. As a stock price falls toward its lower channel or support level, begin watching intraday charts for indications that the stock is changing direction and heading higher. If you see an intraday low near the location of the support channel line, followed by a higher high and a higher low, you can use that situation as an entry signal. After entering a long position, you place a stop-loss order just below the support channel line.

You hold this long position until it either is stopped out or the stock approaches its upper channel resistance level. Again, you need to monitor the intraday charts for hints of a change in direction and exit the trade whenever you see the reversal. After that, you wait for the stock to head back toward the lower channel line to initiate a new long trade.

Trading range-bound stocks

Unlike the typical position trader, a swing trader is more likely to use counter-trend strategies (see Chapter 15) and actively participate when a stock is range bound. The swing trader tries to make trades based on price movements from the bottom to the top of the range and back down again. You can use either daily or weekly charts to identify the trading range. An example using a daily chart is shown in Figure 16-4.

Your trading approach to range-bound stocks is similar to the one for trading a channeling stock that we describe in the previous "Surfing channels" section. As the stock price approaches the support level, which is just below $11.50 in Figure 16-4, you have an opportunity to take a position. You can use the following approaches to enter a position.

You can, for example, simply choose to place a buy order using a limit price just above the support line. Another approach that may give you a little more control and provide better entry and exit points is to monitor the stock to find pivot points as it trades near the support line. A *pivot point* is a three-bar pattern in which the low price of the middle bar is lower than the lows of the bars on either side of it. The entry and exit points for this kind of trading are similar to the ones used for trading based on a pullback pattern. After identifying a pivot point, you enter an order on the next bar. The protective stop is placed either immediately below the low of the pivot bar or just below the support channel line.

Figure 16-4: Chart of DR Horton (DHI) stock prices bound within a trading range.

Using intraday charts is another way to fine-tune your entry point. As the stock approaches the support line, you enter a position as soon as you see a reversal pattern on the intraday charts — for example, a higher high and a higher low, or a gap higher (Chapter 10).

You exit these kinds of positions when the stock price approaches its resistance line. You can then take a short position in the stock — using any of the entry techniques described earlier — or wait for the stock to return to the support line to initiate another long position.

If the stock breaks through its upper resistance level, you interpret that condition exactly the way a position trader does — a very bullish indication that the stock is likely beginning a new trend, immediately closing any open short positions and converting to a trend-following strategy (see the earlier "Trading trending stocks" section).

Swinging with Gann and Taylor

Swing trading has been around in one form or another since the earliest days of markets. The term itself probably originated with W.D. Gann when he invented the swing chart during the 1920s. George Douglass Taylor popularized the phrase, and a short-term trading technique, when he introduced a now classic three-bar trading pattern in his 1950 book, *The Taylor Trading Technique.*

Taylor's ideas serve as the basis for much of today's swing-trading methodology. According to Taylor, trending stocks tend to rally, then rest, and then continue to trend. Swing traders watch for these rest periods and attempt to enter the market just in advance of the thrust of the new trend.

Taylor's method, sometimes called "the book trader's method," was originally developed to trade futures contracts in the grain markets. Taylor theorized that the market cycles through three distinct phases or days. The first phase is the buy day, the second is a sell day, and the third is a sell-short day. Although these three days don't necessarily fall on consecutive days, for the sake of following the discussion, we assume they do.

Taylor first determines the short-term trend, finds the position of the short-term cycle within the trend, and then uses this information to determine when to buy, sell, or sell short. The buy day begins the cycle. A typical buy day begins with weakness, and the trader takes a long position near a previously identified support level based on the weakness. This position is held overnight into the next day, the sell day. The sell day typically opens strong, but the strength fades before the close. The trader sells at the early signs of weakness. The final day of the cycle is the sell-short day. The trader watches for any strength near resistance levels on the third day and sells short into this strength. The short position is held overnight and then covered during early weakness the following buy day. The cycle begins in earnest again with the trader initiating a long position after covering the short position.

Taylor's approach is difficult to execute. Like all swing trading, it requires constant monitoring of the market and an excellent understanding of support and resistance levels. It is a discretionary approach that is difficult to test. Few stocks actually follow a three-day script on consecutive days. Many stocks trend for several days before pulling back or rising, so the three-bar method must be adjusted to account for these differences. Nevertheless, Taylor's thinking is evident in much of today's swing-trading methodology.

Trading volatility

Swing traders try to trade stocks that move up and down more than average. To find these stocks, swing traders spend a great deal of effort measuring and analyzing volatility, usually in the form of historic volatility. Although the math required to calculate historic volatility is complex, the concept is simple. *Historic volatility* measures a stock's price movement. The faster it moves, the higher the historic volatility. Fortunately, many charting and analysis programs include a method for calculating historic volatility, so you don't have to program in the formula.

Historic volatility isn't concerned with the direction of a stock's price movement. A high historic volatility value doesn't reveal whether a stock's price is rising or falling. Although swing traders want to know that a stock trends in one direction or the other, they don't really care which direction. Downside movement is just as attractive as upside movement to the swing trader.

You can use historic volatility for swing trading in several different ways. One popular approach uses historic volatility for finding stocks that have been very volatile but currently are experiencing quiet periods. These temporarily quiet stocks are likely to return to previous levels of historic volatility, and that presents a swing-trading opportunity. Swing traders identify these stocks by comparing measurements of historic volatility across longer and much shorter periods of time and expressing that comparison as a ratio. The ratio looks like this:

> Historic volatility ratio = Short-term historic volatility ÷ Long-term historic volatility

One common ratio compares a 6-day historic volatility with a 100-day historic volatility. Whenever the value of that ratio is less than 50 percent, then the stock is a candidate for a swing-trading position.

After this stock takes a short low-volatility rest, it is likely to return to its historic level of volatility with a fast move. Remember that volatility tells you nothing about the direction of price movements, so to get around this limitation, be sure to place buy and sell-short stop orders respectively above the high and below the low of the current bar. When the stock decides which way it will go, one of your stop orders is filled and that should get you pointed in the right direction. Using more traditional technical analysis tools is another approach to evaluating a stock's current trend, so you can then trade in the direction of that trend.

Risks accompany both approaches. Using the first approach, the stock may take off in one direction and quickly reverse course, and you may end up holding a position with a highly volatile stock heading the wrong way. This same scenario also can happen with the second approach. Another potential problem occurs when the stock price gaps through your entry order, and your order may end up getting filled at a price that's significantly different than you expected.

Money management issues

Because of the short duration of each trade, swing trading generates a large volume of trades. Execution and slippage costs (Chapter 12) can be very high. Profits are relatively small when measured on each trade, so losses must be carefully controlled.

You need to adhere closely to the money management rules we discuss in Chapter 12. In addition, each swing trade must represent only a small percentage of your trading capital. Ten percent of your capital per trade is too much. Risking less than 5 percent — and perhaps as little as 2 percent — of your trading capital on any one swing trade is a more conservative approach. This approach is similar to the one used by professional traders. When profit potential is small, don't take big risks, or you won't be a swing trader for long.

Using Options for Swing Trading

Stock options can be used as substitutes for the underlying stocks when swing trading. A *stock option* is a limited duration contract that grants the *option buyer* the right to either buy or sell a stock for a fixed price. The *option seller,* usually called the *option writer* or the *option grantor,* is granting the right to the option buyer to either buy or sell a specific stock for a fixed price.

Each option represents 100 shares of stock. A *call* is an option to buy 100 shares of a specified stock. The call buyer is acquiring a limited duration right to buy 100 shares of a stock from the option grantor at a fixed price, called the *strike price.* A *put* is an option to sell 100 shares of a specified stock. The put buyer is acquiring a limited duration right to sell 100 shares of a stock to the option grantor at the specified strike price. Options are discussed in more detail in Chapter 18.

You can, for example, substitute a call option for a long stock position or a put option for a short stock position. You realize any profits by selling the options outright, or you can exercise an option and take possession of the shares of stock. Swing traders, however, are more likely to sell the option than exercise it.

Although using options as stock substitutes has several advantages, it also has risks of its own. The primary advantage: An option costs far less than the underlying stock, which enables you to limit your risk to the price of the option.

Each option is a substitute for 100 shares of stock. One call option, for example, gives you the ability to buy 100 shares of a stock at a fixed price for a certain length of time. As an example, assume that the QQQ exchange-traded fund is trading at $36.60 per share. At the time of the example, you can buy one call option with a $36 strike price for $1.70 per share, or a total of $170, before transaction costs. That one option enables you to buy 100 shares of QQQ for $36 before the option expires.

Say that the option in this example has approximately two months before expiration. Your option position is therefore profitable as long as QQQ exchanged traded fund trades above $37.70 (excluding transaction costs) before the expiration date. (We determined the break-even price by adding the $36 strike price to the $1.70 cost of the option, which totals $37.70.) Your risk is the price of the option. In other words, you can't lose any more than $1.70 per share, or $170, on this trade.

Unfortunately, option pricing is not as straightforward as stock pricing. The pricing example above is merely a snapshot that varies with changes in the price of the QQQ exchange traded fund. The following factors affect option prices:

- ✔ Options expire and their prices decay as the expiration date draws closer.

- ✔ The prices of current-month options decay at faster rates than longer-dated options.

- ✔ In percentage terms, *out-of-the-money* options often move at a faster rate than *in-the-money* options. (An option is said to be in the money if it has intrinsic value and out of the money if it has no intrinsic value. For a call option, that means the price for the underlying stock is greater than the specified strike price. For a put, that means the price for the underlying stock is less than the strike price. See Chapter 18 for additional details.) *Note:* Trading options that are far out of the money is rarely a good strategy.

- ✔ Volatility is a component of option pricing. Option prices rise and fall as the volatility of the stock rises and falls.

- ✔ Except in a few unusual circumstances, an option's price doesn't move in lock step with the underlying stock's price. If a stock moves $1, the option, in general, moves some amount less than $1. The more an option is in the money, the closer the change in an option's price will be to the change in the underlying stock's price.

Another factor to consider when substituting options for stocks is that the option's *spread,* or the difference between the bid price and the ask price, is extremely wide when considered as a percentage of the option price.

Before you decide to substitute options for your stock trades, make sure that you understand the option-pricing model. We discuss it in Chapter 18. And be careful that you don't overtrade with options. If you normally buy 100 shares of a stock, then you need to buy only one option contract. Although the price of 10 option contracts may be attractive when compared with the price of the stock, 10 option contracts nevertheless represent 1,000 shares of stock. When buying options for 10 times the number of shares that you normally trade, you're increasing your exposure to risk by a factor of 10.

When trading options, you can't make money in as many ways as you can lose it. Being right on the stock's direction but still losing money on an option trade is still possible because of pricing issues. That's why gaining an understanding of the option pricing model is so important before you try to substitute an option for a stock. We discuss options more fully in Chapter 18.

Getting a Grip on Swing-Trading Risks

Swing trading is risky and demands a great deal of time. As a swing trader, you must monitor the market during every trading hour. You also must be able to control your emotions so that you stay focused and trade within your plan.

Ask any swing trader and you're likely to hear him or her say that strict adherence to money management reduces risk. The counterargument is that swing trading exposes a great deal of capital to risk but makes only small profits. Some traders are able to swing trade profitably, but you need to realize that the odds are stacked against you. Only you can decide whether it's worth the effort.

Some wags argue that swing trading combines the worst aspects of position trading with the worst aspects of day trading. Like day trading, swing-trading profits are small and slippage costs are high. Swing-trading positions are held overnight, so swing traders can't take advantage of the special margin provisions that are available to day traders who close all positions by the end of the trading day. And swing traders are subject to the same account restrictions as day traders, but they may not qualify for the special tax advantages afforded to full-time day traders.

Taxes (of course)

Special tax treatment is available from the IRS for full-time traders. The benefits enable full-time traders to be taxed as a business rather than an investor, and that means you can deduct the cost of the computer hardware and software used for trading, and you can treat your home-office expenses, including the costs for data acquisition, as ordinary business expenses. Furthermore, you can convert capital gains and losses to ordinary gains and losses under the Mark-to-Market accounting rules in the IRS Code Section 475. Mark-to-Market rules enable you to avoid wash-sale regulations and deduct all losses against other income, without hitting the $3,000 cap imposed on other investors.

Unfortunately, swing traders do not necessarily trade every day, so some swing traders have a difficult time qualifying for these special tax provisions. If you are unable to qualify as a full-time trader, then your swing trades will be taxed in the same way as every other investor. You must report gains and losses on IRS Schedule D, and you must adhere to wash-sale regulations. You may also run into difficulty if you try to report your trading expenses as a business deduction.

The rules are complex. You need to consult with your tax advisor to determine your eligibility. Information about the rules is in IRS Publication 550, Chapter 4, "Special Rules for Traders." We provide more information in Chapter 17.

Pattern day-trading rules apply

Swing traders are subject to the same rules as day traders. If a swing trader opens and closes a position in a single stock during one day, and does this more than four times in a five-day period, the swing trader is categorized as a pattern day trader. If this occurs, you must maintain an equity balance of $25,000 in your account or your broker will prohibit you from making any day trades. Additional information about the pattern-day-trading rules is provided in Chapter 17.

This scenario actually is quite likely for the swing trader, because of the number of stops that are hit. You may as well plan to maintain a minimum equity balance in your trading account in excess of $25,000.

Chapter 17

Day Trading

In This Chapter

▶ Exploring day trading

▶ Deciphering account restrictions

▶ Reviewing day-trading strategies

▶ Assessing day-trading risks

Day traders enter and exit trading positions sometimes more than a hundred times within a single day. Day traders may even get into and out of a position within the span of only a minute or two.

Some players compare watching the charts and jumping quickly in and out of positions to the rapid-fire action and excitement of a video game. However, much more is at risk. Instead of merely losing a game, a bad move can mean the loss of your entire portfolio, or maybe even more. Yes, day traders sometimes end up in negative positions, owing money to the firms with which they're trading. We explain how that can happen later in this chapter.

For now, you need to know that day traders rarely hold a stock overnight and that watching a computer screen for hours at a time is a critical part of the day for this high-stress type of trading. Although neither of us is or ever has been a day trader, in this chapter, we nevertheless explain how this type of high-risk trading works, give you some common strategies used by these types of traders, explore restrictions the United States Securities and Exchange Commission (SEC) places on day traders, and show you the high levels of risk day traders face.

What Day Trading Is All About

Day traders try to fashion a career out of buying and selling stocks quickly throughout the day. A certain amount of day trading is critical to maintaining the liquidity of the stock market, because the techniques they use keep the market moving. They're known as *institutional day traders* — specialists and market makers.

Retail day traders, on the other hand, are a different bunch. They make dozens or even hundreds of trades a day, but they also close out all their positions at the end of each day. Retail day traders use technological developments that first became available in the late 1990s to get in on the action that used to be the sole province of the institutional day traders.

Institutional day traders (market makers and specialists)

Specialists are a critical part of the New York and American stock exchanges. All are members of an exchange either as an individual, a partnership, or as part of a corporation. They're responsible for making markets in certain exchange-traded securities, maintaining inventories of the securities for which they're responsible, and making sure the market for those securities is orderly.

Market makers play a critical role in maintaining the liquidity and efficiency of NASDAQ-listed stocks and stocks that are sold over-the-counter and not listed in a particular market. They're usually part of a brokerage firm or bank that facilitates the buying and selling of stocks in these markets. A market maker must be ready to buy and sell stock on a regular and continual basis. More than 500 firms operate as NASDAQ market makers.

Specialists and market makers trade into and out of positions throughout the day, often executing orders in a matter of seconds. We discuss these types of traders in greater detail in Chapter 2.

Retail day traders

Retail day traders try to make money in a totally different way. The playing field of day trading opened for retail day traders in the late 1990s when computer software was developed that enabled individual investors to have direct access to securities markets in ways that previously were only technologically available to licensed and registered professionals. We talk more about licensing and registration in Chapter 20. Today, regulators believe retail day traders are responsible for about a third of NASDAQ's trading volume. Although stocks listed on the NASDAQ are a common choice for day traders, the preferred trading platform for most day traders is the electronic communications network, or ECN, because being connected to the markets in this manner makes becoming the highest bid or lowest ask price easier than doing so via directly trading on the NASDAQ (see Chapter 2).

It's all about access

Brokerage firms that promote day trading provide their customers with real-time links to the major stock markets and the NASDAQ system, which, in turn, gives them information not readily available to average retail investors. Brokerages also provide customers direct entry into their order-processing systems. This direct access enables day traders to send their orders to a particular market or market maker and to determine the order route — a task that only licensed professionals previously were able to accomplish. Although other online and traditional brokerage houses may provide real-time quotation information, they don't offer their customers linkages to markets and market makers. Instead, some have preset algorithms that determine where a customer's order is routed for execution, which may or may not be the cheapest way to go. Many times the algorithms are set based on trading agreements among firms without regard to cost effectiveness.

Why does direct access matter so much? Speed and, again we say, speed! Systems that provide more and more direct access give day traders the opportunity to execute their trades within seconds. Without speedier access, even the most responsive brokerage systems can take several precious minutes to execute the trades that customers make via their respective Web sites. In addition, by using a more direct route, traders can choose market makers whose bid or ask prices look the best and fill their orders instantly.

Traders also can post bid or ask prices directly on an ECN or cancel orders with the click of a button, all because they have direct access. When establishing a position using a limit order through a traditional online broker, traders must fill out another ticket to cancel their trades, and under those circumstances, they can't know whether their orders have been filled until they receive a trade or cancel confirmation.

Day traders aren't looking to make a large profit on one huge sale every day, but instead they seek smaller profits on much more frequent changes in the positions they establish during the day. Mere seconds are critical when you're trying to get in and out of a position, trying to make money on small stock price differences that may be much less than a single point, which, in trading lingo, translates to a dollar in the nontrading world. Although swing traders and position traders seek profits of several points (dollars) with each position they enter, day traders may exit their position after earning a profit of only a few cents. Traders usually buy or sell at least 1,000 shares at a time, so 25 cents translates into a $250 profit for every 1,000 shares traded. *Note:* In only a matter of seconds, what looked like a good price to a day trader can be lost.

By controlling where their orders are sent, day traders also gain better control over the costs of their trades. One of the ways that some traditional brokers make money on trades they execute for customers is charging a fee called a *payment for order flow*. These fees usually range between one and four cents per share of stock, providing something of a kickback to the brokerage house and enabling deep discount brokerages to charge smaller upfront commissions that barely cover the cost of their trades. Although online discount brokers send trades to particular markets or market makers through which they've established trading deals, day traders have the inside information to select the routes that give them the best prices.

Day-trading firms

In addition to direct access, day-trading firms provide (for a fee of course) their customers with training in how to participate in this rapid-fire, price-sensitive buying and selling and then encourage their trainees to use their strategies and their software. These firms developed proprietary software and systems that day traders use to analyze and chart activity and execute orders. This software usually is available only at on-site trading facilities or downloadable to your home computer rather than being used through Internet Web sites.

Day trading through an Internet Web site isn't possible, because the added seconds it takes to download price information and then send back an order is likely to result in the loss of your order to some other trader. Even when a trader has high-speed Internet access, too much time can be spent waiting for pages to load and sending orders. So to be successful, day traders need the instant access they get through proprietary software.

Day-trading firms are organized in one of two ways — as *traditional broker-dealers* (day traders open accounts with the firm and trade using their own accounts) or as *proprietary trading firms* (or a prop firm for short) that either sell interest in the firms to traders who want to day trade or hire traders as independent contractors. Typically, a proprietary trading firm is organized as a limited liability company (LLC), which is corporate structure used to minimize the legal exposure of the firm. LLCs are not a separate entity for tax purposes, but still enjoy many of the legal protections offered to C Corporations.

As part owners or contractors rather than customers, day traders are associated with the firm, and as such, they can trade using a portion of the firm's capital. Most of these arrangements require traders to put up at least $25,000 to buy in. More often, however, the buy-in required is closer to $100,000. This arrangement enables day traders to use much more leverage than traditional broker-dealer arrangements, where borrowing on margin is limited to amounts held in individual traders' accounts under Regulation T margin requirements. We explain how margin accounts work in Chapter 14. In addition to buying into the LLC, traders for these firms also are required to get a Series 7 license, which we discuss in Chapter 20.

Understanding Account Restrictions

Regulation T is one of the key restrictions in the SEC arsenal of tools for controlling day trading. Rules related to the settlement of stock transactions and borrowing from others to meet margin requirements also limit what day traders can do.

The Fed's Regulation T: Margin requirements

The world of day trading became much more restricted in August 2001 when the SEC approved amendments to Regulation T that focus on pattern day traders. Your broker and the National Association of Securities Dealers (NASD) consider you a *pattern day trader* whenever you buy and sell (or short and cover) any security on the same day within a margin account four or more times during any rolling five-day period. Days when the markets are closed — Saturday, Sunday, and market holidays — are not included when calculating the rolling five-day period.

After you're designated a pattern day trader, you're required to maintain a minimum of $25,000 of equity in your margin account before you're ever permitted to do any more day-trading. For most day traders, that means having at least $25,000 in cash at the end of every trading day. This limitation can impact other investing activities in your account, so if you're considering day trading, be sure to talk with your broker to gain an understanding of the impact that margin account minimums have on other stock transactions you may want to make within your account.

After you've been designated as a pattern day trader and maintain the $25,000 minimum in your margin account, you're entitled to borrow up to four times any amount you maintain in your margin account. For example, if you maintain $50,000 in your account, this gives you up to $200,000 of *day-trading buying power*. But remember, this extra buying power is limited only to intraday trades. If you hold positions overnight, you cannot take advantage of the day trading margin when opening a position. You must adhere to the traditional 50 percent initial margin requirements.

Typically, day traders are *flat,* or back into a cash position by the end of the trading day for all day trades; otherwise, you risk a margin call (see Chapter 14). Whenever your day-trading activities result in a margin call, you have five days to deposit cash or securities in your account to meet the call. If you fail to meet the margin call, your account will be restricted to traditional margin requirements.

Although brokerage firms are not required to monitor whether day-trading accounts fall below the $25,000 minimum throughout a given trading day, customers must cover any losses incurred in their accounts from the previous day's trades before they're allowed to continue day trading. If a day trader exceeds the four times–leverage rule during the day, a brokerage firm can impose additional restrictions on the account to protect itself from additional risk and prevent any recurrences of such activities.

Members of the NASD are required to issue day-trading margin calls to pattern day traders who exceed their day-trading buying power. Traders then have five days to meet these calls. Until a margin call is met, the day-trading account's buying power is restricted to traditional margin requirements, which allows the day trader to leverage equity only two times. For example, if a day trader has $50,000 of equity, but the account is restricted due to exceeding buying power constraints, the day-trading buying power is only $100,000. These stricter requirements begin on the trading day after buying power is exceeded and stay in place until the trader either meets the call by depositing the necessary cash or securities or until five business days have passed. After five business days have passed and the day trader still has not met the call, the day trader is limited to trading only on a cash-available basis for 90 days or until the call is met.

Traders can't meet the call and then just take the money right out again. Funds deposited to meet the call must be left in the account for at least two business days. Traders also can't use *cross-guarantees* (guarantees from third parties) for the margin call. The cash or securities must be deposited directly in the account.

Settlement: No free rides

An official stock transaction is settled three days after the date of the trade, meaning that day traders frequently are buying and selling stocks before their transactions are officially settled. Day traders can't *free ride,* meaning they can't buy a security and sell it an hour later without first having enough funds to cover the settlement of the initial trade. If a trader buys a stock or other security, he or she must have the funds to cover the initial trade even if the security is sold for a profit within the same day.

A margin account with leverage of four times excess equity is what enables day traders to get around this rule. To play within these rules, all the trader needs to have is sufficient cash to pay for the shares or sufficient reserve in his or her margin account. Brokers can restrict use of margin funds for three days until a stock transaction is settled, but they're not required to do so.

Before trading, be sure that you understand the restrictions your broker imposes on margin accounts related to stock transaction settlements. The settlement time for options is the next day, as opposed to the three-day waiting period for stocks. To trade using options, funds must be in the account before you place the trade or you'll be stuck wiring funds around, which can add plenty to the costs of your trading.

Strategies for Successful Day Trading

As mentioned throughout this chapter, day traders trade stocks in lots of 1,000 shares or more, putting large portions of cash at risk with every trade. Although the profit potential is great, so is the risk of losing all your money and maybe even owing money if you use borrowed cash in your margin account.

Before you ever considering day trading, you need to understand the risks you're taking and how to control them. Otherwise, money can flow out of your account very quickly. Studies show that it generally takes six months to learn how to be a successful day trader, and during that learning curve, you can count on losing money. Success rates for day traders range from 10 percent to 30 percent of those who try it. In other words, 70 percent to 90 percent of the people who attempt day trading don't succeed and frequently end their day-trading careers in debt. We explain more about risks in the "Risks Are High; Rewards Can Be Too" section, later in the chapter, but first we need to review some of the basic strategies that day traders use.

Technical needs

Number one on the list of things you need to become a day trader is a basic computer and Internet setup. They're necessary for successful day trading. Most traders have two or more monitors with a PC built to handle a large number of data feeds at one time. Windows NT or Windows 2000 are the preferred platforms of day traders, because these operating systems are considered the most stable with the programs that are used, and they're better able to handle multiple monitors.

Daily computer maintenance is critical for day traders. Computer problems are the last thing you want to experience in the middle of your trading day, especially when buy positions are left open. You can lose a lot of money if you're waiting for your computer to reboot and a trade goes sour. Traders recommend that you clear the cookies (files that Web sites send to your computer when you're using them) from your Internet cache on a daily basis and that you *defragment* (reorganize your files so the computer runs more efficiently) your computer at least once a week.

Another key step is finding an Internet service provider (ISP) that is reliable and offers high-speed access to the Internet. Many traders have more than one ISP lined up, so they have a backup in case the first one goes down. Again, you don't want to lose even mere seconds when you're in the middle of your trading day, especially when you have open positions.

Trading patterns

Day traders make use of patterns seen in technical analysis that are similar to the ones we discuss in Part III of this book. One common pattern that day traders look for is a price gap in a stock at the opening of the market. They find that prices usually move in the same direction as the opening price gap during the first few minutes that the market is open and then the market tends to reverse and fill the gap (see Chapter 10). Trading that doesn't fill the gap during the first five to ten minutes can signal a dominant trend for the day for that particular stock. Some traders watch this action to find their targets for the day and the directions they plan to play them. Others believe early market moves give false signals and that using those moves for planning your trading day can be dangerous.

Traders watch for many of the same patterns they find when looking for breakout signals and signs of reversals (see Chapter 10). The key difference is that a day trader looks for intraday signals, while longer-term traders format their charts for longer periods of time.

Scalping

Scalping basically means you move in and out of a position for a very limited profit in an extremely short time frame, usually just a few minutes or possibly only a few seconds. The scalper's objective is to make profits of only fractions of a point on any given trade, rather than the several points profit that most traders seek. Day traders execute their trades in a much narrower time frame, so scalpers look for only an eighth of a point or a quarter of a point, hoping to make small gains as often as possible.

When scalping with higher-priced or faster-moving stocks, one point can be considered a scalp. For most stocks, however, scalping doesn't pay if you trade any fewer than 1,000 shares, because an eighth of a point profit on 1,000 shares is $125 minus any fees or commissions you have to pay.

Trend traders

Not all day traders use the scalping technique. Some are trend traders. Instead of jumping in and out of a trade for a fraction of a point, they look for profits of at least 1 or 2 points and may stay in a position for minutes or even as long as an hour. *Trend traders* make fewer trades than scalpers, but seek higher profits per trade and may trade in blocks of less than 1,000 shares, because they can make a nice profit as trend traders with considerably less share volume. In fact, traders who look for more than a 1 point profit sometimes hold a stock for several hours, unless the stock is high priced or its price is moving fast.

Bandits

Other day traders are known as *bandits*. These traders watch the bid and ask prices of NASDAQ market makers and initiate trades that take advantage of differences in these prices. For example, if one market maker offers to buy a stock at 10⅛ (the bid) and will sell at 10¼ (the ask) while others have increased their bids to 10⅜ and their ask to 10½, the bandit buys at 10¼ from the first market maker and then sells at 10⅜ to another market maker in only a matter of seconds. Bandits used to be more common when the old order system known as SOES (Small Order Execution System) was available. Today's market maker systems are much better, and finding market makers who make the kinds of mistakes that bandits profited from is rare.

Risks Are High; Rewards Can Be Too

Reading about trading patterns and the high volume of stock trading, you've probably already figured out for yourself that the risks are high. Within a matter of minutes, trading in and out of stocks in 1,000-share blocks can be costly whenever a stock quickly moves in a direction you weren't anticipating.

In fact, the U.S. Senate investigated the risks of day trading after a shooting spree at an on-site day-trading facility in Atlanta, Georgia, left nine people dead in July 1999. The shooter, Mark Barton, was a chemist before getting involved in day trading and losing $105,000 in just one month. He killed himself after the shooting spree.

Senate investigators found that the revenue of the 15 largest firms that specialize in day trading for 1999 was $541.5 million, or 276 percent higher than their revenue in 1997. Profits went up by more than $66 million, and by 1999, the 15 firms had opened 12,000 new accounts. Investigators also found that the 4,000 to 5,000 most active traders were borrowing huge sums of money and losing it. In that year traders paid an average $16 per trade and made an average 29 trades per day. Using these statistics, investigators concluded that a trader needed to make more than $111,000 a year in stock market gains just to break even with that level of costs.

Liquidity

In order to be considered liquid, a trader must have the ability to change holdings quickly into cash. Although you can see that a day trader must trade a large number of shares to make a profit, he or she must also have a significant amount of cash and securities in his or her account to be able to continue trading activities. Many traders accomplish this financial feat by borrowing from family and friends, putting not only their own money at risk but also the money of others, all for the sake of keeping their day-trading businesses alive.

Slippage

Slippage can cost day traders significantly if they're not careful how they execute their trades. *Slippage* relates to the difference between what you expect your exit or entry stock prices to be and what you actually end up paying for and getting out of that stock when your order is finally executed. Depending on the volatility of the market, a stock price sometimes can vary by as much as one or two points from the time you see the stock quotation until the time your order is actually executed.

Traders can control slippage, if they use the right type of order. The three basic ways you can enter a position are at market, with a stop order, or with a limit order. Day traders rarely use market orders, which means buying or selling a stock at the market price. Instead they use stop or limit orders to have better control over when their orders are filled and how much they pay for the stock. We discuss various types of orders and the advantages and disadvantages of each in Chapter 2.

Most traders recommend that you never enter a position without immediately placing a stop-loss order at an exit price that you decide is the most you're willing to lose on a particular position. Although a stop order means that once a stock hits the exit price, the order changes to a market order and may result in your selling the stock at less than that price, it nevertheless is safer than placing a limit order, which can mean that you miss the exit point altogether and possibly lose even more. Stop-loss orders can cause some slippage, but you usually lose less with these types of orders than you do with limit orders. A limit order can be completely missed when your stock breaks into a downward trend, because the fall in price was too abrupt or rapid for it to be executed.

When buying stock, traders use limit orders, because they place limits on the entry prices traders are willing to pay. Traders certainly don't want to end up paying higher prices than they intend, which, in turn, raises the bar for making a profit higher than is reasonably possible to attain.

Trading costs

Trading costs vary significantly depending on the amount of trading you do or don't do each month. Just to give you an example of the types of fees you can expect, the minitable below provides a breakdown of the commissions charged by one of the top day-trading firms.

Number of Trades per Month	Commissions
0–399 trades	$12.95 per trade
400–999 trades	$9.95 per trade
1,000 or more trades	$7.95 per trade

The cost of trading is the same whether you have Level I or Level II access (see Chapters 3 and 14 for information on Level I and Level II quoting alternatives). The number of trades you do will impact whether or not you have to pay for Level II access. To get Level II access for free, you must make at least 20 trades per month; otherwise, the monthly fee for Level II access is $125.

Options trading fees are $14.95 per trade, plus $1.95 per contract. In addition to these fees, per-share charges can range from $0.002 per share to $0.01 per share, depending on the exchange on which you choose to trade. If your computer crashes or your Internet access goes down, phone orders (for the company cited in the minitable) can cost you $30 per trade.

So if you trade 30 times a day for 20 days a month, the number of your trades totals 600. At $9.95 per trade, your commission costs are $5,950 per month, and if you trade 1,000 shares with each trade, that adds up to a total of 600,000 shares per month. Even at the lowest per-share exchange cost of $0.002, that means an additional $1,200 in per-share charges. Thus, your monthly cost for this volume of trading would be $7,150.

In addition to these costs, many traders also pay for newsletters or join trading chat rooms that give them alerts for the best opportunities each day. These services can add another $200 to $250 to your monthly costs. So before you see even one penny of profit, your monthly outlay can be $7,400 (that's $88,800 annually). Looking at numbers like these, you can easily understand why so many day traders never see a profit for at least six months and why such a high percentage of day traders actually give up before their businesses turn profitable.

Taxes (of course)

On top of all these costs, you must consider taxes that you'll have to pay on any short-term profits at your current individual tax rate and not the preferred tax rates given to long-term investments that are held more than a year. However, full-time day traders have tax advantages that other traders and investors don't have, but to qualify for these special breaks, day traders must:

✔ Buy and sell a high volume of stocks every day. If you're day trading full time, proving that you're meeting the requirements to qualify for the special day-trading tax breaks is easier. If you work full time and trade part time, proving that you qualify for the tax break may be more difficult.

✔ Establish (in their accounts) that they regularly and continually make numerous trades just about every day the market is open. A broker designating you as a pattern day trader and requiring you to maintain a margin account minimum of $25,000 may help prove you're a day trader in the eyes of the Internal Revenue Service (IRS).

✔ Have a goal of making a profit buying and selling stocks with short-term horizons rather than making profits by holding stocks for long-term gains or dividend income.

If you successfully prove to the IRS that you're a day trader, you can consider your day-trading activities as a business and thereby write off all your trading costs as a sole proprietor on Schedule C of your tax return. The reason doing so gives you such as great tax advantage is that other investors are able to write off only the costs that exceed 2 percent of their adjusted gross incomes. Any losses reported on your Schedule C business return can be written off against your adjusted gross income and thus reduce your tax bill, which, in turn, can help you qualify for other tax breaks.

In addition to the costs of making your trades, you can write off many more items against your business on Schedule C. You also can write off any interest you pay on your margin account and possibly depreciate up to 100 percent of any equipment that you bought to start and continue to run your trading business as a Section 179 business deduction (this deduction could be as much as $102,000 in 2004). If you use a space in your home exclusively for your trading activities, you also can take a home-office deduction.

Any gains that you make on your trading activities are considered capital gains, and as such, are exempt from any self-employment taxes that other sole proprietors must pay on their business profits. You still have to report your gains and losses on Schedule D, and to avoid additional scrutiny, you may want to attach a note to your Schedule C explaining why you have losses and no income. The IRS red flags returns from people who report losses on Schedule C for several years in a row, a factor that also can trigger an audit.

Avoiding the Most Common Mistakes

If the risks and costs don't scare you away from day trading, then you need to become familiar with some of the more common mistakes that lead to failure for many day traders. Some traders talk about their more common mistakes, especially the ones that cost a lot of money while they were building their businesses. Here are some of the more serious mistakes new day traders make:

- ✔ **Breaking your stop loss rules:** When a stock starts dropping, newer, not yet disciplined, traders tend to panic as their picks begin losing money, so they decide to hold the stock rather than exit when their initial stop loss is reached. However, traders go broke using that strategy, because they don't stop their losses as planned. You must set your exit prices based on your technical analysis for both losses and profits when you first buy the stock. Follow those rules mechanically when the target price is hit, and don't let your emotions get in the way.

✔ **Chasing trends:** New traders who aren't yet confident in the way they read patterns often wait to see confirmation that they're right before they enter a position. That hesitation causes them to miss planned entry points and, if they're right, can end up forcing them into buying at a stock price that's higher than they intended when an upward trend is expected or selling at a lower price than they intended when a downward trend is expected. By missing intended entry prices, traders end up chasing the trends and finding that their original entry and exit points no longer are valid because many others already acted on the trend and the stock is no longer available at the planned prices. Experienced traders just walk away from that particular trade instead of getting caught up in trading points that don't match technical analysis and thereby chasing a trend.

✔ **Not waiting for the right trade:** A new day trader must exhibit the patience required in waiting for the right trade to match what the technical analysis indicates. Experienced traders know to wait for the right timing instead of forcing a trade and entering at the wrong price.

✔ **Not establishing set rules before your trading day begins:** To avoid getting caught up in the emotions of a big win or loss, you need to decide your entry and exit points before the trading day begins and never deviate from them after the day begins. Experienced day traders know that you either focus on your trades or think about your rules. You don't have time to do both and trying to do so can be a recipe for disaster. Staying objective and following your rules is crucial to maintaining the control a day trader needs.

✔ **Forgetting that fundamentals don't matter:** New day traders get caught up in the idea that the company whose stock they've purchased is a good company and when its stock loses ground, it's therefore bound to head back up. Experienced traders know that how good the fundamentals look doesn't matter and that when the market is selling down, even the price of a good stock goes down. Day traders must follow market signs and not worry about how good or bad the fundamentals of the company they're trading may appear.

✔ **Averaging down:** Although investors may *average down,* meaning they buy a stock and if the price goes down they buy even more shares believing that it's a good stock that will recover, this technique doesn't work at all for day traders, and most experienced traders of every variety will tell you that using it is a fatal mistake. Day traders instead believe that you need to set a stop price and get out (called stopping out) of a losing stock and possibly reenter again at a lower price. Doing so gives you time to look objectively at what is happening with the stock and determine whether getting back in is worthwhile. Stopping out also is likely to cost you less than averaging down, and you won't risk getting caught with a margin problem. Averaging down can tie up too much money that otherwise can be used for a more profitable trade with a different stock. The worst feeling, even for an experienced trader, occurs when a stock plunges far below the stop position, because deciding whether to take the large loss is difficult. In most cases, if you're uncertain of your next move, experienced traders recommend that you get out of the position before the situation grows worse or out of control.

✔ **Not knowing when to take profits:** New traders sometimes make the mistake of either taking profits too early or not taking profits at all. Both can result in unnecessary losses. Most of the time, indecision strikes when traders are afraid they'll lose a profit if they hold it too long or miss a profit if they exit too soon. Just like with losses, exit points need to be determined before entering a position and rules need to be followed. Remember that as a day trader you must focus either on your trade or on your rules. Day traders who move into and out of positions within seconds or minutes don't have time to do both.

✔ **Walking away from the computer with open positions:** Experienced day traders never walk away from their computers when they still have an open position. Although we touch briefly on holding open positions overnight in the introduction to this chapter, this rule is even stricter. Because experienced day traders respond to price changes that occur in mere seconds or minutes, they definitely don't want to be away from the screen while a position is still open.

Day trading is a high-risk career choice that you should consider only after doing a considerable amount of initial research, hunting down good resources for educating yourself about the risks and rewards, and finding all the techniques you need to use to day trade successfully. Even before you get started, be sure to check out the firms you're planning to use as resources by calling up their disciplinary records and complaint histories through the SEC or state regulators. You're putting a good deal of money at risk, so take the time to find out all you can before spending even that first dime.

You also may want to consider taking your Series 7 exam, the exam all stockbrokers are required to pass. Although you must be sponsored to take the exam, many training centers near your home or online can help you find a sponsoring broker. Even though you may never want to work as a broker, the information you're required to know for the exam gives you a much stronger awareness of the securities markets and the laws by which they're governed. Studying for the test, you'll also discover more about the various investment products on the market and the risks you take when buying and selling each type. We discuss the Series 7 exam in greater detail in Chapter 20.

Chapter 18

Doing It by Derivatives

· ·

· ·

Traders can raise the bar on the leverage they're allowed by opening the door to the derivatives markets. *Derivatives* are any financial instruments that get or derive their value from another financial security, which is called an *underlier*. This underlier is usually stocks, bonds, foreign currency, or commodities. The derivative buyer or seller doesn't have to own the underlying security to trade these instruments.

Derivatives traders use futures and options, which are the two most common types of derivatives, to make money in a highly risky venture. In this chapter, we introduce you to a variety of derivatives, how they're traded, and the risks involved in trading futures and options. However, you need to seek additional training before jumping into this kind of trading.

Types of Derivatives: Futures and Options

Derivatives are marketable instruments, which over time acquire and relinquish value based on an underlying asset (see the later section on "Options lingo"), including such commodities as coffee or soybeans, bonds, and even stocks. They are commonly used by commercial and institutional organizations to *hedge* against the risks of financial losses suffered by the underlying assets that they hold. Buying or selling a derivative, for example, can minimize your financial loss, whenever a major change occurs in the price of an asset that you own. *Hedging* is a popular tactic used by growers, producers, portfolio managers, and users of the commodities.

The two basic and most common types of derivatives are contracts for options and for futures. Traders buy and sell them as a way to speculate on the direction that the volatile prices of underlying assets will take farther down the road. If their hunches are right and the prices move in the directions they expect, traders can make a significant profit. If, on the other hand, they're wrong, they can either lose the amount they paid for the derivative and possibly even quite a bit more. Before we explain all the risks, we need to more accurately define futures and options.

Futures

Futures are legally binding contracts between two parties, one of whom agrees to buy and the other who agrees to sell an asset for a specific price at a specified time in the future. The specific price is known as the *strike price.* The specified date in the future is known as the *settlement date.* Futures first were used in the 18th century in Japan as a means of trading rice and silk, but they didn't appear in U.S. markets until the 1850s, when futures markets were developed for buying and selling commodities, such as wheat, cotton, and corn.

Future contracts are one of the more volatile trading instruments. Prices can change rapidly, causing traders to face sudden and sometimes huge losses or gains. Future contracts are traded based on the prices of underlying commodities, indexes, bonds, and stocks. Most people who enter futures markets do so not to actually buy and sell the actual goods, but rather either to speculate on or to hedge the risks of the changing prices of the assets that they do hold.

What's your position?

When people talk about futures, they're bound to say something about their positions. Here's what they mean:

- **Short positions:** The party in the contract who agrees to deliver the commodity, stock, or bond holds a short position. Traders who take short positions are expecting the price of the underlying commodities to go down.

- **Long positions:** The party in the contract who agrees to buy the commodity, stock, or bond in a futures contract holds a long position on the security. Traders who buy long positions are expecting the price of the underlying commodities to go up.

Making money using futures

Traders can make money from trading futures on the basis of the daily movements of the markets for the various types of underlying commodities, stocks, bonds, or currencies involved in the contracts they buy and/or sell.

For example, typical future contracts for wheat are signed between wheat farmers and bread producers. On one side of this contract, farmers agree to sell a specific amount of the wheat they grow at a specific price and a specified time, and on the other side, producers agree to pay that price for the contracted amount of wheat to be delivered to them by the specified time. Farmers benefit by ensuring that they can get a specific price or income from their wheat, and bread producers benefit by knowing how much they have to pay for the wheat they need to make the bread that they, in turn, sell to earn a living.

The value of that future contract is calculated daily. Assuming the farmer agreed in February to sell 10,000 bushels of wheat to the bread maker at $4 per bushel in July, and assuming that before the July settlement date the price of wheat raises to $5 per bushel, the farmer holding the future contract has lost $1 per bushel of wheat or $10,000. These types of price adjustments actually are calculated daily throughout the time that the future contract is in force, and that means the farmer's or bread maker's accounts are credited or debited as wheat prices fluctuate.

The farmer and bread maker will probably never actually exchange their goods. Instead, the obligations of the future contract eventually are settled with cash. In this scenario, the bread maker will probably buy his wheat at the current price of $5 per bushel when he needs it, but because he speculated correctly on the price, it's only really costing him $40,000 (instead of $50,000 at the current market price) to buy the wheat. Although the bread maker pays $50,000 for 10,000 bushels of wheat, he has saved $10,000 because of the money he made on the wheat future contract. The farmer, on the other hand, sells his wheat at $5 per bushel and gets $50,000 cash, but actually keeps only $40,000, because he has to cover his loss from the futures contract.

You can see from this example that future contracts are actually financial positions. This financial position, or the buying and selling of future contracts, is what traders are speculating about. If futures traders believe the price of wheat is rising, they buy futures contracts so they can benefit from the gain made by the price. But when the situation is reversed and the price of wheat drops to $3 per bushel, then the trader who buys can be on the losing side of that future contract and be liable for a $10,000 loss. The costs of buying into a futures contract is called the *premium* paid for that contract, which is only a small percentage of the price of the actual commodity, stock, bond, or currency underlying the contract.

Commodities futures

People who buy commodities futures basically are agreeing to buy a certain amount of a commodity at a set price at some point in the future. Conversely, people who sell those same futures are agreeing to provide a certain amount of a commodity at the agreed upon price by the agreed upon time. Buyers or sellers can enter into futures contracts on many commodities, including farm products (pork bellies, wheat, corn, or soybeans), precious metals (gold, copper, and silver), and many others.

Traders usually don't get directly involved as buyers and sellers of the actual commodities, because they usually get out of their futures contracts before the underlying commodities upon which their trades are based ever change hands. Instead, they're speculators, buying and/or selling futures contracts based on which way they think the commodity price is going to move. Speculation, as you know, is wrought with risk, and the reason the risk is so great is that a commodity contract controls a large amount the commodity (or commodity value) compared with the relatively small price that it takes to buy or sell the contract. The result is extensive leverage, which means controlling a large position with only a small cash deposit. If the price moves in a direction that's the opposite of what the trader anticipates, he or she may have to take a huge loss to get out of the contract.

Index futures

Index futures are based on the expected direction of the value of indexes like the S&P 500 and the New York Stock Exchange Composite indexes. They can be the riskiest types of futures. No underlying commodities, stocks, or bonds ever change hands with these futures contracts. Any differences in these contracts must be settled with good old, cold hard cash. Leverage also is high on these types of futures. For example, a NYSE Composite Index futures contract has a value that's 500 times the value of the underlying NYSE Index.

Smaller index futures contracts, known collectively as *e-minis,* are targeted at individual traders. These minicontracts are available for indexes such as the S&P 500, the NASDAQ 100, the S&P mid-cap, and the Russell 2000. Their respective individual values range from 20 times to 50 times those of the underlying indexes.

The S&P 500 e-mini contract, for example, is $50 times the value of the S&P 500 index. In other words, if a trader takes a position in the S&P 500 e-mini contract, every time the underlying S&P 500 index moves one point, the value of the S&P 500 e-mini contract changes by $50. Another way to think about this is for every .01 points, the value of the S&P 500 e-mini contract changes by 50 cents. If you take a long position in the S&P 500 e-mini contract when the underlying index is at 1,000, and the index moves to 1,010, you have a $500 profit. The trader who took the other side of this trade, the short position, is in exactly the opposite position, losing $500.

Bond futures

Bond futures are based on the price of future delivery of a specific type of bond in a specific denomination at a specific interest rate on a specified date. Speculators basically are betting on whether the price of that bond goes up or down. Changes in interest rates have a big impact on the values of bonds. In general, when interest rates fall, bond prices go up, and when interest rates rise, bond prices go down. Speculators in bond futures basically enter positions based on whether interest rates will go up or down. For example, a speculator who thinks interest rates will go up sells contracts for the future delivery of bonds. If interest rates, indeed, go up as expected, the price for the underlying bonds goes down, and speculators can do one of two things:

- ✔ Buy the lower-priced bonds, and, in turn, earn a profit by selling them to the buyer to settle at the higher price named in the original futures contract.
- ✔ Close the contract to realize a profit.

Stock futures

Stock futures are contracts in which you either agree to deliver or purchase upon delivery 100 shares of a particular stock on or before a designated date in the future that's known as the *expiration date*. For example, a trader who enters into a contract to buy 100 shares at $30 a share for a total of $3,000 and expects the price of that stock to go up, can lock in the lower price and then can buy the actual stock at that lower price on the settlement date or close the contract and realize a profit. Traders who enter into this type of contract generally must have about 20 percent of the cash value of 100 shares of the underlying stock in their brokerage accounts, so a trader in the earlier example would have to have $300 in a brokerage account.

Foreign currency futures

Future currency contracts are contracts that involve the future delivery of certain foreign currencies. We discuss these types of futures in Chapter 19.

Yes, future contracts are riskier than options, because you actually have to come up with the underlying commodity, bond, stock, or currency to satisfy the contract, sell the future at a loss before the settlement date, or pay the difference in cash to settle the contract. Futures are binding contracts that require you to fulfill the obligations specified in the contracts. Options are less risky, because they're not an obligation to perform, but instead give the buyer of the option the right to exercise the option, but the buyer is not obligated to do so.

Options

Although futures have been available in the United States since the 1850s, options did not become available until 1982, when they were part of a government pilot program. The big advantage options have over futures is that you buy the right to exercise the option contract, and yet you still can decide simply to allow the option to expire without ever exercising that right. When you let an option expire, you lose only the amount you paid for the option and not the full amount that otherwise can be lost in trading the underlying asset. Option sellers take the riskier stance, because they can lose the value of whatever asset they promised to sell or buy if the option buyer decides to exercise the option.

Options are financial instruments that give the buyer the right, but not the obligation, to buy or sell a particular asset at a predetermined date in the future at a specified price.

Options lingo

Trading in options has a language all its own, and you'll need to understand it before we get into the mechanics, so here are some key terms:

- **Puts:** A *put option* is a contract that gives the buyer the right to sell a particular asset at a specified price at any time during the life of the option.

- **Calls:** A *call option* is a contract that gives the buyer the right to buy a particular asset at a specified price at any time during the life of the option.

- **Option grantor:** The person who writes or sells any option is called the *option grantor*. This person or financial entity must come up with the underlying asset promised in the option, even if doing so means a loss, whenever an option buyer decides to exercise an option. For example, if an option grantor agrees to sell you 100 shares of ABC stock for $50 per share on or before May 1, and the stock price rises to $60 on April 20, then the grantor must sell you that stock for $50 and take the $10-per-share loss. You get to sell ABC at the current price and reap the benefits.

- **Covered calls:** If an option seller holds an *equivalent position,* or owns the same number of shares of the underlying asset that is offered in the call, then the contract is considered a *covered call.* Options traders selling covered calls are trying to take advantage of a neutral or declining stock. If the option expires unexercised, the writer (seller) of the option keeps the premium. If, on the other hand, the holder (buyer) of the option exercises it, the stock must be delivered. However, because the option writer already owns the stock, the risk is limited. The opposite scenario is an *uncovered call,* which is when the writer sells a call for a stock that he or she doesn't own. The seller of an uncovered call is taking virtually unlimited risk.

✔ **Covered puts:** When the seller of a put option also has sold short an equivalent amount in the underlying security, then this option is considered a *covered put.* If the writer has neither established a short position in the underlying security nor deposited a corresponding amount of cash equal to the value of the put, then the put is called a *naked put.* The seller of a naked put also is taking virtually unlimited risk.

✔ **Option holder:** The person who buys the option is called the option holder. If the option buyer buys the right to sell an asset at some time in the future, then he or she buys a put option. If the option buyer buys the right to purchase an asset at some time in the future, then he or she buys a call option. The most an option holder can lose is the amount paid for the option contract.

✔ **Underlying asset:** An option contract is based on an underlying asset — usually either a futures contract or specific number of shares of stock — that can be bought or sold.

✔ **Premium:** The actual price paid for the option is called the *premium,* which is what the option holder pays to the option grantor to gain the right to either buy or sell the underlying asset. Premiums for options are set by the open market. Option buyers must pay the premium plus whatever fees their brokers charge for such transactions.

✔ **Expiration date:** The *expiration date* is the last day that an option buyer can exercise the rights specified in the contract. Options based on futures contracts usually expire one month before the settlement date of the underlying future contract. After an option expires, the option holder no longer has any rights and the option has no value. So option buyers lose whatever premium they paid plus any commissions or transaction costs that had to be paid when the option was purchased. In that case, the option is said to expire worthless.

✔ **Exercise:** Option buyers can exercise the rights they purchase with the option any time before the expiration date, if, that is, the option they purchased is an *American-style option. European-style options,* on the other hand, can be exercised only on their expiration dates. Exercising a call option means the option buyer buys the underlying asset at the price set in the option regardless of the current market price for the asset. Exercising a put option means the option buyer sells the underlying asset at the price set in the option. An option buyer can always decide not to exercise the rights set forth in his or her option and simply let it expire. The option holder also can sell the option contract at its current market value.

- ✔ **Strike price:** The *strike price* is the price of the underlying asset at which the option can be exercised.

- ✔ **Offset:** If option buyers or sellers want to realize their profits or limit their losses, they can *offset* their option through a sale or purchase that also is called liquidating an option or closing an option. When an option is liquidated, no position is actually taken in the underlying asset. Offsetting is usually done on the same exchange where the buyer first bought or sold the option. If they can sell the option for more than they bought it, then they will realize a profit. If they sell the option for less than they paid, then they will take a loss.

- ✔ **In-the-money:** An option is said to be *in-the-money* when it is worthwhile to exercise the option and buy or sell the underlying asset. A call option is in-the-money when the market price for the underlying asset is above the strike price set in the option contract. A put option is in-the-money when the price for the underlying asset is lower than the strike price set in the option contract.

- ✔ **At-the-money:** An option is deemed to be *at-the-money* when the strike price for the option is the same as the market price for the underlying asset.

- ✔ **Out-of-the-money:** An option is said to be *out-of-the-money* when it's not worthwhile to exercise the option. A call option is out-of-the-money when the strike price is higher than the market price for the underlying asset. A put option is out-of-the-money when the strike price is less than the market price for the underlying asset.

Option pricing

The three factors affecting the price of an option premium are the:

- ✔ **Date of expiration:** As the option moves closer to its date of expiration, the value of the option declines, and that's why an option is considered a *wasting asset*. The more time that you have until an option expires, the greater possibility you have for the option to reach the point of being in-the-money. Longer options therefore have higher premiums.

- ✔ **Strike price:** For out-of-the-money options, when the current market price moves more and more out-of-the-money and away from the strike price, the premium price gets lower and lower. The premium for an in-the-money option, on the other hand, rises in value if the underlying asset moves further into the money in relationship to the strike price.

- ✔ **Volatility:** The more volatility that's in the market for the underlying asset, or stock, the greater the chance that the option will become worthwhile to exercise. When the market for an asset is volatile, premiums for options on that asset are higher.

Option pricing techniques are considered to be among the most mathematically complex of all applied areas of finance. One common example, the Black-Scholes option-pricing model (named for its developers Fischer Black and Myron Scholes), takes into consideration the stock's price, the option's strike price and expiration date, the risk-free return, and the standard deviation of the stock's return, which are measures of volatility.

When you get a quote for an option, you may have to choose from numerous strike prices and expiration dates that are available. When you're thinking about buying a call option and its strike price is low and yet close to becoming worthwhile to exercise, the premium price (the price you pay for the option) will be much higher than for an option with a higher strike price. If you're thinking about buying a put option, then you'll pay more of a premium for an option with a high strike price than you will for one with a lower strike price.

Just to give you an idea of how the pricing of options is affected by strike price and time, Table 18-1 is an options quote for an imaginary stock we call ABC. Settle is the time of expiration for the option.

Table 18-1	ABC Stock Sample Option Quotation (In Dollars)					
Strike Price	**Calls/Settle**			**Puts/Settle**		
	Apr	**May**	**July**	**Apr**	**May**	**July**
$50	4.50	4.60	5.40	0.25	0.50	1.50
$52	3.50	3.60	4.40	0.50	1.00	3.50
$54	2.50	2.60	3.40	0.75	2.00	5.50
$56	1.50	1.60	2.40	2.00	3.00	7.50
$58	0.50	0.60	1.40	4.00	5.00	9.50

You can see from the options quotes for ABC stock that a May call with a strike price of $54 commands a premium of $2.60 per share. To buy an option for 100 shares, the premium would be $260 plus whatever fees your exchange or broker charges. Buying a call is much less of a cash outlay than if you were to buy 100 shares of ABC stock at $54. That would cost you $5,400. The premium of $260 is paid to the option seller, minus any fees charged by the broker or exchange.

Fees include commission charges plus any costs involved in executing the order on the trading floor of the exchange. Commissions vary greatly from broker to broker, so be certain you understand all the possible fees before initiating a trade. Some brokers charge commissions per trade, but others charge on the basis of a *round trip,* including both the purchase and the sale of the option. Some brokerage firms charge per-option transaction fees, while others charge on the basis of a percentage of the option premium that's usually subject to a minimum charge.

Commission charges can have a major impact on whether you're able to earn a profit or have to suffer a loss on an option. A high commission charge reduces your potential for making a profit and can even drive what little profit you make into a loss. So be careful. Know what charges you have to pay and compare them with other brokers before you trade.

Options and futures are quoted with bid and ask prices just like stocks, and the spreads with options can grow pretty wide as a percentage of the option's premium, which, in turn, can have a significant impact on the profitability of your option position. The wider the spread, the harder it is for you to make a profit. As an option trader, you typically buy at the ask, the higher price, and sell at the bid, the lower price. That means that any trade must recover the difference between the bid and the ask before you can earn a profit. As with stock trading, you can use a limit order to put your order between the bid and the ask, but there is no guarantee that your order will be filled. See Chapter 14 for more about bid-ask spreads.

Buying Options and Futures Contracts

All types of options and futures are traded on a commodities exchange. In addition, some types of options can be traded on stock exchanges. The American Stock Exchange (Amex) trades stock options, index options, and options on exchange-traded funds. The Philadelphia Stock Exchange trades index and currency options. The Chicago Board Options Exchange (CBOE) handles stock and futures options. You can trade stock options and some index options in a traditional stock account. Special risk release forms must be signed, but otherwise, the account remains the same. (For more about establishing an account, see Chapter 3.) Covered options and naked short positions require a margin account.

Opening an account

If you want to buy futures or options on futures, you must do so through an individual account that you open with a registered futures commission merchant (FCM) or through your broker. Your broker transmits any transactions through an FCM as an introducing broker. Your broker won't collect the funds from you for your options trades. You have to deposit them directly with the FCM.

You have the choice of opening either a discretionary account or a nondiscretionary account. A *discretionary account* is an account in which you sign a power of attorney over to either your FCM, your broker, or a commodity trading advisor (CTA) so he or she can make trading decisions on your behalf. A *nondiscretionary account* is an account in which you make all the trading decisions. You also may want to consider trading through a commodity pool. When trading through a *commodity pool,* you purchase a share or interest in a pool of other investors, and trades are executed by an FCM or CTA. Any profits or losses are shared proportionately by the members of the pool.

When you open an individual account, you need to make a deposit that amounts to a *margin payment* or *performance bond* for the options or futures you trade. This payment is relatively small compared to the size of your potential market position, and it gives you the opportunity to greatly leverage your money. Small changes in options and futures prices can result in large gains or large losses in relatively short periods of time.

Your broker calculates the values of the future and option contracts in your account on a daily basis, and you need to maintain a margin level that's approximately 75 percent of the amount required when you originally enter your positions. If your holdings fall below that level, you'll be asked to come up with the cash to restore your margin account to the initial level, a situation that's known as a *margin call.* If you can't meet the margin call in a reasonable period of time, which can be as little as an hour, your brokerage firm closes out enough of your positions to reduce your margin deficiency. If your positions are liquidated at a loss, you can be held liable for that loss, which sometimes can be substantially more than your original margin deposit.

Calculating the price and making a buy

Before buying an option, you first must calculate the break-even price, but you must know the option's strike price, the premium cost, and the commission or other transaction costs to be able to do it. With those three details in hand, you can determine a break-even price for a call option using this formula:

> Option strike price + option premium costs + commission and transaction fees = break-even price

Using the example in Table 18-1, here is the per-share break-even price for buying a May call option with a strike price of $54 and a commission of $25, or 25 cents per share:

> $54 + $2.60 + $0.25 = $56.85

To make a profit on this call option, the stock price of ABC has to rise above $56.85. If the stock price doesn't rise above $56.85, you won't make a profit on this option purchase (unless you're somehow able to sell the option for more than $2.85 before the expiration date — see the next section). These calculations are correct only when your broker has one fee for a round-trip option exchange. If you have to pay fees in both directions, which is common, then you need to double the fee in the calculation. Most brokers do charge fees in both directions. The fees are the same in each direction, so the cost for trading would be double.

When calculating the break-even price for a put option, you subtract the premium, commission, and transaction costs. Here is the break-even calculation for a May put option for ABC stock at a strike price of $54 with a commission of $25, or 25 cents per share:

$$\$54 - \$2.00 - 25 \text{ cents} = \$51.75$$

In this scenario, ABC stock has to drop below $51.75 for this put option to be worthwhile.

If you're expecting a stock price increase, you want to consider purchasing a call option, but if you expect a price decline, you want to consider purchasing a put option. In both scenarios, you need to check the fundamental and technical analyses information you gathered on the underlying stock or asset, so you can be certain that any break-even prices you've calculated reasonably match what your analysis indicates.

Options for Getting Out of Options

After you buy an option, you have to decide how you want to opt out of that position. You can choose one of the following three alternatives:

✔ Offset the option.

✔ Continue holding the option.

✔ Exercise the option.

Offsetting the option

You offset an option by liquidating your position in the option, usually in the same marketplace that you bought the option. If you want to get out of an option before its expiration date, you can try to sell it for whatever price you can get. Doing so either enables you to take your profits or reduces your potential loss by the amount you receive for the option. As long as you bought your option in an active market, other investors usually are willing to pay for the rights your option conveys. The key, of course, is how much they're willing to pay.

Your net profit or loss for this option is determined by the difference between what you originally pay in premiums, commissions, and other transaction costs minus the premium you receive when you liquidate the option after deducting commissions and other transaction costs.

Holding the option

If your option is not yet in-the-money, but you still believe it may get there, you can continue to hold the option until the exercise date. If you're right, you can exercise the option before the expiration date or liquidate at a later date, which means to buy or sell the option before the expiration date at some time in the future. If you're wrong, you risk the possibility that you won't find a buyer or that you'll have to let the option expire and take a loss that is equal to the amount of the premium, commission, and transaction costs you paid. Some traders take an even more risky position by buying options that are deeply out-of-the-money for just pennies a share. Even if these options never grow any nearer to being in-the-money, as long as they move in the right direction, the premiums will rise. Although we don't recommend using this strategy, profits can be made as long as you're able to sell the option before its expiration date.

Options decline in value as they get closer to their expiration dates, so if you think you've made a mistake and the market moves against your position, bite the bullet as soon as possible and try to liquidate your option to minimize your losses.

Exercising the option

You can exercise an option any time prior to its expiration date, as long as you're trading in American-style options. You don't have to wait until the exercise date to exercise an American-style option. (Some option contracts sold in the United States are European-style, which can be exercised only on the expiration date.) Exercising an option means:

- ✔ Buying the underlying asset when you own a call
- ✔ Selling the underlying asset when you own a put

In general, call options are exercised only when the trader plans to hold the underlying asset, and put options are exercised only when the trader owns the underlying asset and wants to sell it. Option traders are more likely to realize any gains or losses by closing their option positions rather than exercising them.

The Risks of Trading Options and Futures

Trading in options and futures is risky business, and regulations governing those trades are stringent, even with regard to allowing you to open an account. Before opening an account for you, a broker must provide you with a disclosure document that describes the risks involved in trading futures and options contracts. The document gives you the opportunity to determine whether you have the experience and financial resources necessary to engage in option trading and whether option trading is appropriate for meeting your goals and objectives.

Topics that must be covered in the disclosure statement include the risks inherent in trading futures contracts or options and the effect that leveraging your account can have on potential losses or gains. The statement also must include warnings about trading futures in foreign markets, because those types of trades carry additional risks from fluctuations in currency exchange rates and differences in regulatory protection.

Commodities options and futures also can be risky, because many of the factors that affect their prices are totally unpredictable, such as the weather, labor strikes, inflation, foreign exchange rates, and governmental policies. Because positions in futures and options are so highly leveraged, even a small price movement against your position can result in at least the loss of your entire premium payment and possibly even much greater liability for additional losses.

After you begin trading options and futures, you can't close your account until all open positions are closed, if, that is, you're trading through an account with a commodities exchange. This restriction does not apply to options traded in a stock brokerage account. Any accruals on futures contracts are paid out daily. Any funds in your margin account that are beyond your required margin or account-opening requirements can be withdrawn, but other such funds have to remain in the account until all your positions are closed. Any restrictions on the withdrawal of your funds is stated in the original disclosure document. Be sure that you understand those restrictions before committing your funds.

After opening your account, your broker usually mails you confirmation of all purchases and sales and a month-end summary of transactions that show any gains or losses and an evaluation of your open positions and current account values. You need to be able to get this information from your broker on a daily basis after you begin to trade.

Brokers are required to segregate any money you deposit in your account from the brokerages' own funds. The amount that is segregated either increases or decreases depending on the success of your trades. Even if the brokerage firm segregates your funds, you still may not be able to get all your money back if the brokerage firm becomes insolvent and is unable to cover all the obligations to its customers. In other words, the money you put into your brokerage account is not insured.

Whenever problems with your broker arise and you can't resolve them without help, you have several dispute-resolution options. You can contact the reparations program of the Commodities Futures Trading Commission (CFTC) and ask for an industry-sponsored arbitration, or you can take your broker to court. Before deciding how you want to proceed, you must consider the costs involved with each option, the length of time it may take to resolve the problem, and whether you want to contact an attorney. You can get more information about dispute-resolution alternatives by calling the CFTC's Office of Proceedings at 202-418-5250.

Minimizing Risks

In a nutshell, the best way to minimize the risks of derivative trading is to take the time to find out as much as you can about the inherent risks of the derivatives you're trading and how others have dealt with them. The first step you can take is to check out the firms or individuals with whom you plan to trade. All firms and individuals that offer to trade options or futures must be registered with the CFTC (www.cftc.gov) and be members of the National Futures Association (NFA — www.nfa.futures.org). You can check out firms and individuals online at the NFA site by using its Background Affiliation Status Information Center (BASIC). On BASIC, you'll find the status of the firm or individual and any disciplinary actions taken by the NFA, the CFTC, or any U.S. exchanges.

Next be sure that you're familiar with the firm's commission charges and how they're calculated. Compare one firm's quotes with those of other firms you're considering. Whenever a firm has unusually high commission charges, ask for a detailed explanation for the higher charges and what additional services justify the higher cost.

Always make sure that you calculate the break-even price for any option you're thinking about purchasing, because you have to know at what point the option you're planning to buy will be profitable and whether the data you've collected justifies the option's premium costs.

You also need to understand the market for the underlying asset of the option or future you plan to buy and what can impact the market price of that asset. Be sure that your expectations for the potential profits from the option or future contract you choose are reasonable.

You don't ever want to buy an option without first coming to a full realization that you can lose the entire value of your trade. If you want to take the riskier position as an option writer, be sure you can accept the possibility that your losses may exceed the premium you initially received for the option. Option writing comes with the potential of unlimited losses, and so does futures trading.

Just like with stock trading, you can limit your losses by carefully setting your risk limits before you start to trade. Don't let yourself get caught up in the emotions of futures and options trading. Develop a plan before you buy that first option or future and stick with that plan, and be sure to diversify your holdings not only by asset types but also by time of expiration.

After you determine how much capital you want to put into trading derivatives, make sure that you know how much you can afford to lose on just one trade to be able to stay in business. You don't want to overexpose your cash position on one trade and risk the possibility that you won't have the money you need when the next opportunity comes along. By exposing your capital to a variety of markets, you also have a better chance that some of your trades will end up succeeding — how bad can that be?

Be wary of firms that lead you to believe you can make lots of money trading options or futures with very little risk. That's never true. If a firm is using high-pressure tactics to get you to trade, that's a sure sign of a problem, so don't allow yourself to be rushed into a trading decision. If you aren't being given enough time to construct your own fundamental and technical analyses before you make a purchase, walk away from the deal.

The risks associated with trading futures and options can be more than you initially paid for the trade, so be careful out there! We've given you an overview of the options and futures trading arena, but before you jump in, be sure you get significantly more training.

Chapter 19

Going Foreign (Forex)

In This Chapter
▶ Understanding foreign exchange markets
▶ Using money market instruments
▶ Trading with money
▶ Discovering risks of money trading

*T*rading money in the global markets can be a great way to make more of it, but beware that it also can be a lesson in how to lose money quickly. More than $1 trillion is traded every day on the *foreign currency exchange* (Forex), and yet no centralized headquarters or formal regulatory body exists for this form of trade. Foreign currency exchange is regulated through a patchwork of international agreements between countries, most of which have some type of regulatory agency that controls what goes on within their respective borders. Thus, the foreign currency exchange actually is a worldwide network of traders who are connected by telephone and computer screens.

Although more international policing of money trading has occurred in recent years, authorities have had some successes exposing scams and frauds that victimize traders, especially newer ones. So if you want to try this wild world of trading, you need to be wary and not depend entirely on what we discuss here in this chapter. Sure, we explain the workings of foreign exchange markets and how the language of the Forex and its risks are unique, but you need to do a whole bunch more training before you ever consider entering this extremely risky trading arena.

Exploring the World of Foreign Currency Exchange

If you've ever traveled outside the United States, you've probably traded in a foreign currency. Every time you travel outside your home country, you have to exchange your country's currency for the currency used in the country you're visiting. If you're a U.S. citizen shopping in England, and you see a sweater that you want for £100 (100 pounds — the pound is the name of the basic unit of currency in Great Britain), you'd need to know the exchange rate. In April 2004, for example, the rate was $0.55 U.S. for £1 (one pound). So a £100 sweater would cost you $181.60 in U.S. dollars.

We include this example here to show you how foreign currency exchange is used by the average shopper, but foreign currency traders trade much larger sums of money thousands of times a day. The majority of trades take place in three main centers of currency trading — the United States, the United Kingdom, and Japan. The rest of the trading takes place primarily in Singapore, Switzerland, Hong Kong, Germany, France, and Australia. The United Kingdom manages the largest share — about 32 percent. The United States is second with 18 percent, and Japan is third with 8 percent.

Currency trading is ongoing, 24 hours a day, with some countries just getting started as others are finishing up their business day. For example, when the trading day opens at 8 a.m. in London, the trading day is ending for Singapore and Hong Kong. When New York opens its trading doors, it's already 1 p.m. in London. Thus, traders must be alert around the clock, because a major event at an off hour anywhere in the world can shake the markets at any time.

Individual trades in the range of $200 million to $500 million are not uncommon. In fact, the U.S. Federal Reserve estimates that approximately $1.5 trillion dollars are traded every day, and that represents more than $200 every business day of the year for every man, woman, and child living on the planet. Wow! That's several times the daily turnover in U.S. government securities, which is the world's second largest market. In fact, estimates indicate that quoted price changes occur as frequently as 20 times per minute, and the most active currency rates can change as many as 18,000 times in a single day, according to the Federal Reserve.

Types of currency traders

Traders can be grouped into one of four basic types — bankers, brokers, customers, and central banks. Each plays a different role in the foreign currency exchange market.

- **Bankers, banks, and other financial institutions** do the lion's share of trading. They make profits buying and selling currency to each other. Approximately two-thirds of all Forex transactions involve banks dealing directly with each other.

- **Brokers or dealers** sometimes act as intermediaries between the banks, helping them, or other traders looking for a good deal, find out where they can get the best currency trade. Buyers and sellers like working through brokers or dealers, because they can trade anonymously through intermediaries. Brokers make profits on currency exchanges by charging a commission for the transactions they arrange.

✔ **Customers,** which primarily are major companies, trade currency so they can operate globally or invest internationally. For example, if a U.S. car manufacturer buys parts from a manufacturer in Japan, then the U.S. car manufacturer needs to buy and pay for the parts in Japanese yen. Companies that trade currencies regularly have their own trading desks, while others conduct their currency trading through brokers or banks.

✔ **Central banks,** like the U.S. Federal Reserve, that act on behalf of their governments, sometimes participate in the Forex market to influence the value of the currencies of their respective countries. For example, if the Federal Reserve believes the dollar is weak, it may buy dollars, and even encourage central banks of other countries to do the same in the Forex market, to boost, or increase, the value of the dollar.

Why currency changes in value

Among the many factors that impact the value of a nation's currency are

✔ Business cycles

✔ Political developments

✔ Changes in tax laws

✔ Stock market news

✔ Inflationary expectations

✔ International investment patterns

✔ Policies adopted by governments and central banks

Traders must monitor all these potential factors so they can stay on top of political or economic changes that impact the value of the currencies they hold. Currency trading, like other forms of trading, is affected by the basic economic principle of supply and demand. When a whole bunch of one type of currency is available for sale, the market can be flooded with it, and the price of that currency drops. When the supply of currency is low and the demand for it is high, then the value of that currency rises. Governments influence the value of their respective currencies by flooding the market whenever they want the value to fall or making the supply scarce (by buying their own currency) whenever they want the value of their currencies to rise.

What traders do

Currency traders look for a currency that offers the highest return with the lowest risk. For example, if a nation's financial instruments, such as stocks and bonds, offer high rates of return with relatively low risk, then traders who are foreign to that nation want to buy that currency, thus increasing the demand. Currency is also in demand when its country is going through a growth segment in its business cycle highlighted by stable prices and a wide range of goods and services available for sale. Forex traders who speculate on the values of currencies to earn their keep look for specific signs to indicate when exchange rates may change, including the following:

- **Political instability.** Unrest in a country drives up demand for currency in safer markets, such as U.S. dollars, as speculators race to find safe havens.

- **Rising interest rates.** Higher interest rates encourage foreign investments in countries where native investors are seeking better rates of return than they can get at home.

- **Economic reforms.** Economic reforms in developing countries may help improve their currencies. As a result, investors see new opportunities for investing in the currencies of those successfully developing countries.

Traders try to predict these moves in advance, so they can get in or out of a currency before others. Correctly guessing where a currency is going and taking a position in that currency at the beginning of the trend can mean huge profits for a trader. Traders make money either by buying the currency at a lower price and then selling it later at a higher price or by selling their holdings in currencies of other countries at higher prices before they have time to react negatively to improvements in the first currency. After the markets for their original holdings fall, they simply reestablish positions in them at bargain prices.

When a trader purchases a large amount of a particular currency, then he or she is *long on the currency.* Conversely, when a trader sells a large amount of a currency, then he or she is *short on the currency.*

The Forex market is dominated by four currencies, which account for 80 percent of the market — the U.S. dollar, the Euro, the Japanese yen, and the British pound. These currencies always are liquid, which makes finding someone willing to buy or sell any of them easy for traders. Other currencies are not as liquid, and as is true with the stocks of small companies, you're sometimes unable to find any buyers or sellers when you're ready to trade for the currency of a smaller country. Currencies of developing countries are softest, usually facing lower demand than the currencies of developed countries. Soft currencies at times can be difficult to convert.

Understanding Money Jargon

The world of foreign currency exchange has a unique language of its own. Prices are quoted two ways, meaning that when one trader talks price with another, they state their respective prices in terms of what *exchange rate* they'll pay to buy it and what they'll take when selling it. Bid and ask price differences, or *spreads,* usually are stated in *pips* or hundredths of a currency unit. Spreads normally are no more than ten pips.

Pips are the smallest incremental price movement permitted in the currency market. Although most transactions deal in thousands or millions of dollars, yen, euro, or other currencies, and a one-cent spread can equal thousands of dollars, most currency price quotes nevertheless are extended out four decimals (1.5432, for example). Many times traders quote only the last two digits, or the small numbers, such as 32 exchange for 22, because the incremental changes are so small only the last two digits matter.

As a trader, you need to think in terms of the host currency when receiving a quote for *direct exchange,* which would be an exchange based on the value of the host country's currency. For example, quotes given to traders on the Chicago Mercantile Exchange are based on the U.S. dollar, because it's the host currency for the CME. You can see how that exchange works at www.cme.com. Quotes for *indirect exchange* are just the opposite. They're based on the foreign currency for which you are seeking a trade rather than the host currency. For example, if you're in the United States and receive an indirect price quote, you'd be getting a price based on buying a set amount of foreign currency in exchange for U.S. dollars. Most exchanges take place on the interbank market, currency exchanges among the world's banks, and are based on the U.S. dollar. The one exception to the rule is the British pound sterling.

Traders use three different types of trades to exchange currency. They're known as spot, forward, and option transactions.

Spot transactions

Spot transactions account for about a third of all Forex transactions and involve trades in which two traders agree on an exchange rate and then trade currencies based on that rate. These transactions usually start with one trader calling another and asking for a price on a particular type of currency without specifying whether he or she wants to buy or sell. The trader on the receiving end of the call gives the caller a two-way price — one if he or she wants to buy and the other one if he or she wants to sell. If they agree to do business, the two exchange their respective currencies.

Forward transaction

Forward transactions are used when traders want to buy or sell currency at some agreed-upon date in the future. A buyer and a seller set an exchange rate for the transaction, and the transaction occurs at the set price at the appointed time regardless of what the current market price is for the currencies. Forward transactions can be only a few days or even years in the future, although most future contracts are for 30, 60, or 90 days. The two types of forward transactions are futures and swaps.

- ✔ **Futures.** *Futures* are forward transactions that have standard contract sizes and maturity dates. These types of transactions are traded on an exchange set up for this purpose.

- ✔ **Swaps.** A *swap,* the more common type of forward transaction, is a private contract through which two parties exchange currencies for a specific length of time and then agree to reverse the transaction at a later date, which is set at the time of the initial contract.

The risk that traders take in using forward transactions is that market rates can change, turning the contract to which they've just agreed into a losing trade. They still have to fulfill the contract at the fixed price, because after the contract is signed the price cannot be revised.

Companies that place orders for products from foreign firms usually use this type of transaction so they can lock in an exchange rate at some time in the future when their orders are ready. Companies placing these orders don't want to lay out the cash upfront to exchange currencies, but they nevertheless want to be able to budget set amounts for their purchases. As such, they'd rather risk missing a better rate for the currency exchange in the future than a major shift in the price of the product (perhaps brought on by a currency shock) that's going to end up costing them much more than they intended to pay.

Options

Option contracts were added to the Forex world to give traders a bit more flexibility than a forward transaction affords them. Like forward transactions, the owner of an option contract has the right to either buy or sell a specified amount of foreign currency at a specified rate up to a specified date. The big difference with option contracts is that traders who hold a contract are not obligated to fulfill the transaction. They can, instead, simply decide to let it expire.

Option buyers have to pay for the right to buy or sell these transactions on or before a specified date. The set price at which the currencies are exchanged is called the *strike price*. When the date for the exchange arrives, the option holder determines whether the strike price is favorable. If it is, the option owner completes the transaction and earns a profit, but if it isn't favorable, the option owner allows the option to expire and absorbs the cost of purchasing the original option, which is less of a loss than actually exchanging the currencies. The two type of options currency traders deal with are

- ✔ **Call options,** which are options to buy currency at some set price in the future

- ✔ **Put options,** which are options to sell currency at some set price in the future

For example, suppose a trader purchases a six-month call option on one million euros at an exchange rate of 1.19 U.S. dollars to the euro. During that six-month period, the trader can (has the option to) either purchase the euros at the $1.19 rate, buy them at market rate, or do nothing at all. As market rates for currencies fluctuate, options in those currencies can be sold and resold many times before the expiration date. Companies operating overseas use options as insurance against major unfavorable market shifts in the exchange rate and thus avoid locking their companies into guaranteed exchanges.

Trades are made using various currency symbols that are similar to the ones you need to know for stocks when seeking price quotes. Some of the more common currency symbols are listed in Table 19-1.

Table 19-1	Common Currency Symbols
Currency Symbol	*Country & Currency Name*
AUD	Australian Dollar
GBP	British Pound
CAD	Canadian Dollar
CNY	China Yuan Renminbi
EUR	Euro
GRD	Greek Drachma
JPY	Japanese Yen
MYR	Malaysian Ringgitt

(continued)

Table 19-1 (continued)

Currency Symbol	Country & Currency Name
MXP	Mexican Peso
NZD	New Zealand Dollar
RUR	Russian Ruble
SGD	Singapore Dollar
USD	U.S. Dollar

You can find current exchange rates for most major currencies online at the Universal Currency converter (www.xe.com/ucc). You merely set an amount, the type of currency you want to convert, and the type of currency to which you want to convert to find out the exchange rate and how much the set amount of your currency is worth when converted or exchanged. Although this site won't give you a rate at which you're guaranteed to find a trade, it certainly gives you a decent estimate that's in the ballpark of what you can expect to find to within six decimal points.

How Money Markets Work

The currency exchange market is made up of about 2,000 dealer institutions that are particularly active in foreign currency exchange. Most of the players are commercial or investment banks that are geographically dispersed in the key financial centers around the world. Among these 2,000 dealers, about 100 to 200 members carry on the core trading and market-making activities. Major players are fewer still.

When a dealer buys a U.S. dollar, regardless of where in the world the transaction takes place, the actual deposit is located either directly in a U.S. bank or in a claim of a foreign bank on a dollar deposit located in the United States. The same is true of the currency of any other country.

Different countries, different rules

The actual infrastructures of the various currency markets and how they operate are determined by each separate nation. Each country enforces its own laws, banking regulations, accounting rules, and tax codes. The method of payment and the settlement system also are determined separately by each country. Yikes, doesn't that mean you have to know a lot about international monetary laws to be able to trade? Yup. Especially if you want to be successful.

Luckily, considerable global cooperation exists among exchange regulators, which minimizes differences and helps protect Forex traders from fraud and abuse. In the United States, the U.S. Commodity Futures Trading Commission (CFTC) sets rules and investigates any problems involving U.S. currency trades. The CFTC reaches agreements, or *Memoranda of Understanding* (MOUs), with most major nations that have active currency exchanges, and these MOUs form a method of cooperation between regulatory and enforcement authorities across international borders that combats fraud and other illegal practices that can harm customers or threaten market integrity.

If you plan to become involved in foreign currency exchange, be sure to visit the CFTC's Web site at www.cftc.gov to bone up on your knowledge of international laws and find information about recently exposed scams and other illegal activities. You certainly don't want to get caught up in a fraudulent deal and lose all your money.

The almighty (U.S.) dollar

The U.S. dollar by far is the most widely traded currency. Based on a Federal Reserve survey, the dollar is one of two currencies that are involved in more than 85 percent of all global foreign exchange transactions. The U.S. dollar wears many hats, serving as an investment currency in many capital markets, a reserve currency for many central banks, a transaction currency for many commodity trades, an invoice currency for many contracts, and a currency of intervention used by countries that want to influence the values of their own currencies.

Organized exchanges

The money market is largely unregulated as a *defined market*. By that, we mean that a commercial bank in the United States doesn't need any special authorization to trade or deal in foreign currencies. Securities and brokerage firms don't need special permission from the SEC or any other regulatory body to carry out foreign exchange activities.

Transactions can be carried out based on whatever terms the law permits and using whatever provisions are acceptable to the two parties, subject to the commercial law governing business transactions. Of course that means the money market is the closest thing to the Wild West you'll find in the trading world. Almost anything goes. Institutions that participate are not inspected specifically for their exchange practices, but regulatory authorities nevertheless look into trading systems as part of their regular examinations of financial institutions, just to be sure they're operating under the country's commercial banking or securities laws.

Although no official rules or restrictions govern the hours or conditions of trading on this over-the-counter (OTC) market in the United States, trading conventions developed mostly by market participants are in place. The OTC market for foreign currency trading is any currency trading done outside the confines of an exchange, such as the Chicago Mercantile Exchange. You can find out what those rules are by contacting the Federal Bank of New York, which produces and regularly updates the *Guidelines for Foreign Exchange Trading*. These guidelines clarify common market practices and offer "best practice recommendations." Before you become a trader, protect yourself by making sure you're working with a dealer or a broker that follows these guidelines. You can access the most current version, published in 1996, at `www.newyorkfed.org/fxc/fx12.html`. The New York Federal Reserve regularly issues updates to the guidelines, which you can find on its Web site at `www.ny.frb.org`.

The OTC currency exchange market accounts for more than 90 percent of the total U.S. foreign exchange market, including spot transactions, forwards, and swaps. If you're new to Forex trading, starting out is much safer on an organized exchange, where you can trade currency futures and certain currency options. The Chicago Mercantile Exchange (CME) is one of the largest, and it offers excellent educational materials to help you get started. Find out more about the CME at `www.cme.com/edu`.

Organized exchanges and regulations governing them are considerably different from the OTC foreign currency market. Trading actually takes place in a centralized location rather than through a network of computers, telexes, and telephones. Hours and trading practices are regulated by each of the respective exchanges, and their products are standardized. Organized exchanges also are equipped with central clearinghouses for payments and cash settlements.

The Risks of the World Money Market

Leverage, which means borrowing money to trade, is the number one risk to your portfolio when trading in money markets. Success on the foreign currency exchange market means having to trade in large sums, because profits are made at exchange-rate differences of only fractions of a cent. Banks or brokers determine the leverage they want to offer you, but you won't find strict regulations like the ones that govern stock margin accounts.

After you're approved for trading, customers are given a set amount or allowance on which they can trade on margin. A common starting allowance for trading on margin is 5 percent (see Chapter 14 for more about margins), which means that if you put $100,000 in the bank, you're allowed to execute transactions of up to $2 million. As you gain success with more experience, that margin may be lowered to 1 percent, which means you'd be allowed to trade as much as $10 million on your $100,000 deposit.

When trading at those high margin levels, even a minor mistake can wipe out your entire deposit.

The most conservative of banks require *full margin,* meaning you have to deposit $1 million to be able to trade $1 million. Be sure that you understand the leverage you're being offered and the loss potential you face if your trade goes sour. Just imagine starting with $100,000, which you can use to trade $2 million dollars, and then losing half of that trading maximum with trades that have gone sour. You could end up $900,000 in the hole. Sure, lots of traders can come up with that — no problem. In reality, as long as you stick to trading, the major currencies' drastic price changes that end up in that type of loss are unlikely, but a loss of 10 to 20 percent of your holding in a matter of minutes can happen. Only trading in third-world currencies could result in losses of the million dollar magnitude described here and only if there was a major uprising in the country and the price of its currency dropped dramatically.

Types of risks

You also face a number of different kinds of risk, including market risk, exchange risk, interest rate risk, counterparty risk, volatility risk, liquidity risk, and country risk.

Market risk

All traders and investors face market risk. Basically, *market risk* is comprised of changes in price that adversely impact your trade or investment. Market risk is in play from the moment you enter into a foreign currency exchange position until the moment you exit it. The foreign exchange rate can change any time during that period, so when you're dealing in foreign currency exchange, two key factors can impact the price of the currency — exchange risk and interest rate risk.

Exchange risk

Foreign exchange traders take on exchange risk the moment they buy or sell a foreign currency. Every time you take on a new foreign exchange position, regardless of whether it's through a spot, forward, future, or option transaction, you're immediately exposed to the potential that the exchange rate will move against your position, making it worth less than when you bought it. In only a matter of seconds, a profitable transaction can turn into an unprofitable one.

Interest rate risk

Foreign exchange positions can change in value not only because of the exchange rate but also because of the currency's underlying interest rate. Whenever a country's central bank (think Federal Reserve) raises or lowers the underlying interest rate for its currency, the impact on any positions you're holding in that country's currency can be a major one.

Counterparty risk

In the currency trading world, a *counterparty* is the other entity involved in a transaction — a bank or banker, a broker, or another trader. When you buy a currency option or execute a forward transaction, you risk the possibility that the counterparty to your transaction won't be able to meet his, her, or its obligations. (**Note:** Whenever you buy the option through an exchange, rather than directly from the counterparty, this risk is not a factor.) When that happens, you run into additional replacement costs, because you're forced to enter into another currency transaction to meet your own foreign currency needs. The key to avoiding this kind of risk is entering into contracts with known entities that have high credit ratings. Additionally, you need to investigate whether the counterparty with which you're trading has had any problems with regulators, insolvency, or questions of ethical conduct. One good place to begin your investigation is the consumer protection section of the CFTC at www.cftc.gov/cftc/cftccustomer.htm.

When evaluating a company, you first need to consider its credit risk. You can find credit rankings for many major banks at the Standard & Poor's Web site (www2.standardandpoors.com). You can research a company's creditworthiness by investigating the requirements and standards it uses when providing credit to its customers. Companies that provide easy credit to their customers run a greater risk of not being able to meet their obligations. Conversely, companies with higher margin limits definitely are safer to do business with when you're entering into a contract.

Volatility risk

Volatility risk relates to the possibility of rapidly changing exchange rates that can impact your positions in foreign currencies. As we mention in the "Exploring the World of Foreign Currency Exchange" section, earlier in this chapter, currency prices can change thousands of times per day. Options on currencies are valued according to volatility and underlying changes in the prices of the respective currencies. If a trader sees an increase of 100 percent in volatility, or a doubling of volatility, then the price of the option can increase 5 percent to 10 percent. If you're trading on credit, which is highly likely, your bank or broker can reevaluate the credit it's extending to you whenever it sees a dramatic increase in the volatility of your holdings.

Liquidity risk

Liquidity risk is not a major factor if you're trading in the more commonly traded currencies, but if you decide to trade in less active currencies, it can become a factor when you're unable to sell a currency you hold at the expressed time you want the sale to take place, especially when the market for that currency is not active. You can avoid liquidity risk by buying currency options or futures on an exchange.

Country risk

Country risks come in several different varieties, all of which you need to consider whenever you trade in foreign currencies. Among those aspects are

- ✔ **Political risk:** This variety relates to the political stability of the country in whose currency you're trading. Although we haven't seen any recent seizures of commercial assets by any nations, it has happened in the past. For example, Venezuela took control of its oil industry by seizing assets of non-Venezuelan oil companies. If you trade in currencies of countries that are at risk of possible *destabilization,* the currency you buy can become worthless if the country changes political leaders.

- ✔ **Regulation risk:** This variety relates to what can happen after you establish a position in a country's currency. Its government can change its regulations, and in effect, put restraints on the ownership established by your position in the currency and by the position of your counterparty — and that can get messy.

- ✔ **Legal risk:** This variety relates to which country has jurisdiction to rule on a contract if your counterparty happens to default. Unfavorable contract law in the host country of your counterparty can end up determining that the contract is invalid or illegal, and you can lose your position. Be sure that you understand from whom you're buying and under which country's laws any disputes will be settled. If U.S. law won't be the overriding law for the contract, be certain you understand contract law in the country of the counterparty with whom you're trading.

- ✔ **Holiday risk:** This variety relates to the possibility that the country in whose currency you're trading has different religious, political, or governmental holidays that can shut down trading in that currency right when you need the money. Be sure you know the holiday schedules for the countries in whose currencies you trade.

Seeking risk protection

Although trading in foreign currencies often is called the modern-day Wild West, forces are in place that can help you minimize the risks — provided you take advantage of them and trade within their boundaries. The primary monitors of foreign currency trading are the world's central banks. They monitor the flow of money between countries and the balance of payments between governments and banking institutions. In the United States, these types of transactions are monitored and regulated by the U.S. Treasury Department and the Federal Reserve Banks. Similar regulatory authorities exist in most major currency markets, but if you decide to do business with a nonbanking institution, you're transacting your business in unprotected waters outside the safe harbor of regulatory oversight and must do so under the often fateful guise of caveat emptor — let the buyer beware.

Internationally, the Bank for International Settlement (BIS — www.bis.org/index.htm) is the leading independent agency for evaluating foreign exchange trading institutions on a global basis. BIS created risk-weighted evaluation and capital requirements for institutions that trade in foreign currencies and money market transactions. Be certain that any institution outside the United States with which you plan to conduct trades meets BIS standards.

A number of common clearing systems assist with the transfer of foreign currencies. The two best-known ones are the Clearing House Interbank Payments System, or CHIPS, and the Society for Worldwide Interbank Financial Telecommunication, or S.W.I.F.T. Be sure you're using one of these systems when you trade, because they code transactions to avoid defaults and help you identify the creditworthiness of transactions. CHIPS is privately owned and operated by the New York Clearing House.

If you're trading in foreign currency futures, your risks are much less, because the futures industry is highly regulated. Clearinghouses for futures are efficient, and future transactions usually are cleared hourly and in some cases even minute-by-minute.

Getting Ready to Trade Money

Your first step as a foreign currency trader is to develop an extensive collection of historical information not only about rate fluctuations for the currencies you plan to trade but also about interest rate fluctuations, economic history, and political stability of the countries whose currencies you're considering. Gathering some background information about the Forex market itself doesn't hurt either.

After collecting this information, you need to consider your own trading goals and how much you want to put at risk. Set your risk limits before you start, so you don't get emotionally caught up in having to making these potentially disastrous trading decisions on the fly. Capital that you risk on foreign currency exchange trading needs to be money that you can afford to lose without impacting your lifestyle. Do not, for any reason, use retirement savings, savings for your children's educations, or savings required to maintain your house and lifestyle.

As is true for stock trading, when trading currencies, you need to develop a plan that determines what you trade and how much you're at risk. When your plan's in place, you need to stick to it for the entire trading day. You should not be developing the plan and executing it at the same time. Foreign currency trading requires a great deal of focus, and you can't risk breaking that focus to do additional planning in the middle of a trading day. Monitor the successes you have in meeting the goals of your plan. If you're not achieving your objectives, you may want to step back and reevaluate your plan and your decision to trade in foreign currency.

Technical analysis is used by foreign currency traders in a way that is similar to stock trading (see Chapters 9 and 10). Bar charts are the most common tools. The basic bar chart shows the opening, the high, the low, and the closing prices for a given period of time.

The key difference between trading currencies and stocks is that in the foreign exchange market, a daily price chart sometimes shows the opening price in the Pacific Rim and the closing price in the United States. Because the foreign exchange market is open 24 hours a day, time periods are different for foreign currency trading than they are for stock trading. You can play with Forex charting online at www.forex-markets.com/charts.htm.

We won't cover the basics of technical analysis for foreign currency trading, because we'd need to take up another entire book to do it right. That's exactly why Wiley Publishing, Inc., also publishes *Technical Analysis For Dummies*. Be sure to check it out, too.

Because we can't say it enough, we repeat: If you truly want to pursue this form of trading, we highly recommend that you seek additional training before you begin trading individually.

Chapter 20

Trading for Others: Obtaining Trading Licenses and Certifications

In This Chapter

▶ Exploring NASD tests

▶ Deciphering financial advisor designations

▶ Knowing what licenses are required

▶ Getting your own licenses

*A*s you become more involved in trading, you hear about trading designations, such as Series 7 or Series 23. Nope, they're not talking about the World Series. These designations refer to examinations administered by the National Association of Securities Dealers (NASD) that you must pass to be able to work in various capacities within the securities field. After passing these examinations, you can become licensed in the securities markets. What tests you need to take depend on where you plan to work and what you plan to do.

You also may hear an alphabet soup of designations like CFA, CFP, or CFS. They are certifications given by different professional organizations to people who have completed coursework, testing, and in most cases, years of work experience.

Typically, investment and trading advisors must be licensed. In this chapter, we discuss the various types of licenses and certifications and the level of training that is required for each. We also describe the types of tests the NASD offers for each of its designations and help you find out about how advisors are licensed and regulated and what requirements you need to fulfill if you plan to make trades for others.

Getting to Know the NASD Series

Brokers can't just hang out a shingle and advertise that they're selling securities. Before ever selling the first share of stock, a broker must complete coursework and pass an examination administered by the NASD to become a registered securities broker, agent, or salesperson.

A number of different types of exams are required for brokers to demonstrate their knowledge of the various types of securities they plan to sell. Each examination indicates whether candidates have an understanding of specific products they want to sell and the laws that govern investing in them.

Failure to register with the NASD can result in hefty fines imposed by the United States Securities and Exchange Commission (SEC) or state regulators whenever you try to sell securities as an unregistered broker. People who plan to supervise other brokers must take additional coursework and training.

Courses to prepare candidates for these exams are available for home study, or they can be taken on-site at various training centers throughout the United States. Tests are given six days a week — Monday through Saturday — through the Prometric (Sylvan) Centers in each of the 50 states.

Two sets of examinations are administered, one for registered representatives, or the people on the front lines, and the other for principals who manage registered representatives. In the sections that follow, we give you an overview of the types of examinations and licenses that people who want to do business in the securities market must take, including what you can expect to find on some of the key tests.

To pass any of the NASD examinations that we discuss in the sections that follow, you must answer at least 70 percent of the questions correctly to become registered or licensed as a broker or principal in the areas evaluated by each specific exam.

Becoming a registered representative

Registered representatives are licensed by the NASD to sell various kinds of securities. The type of security a registered representative is allowed to sell depends on the tests he or she has taken and passed. What follows are discussions of some of the key licensure tests.

Series 3 — National Commodity Futures

The NASD administers the National Commodity Futures Examination (Series 3), but it's actually required by the National Futures Association (NFA), which regulates the futures markets. Topics covered on this test include options and contracts, futures theory, hedging, margins and settlements, rules of the NFA and Commodity Futures Trading Commission, and managing customer accounts and orders.

Test takers are given 150 minutes to answer 120 multiple-choice questions found on the exam.

Series 6 — Investment Co./Variable Contract Representative

The Investment Company Products/Variable Contracts Limited Representative (Series 6) Examination is the NASD's licensing test and is for individuals who want to sell only mutual funds or variable annuities.

Test takers will find 100 multiple-choice questions on this exam and have 135 minutes to complete it. Test questions are grouped under four topic areas:

- ✔ Securities and markets (23 questions)
- ✔ Investment companies, taxation, and customer accounts (36 questions)
- ✔ Variable contracts and retirement plans (16 questions)
- ✔ Securities industry regulations (25 questions)

Series 7 — General Securities Representative

If you want to sell securities, the General Securities Representative (Series 7) Examination is the primary NASD test that you need to pass. Candidates who pass this exam can solicit, purchase, and/or sell all securities products, including corporate securities, municipal securities, municipal fund securities, options, direct participation programs, investment company products, and variable contracts.

In the general information it provides about the exam, the NASD says the primary purpose for this exam is "to safeguard the investing public by helping to insure that registered representatives are competent to perform their jobs. Given this purpose, the Series 7 Examination seeks to measure accurately and reliably the degree to which each candidate possesses the knowledge, skills and abilities needed to perform the critical functions of a registered representative (RR)."

Test takers face 260 multiple-choice questions, ten of which are experimental questions that are being evaluated for future use. The test is given in two 180-minute segments. In designing the test, the NASD focused on the seven critical functions about which registered representatives need to be tested. The number of questions on the test devoted to each function is shown in parentheses below. The registered representative must have the ability to

- ✔ Seek business for the broker-dealer through customers and potential customers (9 questions).

- ✔ Evaluate customers in terms of financial needs, current holdings, and available investment capital, and help them identify their investment objectives (4 questions).

- ✔ Provide customers and prospective customers with information about investments and make suitable recommendations (123 questions).

- ✔ Open, transfer, and close customer accounts and maintain appropriate account records (27 questions).

- ✔ Explain the organization, participants, and functions of various securities markets and the principal factors that affect them (53 questions).

- ✔ Obtain and verify the customer's purchase and sale instructions, enter orders, and follow up on the completion of transactions (13 questions).

- ✔ Monitor the customer's portfolio and make recommendations consistent with changes in economic and financial conditions and with changes in the customer's needs and objectives (21 questions).

Series 9 and 10 — General Securities Sales Supervisor

Branch office managers and regional and national sales managers must take additional testing to supervise the sales activities in corporate, municipal, and options securities; investment company products; variable contracts; and direct participation programs. The General Securities Sales Supervisor (Series 9) Examination focuses on the regulation of options, and the Series 10 exam with the same name focuses on sales supervision. Supervisors must pass these tests to be able to register with the NASD. A valid Series 7 license is required before you can take the Series 9 and Series 10 tests.

The combined exams include 200 multiple-choice questions covering these categories:

- ✔ Regulation of options (55 questions)

- ✔ Sales supervision (38 questions)

- ✔ Account supervision (33 questions)

- ✔ Compliance, recordkeeping, and financial responsibility (19 questions)

- ✔ Regulations affecting the operation of securities markets (10 questions)

- ✔ Municipal securities regulation (45 questions)

Test takers have 90 minutes to take the Series 9 portion of the exam and 240 minutes to take the Series 10 portion. The two sections can be taken in any order, at any time, as long as they're completed within a 120-day enrollment-period window. To pass the exams, candidates must correctly answer 70 percent of the questions on each portion of the exam.

Series 22 — Direct Participation Programs Limited Representative

Representatives who want to sell limited partnerships, limited liability companies, and S Corporation offerings that provide pass-through tax benefits must get a Series 22 license, which can include programs involving oil and gas real estate, equipment leasing and cable, and commodity programs. It doesn't, however, include real estate investment trusts, securities, and options. To sell other types of securities, they would need to take other limited exams, or to sell all types of securities, they must take the Series 7 exam.

Topics covered on the Direct Participation Programs Limited Representative Exam include

- Investment entities for direct participation programs (12 questions)
- Types of direct participation programs (11 questions)
- Offering practices applicable to direct participation (14 questions)
- Tax issues applicable to direct participation programs (20 questions)
- Regulation of direct participation programs (32 questions)
- Factors to consider in evaluating direct participation programs (11 questions)

Test takers need to answer 100 multiple-choice questions within 135 minutes to complete the exam.

Series 42 — Registered Options Representative

Representatives who only want to sell options take the Series 42 exam to become registered options representatives. This exam deals with topics such as options accounts, equity, debt, foreign currency, and index options. In addition to a Series 42 license, registered options representatives must also earn a Series 62 license for corporate securities limited representatives (see the "Series 62 — Corporate Securities Limited Representative" section, later in this chapter), so they can demonstrate a functional understanding of the securities products that underlie options contracts.

The test features 50 questions that must be answered within 90 minutes. Topics covered on the Series 42 exam include

✔ Handling options accounts (17 questions)

✔ Equity options (16 questions)

✔ Debt options (3 questions)

✔ Foreign currency options (6 questions)

✔ Index options (8 questions)

Series 55 — Limited Representative Equity Trader

If you want to trade equity and convertible debt on a principal or agency basis, you must take the Limited Representative Equity Trader (Series 55) Examination. Before taking this exam, you first need to pass either the Series 7 or the Series 62 examination.

Test takers must answer 70 percent of the 100 questions on the exam correctly within 180 minutes to pass the exam. Topics covered on this exam include

✔ NASDAQ and over-the-counter markets (45 questions)

✔ NASDAQ automated execution and trading systems (9 questions)

✔ Trade reporting requirements (18 questions)

✔ General industry standards (28 questions)

Series 62 — Corporate Securities Limited Representative

Representatives who want to sell corporate stocks, corporate bonds, rights, warrants, real estate investment trusts, collateralized mortgage obligations, and securities of closed-end companies must take the Series 62 exam for corporate securities limited representatives to get their licenses.

Test takers face a total of 115 multiple-choice questions and are given 150 minutes to finish the examination. Topics covered on this exam include

✔ Characteristics of corporate securities (28 questions)

✔ Markets for corporate securities (31 questions)

✔ Valuing corporate securities (14 questions)

✔ Handling customer accounts (42 questions)

Series 82 — Limited Representative/Private Securities Offerings

Representatives who sell private placement securities as part of a primary offering must get a Series 82 license. The Limited Representative/Private Securities Offering Exam has a total of 100 multiple-choice questions.

Test takers are given 150 minutes to complete it. Topics covered by this examination include

✔ Characteristics of corporate securities (13 questions)

✔ Regulation of the market for registered and unregistered securities (45 questions)

✔ Analyzing corporate securities (15 questions)

✔ Handling customer accounts and industry regulations (27 questions)

Becoming a registered principal

If you want to manage an office in investment banking or the securities business, you must pass at least one additional exam to be registered as a principal. *Principals* supervise, solicit, and conduct business, and train persons associated with the offices they manage. All principals must have their Series 7 licenses. The principal exam that is required depends on the types of businesses you'll be managing. Some of the key principal exams are covered in the following sections.

Series 23 or 24 — General Securities Principal

People who want to manage or supervise others in investment banking or the securities business, including the sales of direct participation programs, investment company products, and variable contracts, must fulfill either the Series 23 or Series 24 requirements for becoming a general securities principal. Candidates who already have successfully completed the Series 9 and 10 exams take the Series 23 exam, which covers material from the Series 24 exam that was not on the sales supervisor's Series 9 and Series 10 exams. Managers seeking to be a principal who don't have their Series 9 and 10 licenses take the Series 24 exam.

The Series 23 examination includes 100 questions that must be completed within 150 minutes. The Series 24 examination includes 150 questions that must be completed within 230 minutes. Both exams include questions on the topics of:

✔ Supervising investment banking activities (25 questions on the Series 23 exam and 23 questions on the Series 24 exam)

✔ Trading and market making activities (29 questions on the Series 23 exam and 39 questions on the Series 24 exam)

✔ Supervising brokerage office operations (16 questions on the Series 23 exam and 34 questions on the Series 24 exam)

✔ Understanding sales supervision, general supervision of employees, and the regulatory framework of the NASD (19 questions on the Series 23 exam and 38 questions on the Series 24 exam)

✔ Complying with financial responsibility rules (11 questions on the Series 23 exam and 16 questions on the Series 24 exam)

Series 26 — Investment Company Products/ Variable Contracts Principal

Managers who plan to supervise activities limited to the sales of mutual funds and annuities need only to get the Series 26 license instead of the Series 23 or Series 24 license. A total of 110 multiple-choice questions are on the Investment Company Products/Variable Contracts Principal Examination. Test takers have 150 minutes to complete it. Topics covered on this examination include

✔ Hiring and qualification (11 questions)

✔ Training of representatives (19 questions)

✔ Supervision (24 questions)

✔ Sales practices (32 questions)

✔ Business processing and recordkeeping rules (24 questions)

This exam and registration is not required for someone who already has a Series 23 or 24 license.

Series 4 — Registered Options Principal

Managers who supervise options sales personnel or supervise compliance with options regulations must pass the Registered Options Principal (Series 4) Exam. Topics tested on this exam include option strategies, equity options, debt options, index options, foreign currencies, supervision and compliance, and the management of customer accounts and orders.

The test features 125 multiple-choice questions that must be completed within 180 minutes. Principals with Series 23 and Series 24 licenses must take this exam if they plan to manage options sales personnel or supervise compliance with options regulations. The questions cover these three basic areas:

✔ Investment strategies (35 questions)

✔ Supervising sales practices (71 questions)

✔ Trading procedures and business conduct (19 questions)

Series 27 — Financial and Operations Principal

The Financial and Operations Principal (Series 27) Exam tests the candidate's knowledge of applicable rules relating to broker/dealer financial responsibility and recordkeeping and to investor protections under the Securities Investor Protection Act of 1970.

Test takers are given 230 minutes to finish the 145 multiple-choice questions. Principals who have their Series 23 or Series 24 licenses must take this exam if they want to operate as a financial and operations principal. Test questions include these topics:

- ✔ Keeping and preserving records and broker/dealer financial report requirements (16 questions)
- ✔ Net capital requirements (44 questions)
- ✔ Customer protection (37 questions)
- ✔ Municipal securities rulemaking board regulations (10 questions)
- ✔ Federal Reserve Board Regulations (8 questions)
- ✔ Uniform practice rules (15 questions)
- ✔ Other relevant regulations and interpretations (15 questions)

The ABCs of Financial Advisors

When you get a business card from a broker or other type of investment advisor, you may see a long list of initials that indicate professional certifications. Some of these require extensive training, education, and testing, but others require only minimal education and testing. In addition to the initial testing, some require continuing education and offer a disciplinary process and ways to check on a professional's status online. The sections that follow break down the key designations for financial advisors and what getting and keeping the designation takes.

Accredited Asset Management Specialist

The Accredited Asset Management Specialist (AAMS) certification is issued by the College for Financial Planning. It has no work experience requirements. Candidates must take a self-study course that includes 11 modules totaling 96 to 120 hours. Topics include asset management process investors, risk, return, investment performance, asset allocation and selection, investment strategies, taxation of investment products, investment opportunities for an individual's retirement, investment considerations for small-business owners, investment considerations for highly compensated executives, insurance products for investment clients, estate planning for investment clients, and regulatory and ethical issues.

After coursework is completed, candidates must pass a final certification exam. This certification has no continuing education requirements, no investor complaint or public disciplinary processes, and no way to check the professional status of an AAMS designee online.

Chartered Financial Analyst

A Chartered Financial Analyst (CFA) designation is issued by the Association for Investment Management and Research (www.aimr.com). Before you can get this designation, you must meet educational and work experience requirements. Candidates can have either an undergraduate degree plus three years of professional experience involving investment decision-making or four years of qualified work experience.

In addition to the work requirements, candidates must complete 250 hours of self study for each of these three levels of examination:

- ✔ **Level 1,** which focuses on investment evaluation and portfolio management
- ✔ **Level II,** which focuses on applying the analytical tools for valuing investments
- ✔ **Level III,** which focuses on the entire portfolio management process

Many CFA candidates fulfill their work experience requirements as they prepare to take the three required exams.

Certified Financial Planner

A Certified Financial Planner (CFP) designation is awarded by the Certified Financial Planner Board of Standards (www.cfp.net). Candidates must meet work experience and educational requirements. To be recognized as a CFP, candidates must have either three years of personal financial planning experience plus a bachelor's degree or five years of personal financial planning experience.

In addition to the work experience requirements, CFP candidates must complete either a five-course, CFP board–registered program or qualify to take the final CFP examination by having earned one of the following designations:

- ✔ Certified Public Accountant (CPA)
- ✔ Chartered Financial Consultant (ChFC)
- ✔ Chartered Life Underwriter (CLU)
- ✔ Chartered Financial Analyst (CFA)
- ✔ A doctoral (PhD) degree in business or economics, Doctor of Business Administration, or an attorney's license

Courses that must be taken include financial planning process and insurance, investment planning, income tax planning, retirement planning and employee benefits, and estate planning. After earning the CFP designation, planners must complete 30 hours of continuing education every two years thereafter to maintain their CFP status.

Certified Fund Specialist

Certified Fund Specialist (CFS) certificates are issued by the Institute of Business and Finance (www.icfs.com). No work experience is required before getting this designation. However, about 60 hours of coursework are required before you can take the certification exam. Topics covered include understanding mutual funds, fixed income, analysis, when to sell, closed-end funds, money market funds, diversification, global investing, asset allocation, risk, matching clients' goals and portfolios, and retirement strategies. After a specialist is certified, he or she must take 15 hours of continuing education courses only during the first five years after certification.

Chartered Financial Consultant

The Chartered Financial Consultant (ChFC) designation is issued by The American College www.amercoll.edu/Current_students/Designations/chfc.asp. Candidates must complete three years of full-time personal finance or insurance experience and take five core and three elective courses at The American College.

The core courses include insurance and financial planning, income taxation, planning for retirement needs, investments, and fundamentals of estate planning. The three elective courses can be chosen from four offerings that include financial systems in the economy, financial planning applications, estate planning applications, and financial decision-making at retirement. As a candidate completes each course, a final exam is given. The candidate must pass each final exam before being awarded the ChFC designation. After getting the designation, consultants must take 30 credits of continuing education courses every two years to maintain the designation.

Chartered Life Underwriter

The Chartered Life Underwriter (CLU) designation also is issued by The American College and focuses on insurance and coursework. Candidates must complete three years of full-time related business experience, five core courses, and three elective courses.

Core courses include insurance and financial planning, individual life insurance, life insurance law, fundamentals of estate planning, and planning for business owners and professionals. The three elective courses can be chosen from courses on individual health insurance, income taxation, group benefits, planning for retirement needs, investments, and estate planning applications. After earning this designation, consultants must take 30 credits of continuing education courses every two years to maintain their status as a CLU.

Chartered Market Technician

The Chartered Market Technician (CMT) is issued by the Market Technicians Association. Candidates must be a member of the association to enter the CMT program. To become a member, a person must be employed professionally as an analyst or professional investment manager for five years. Membership must be maintained in the MTA to get and hold the CMT certification. Certification is a three-step process that includes three exams. The first is a multiple-choice exam on the basic definitions related to technical analysis. The second exam is also a multiple-choice exam that tests the candidate's ability to apply advanced analytical techniques. The third exam can be satisfied with either a research paper or an essay exam related to portfolio strategies or trading decisions.

Chartered Mutual Fund Counselor

The Chartered Mutual Fund Counselor (CMFC) designation is issued by the College for Financial Planning. No work experience is required for this certification. Candidates must complete a nine-module, self-study course that totals

72 to 90 hours. Course topics include open- and closed-end mutual funds, risk, return, asset allocation, selecting mutual funds for a client, retirement planning, and ethics, integrity, and professional conduct.

Personal Financial Specialist

The Personal Financial Specialist (PFS) is a professional designation issued by the American Institute of Certified Public Accountants (AICPA) (www.aicpa.org). Prerequisites for taking the examination include membership in the AICPA, an unrevoked Certified Public Accountant certificate issued by a state authority, and accrual of at least 100 points in the PFS point system.

Points in the PFS system are awarded for work experience, passing the PFS exam, and continuing education. Topics covered on the PFS exam include professional responsibilities, personal financial planning processes, personal income tax planning, risk management planning, investment planning, retirement planning, and estate planning. In addition, candidates must submit references and other documentation that prove their business experience in personal financial planning–related services.

Initial certification is granted for a period of three years. During that time (and every three years thereafter), PFS designees must earn a combined total of 60 PFS points to maintain their certifications. The PFS points system is based on continuing personal financial business experience and other learning activities that meet the PFS requirements.

Registered Financial Consultant

The Registered Financial Consultant (RFC) designation is issued by the International Association of Registered Financial Consultants (www.iarfc.org). An RFC candidate must have an undergraduate or graduate financial planning degree or have earned an AAMS, CFA, CFP, ChFC, CLU, or CPA designation.

In addition to the educational requirement, candidates must meet licensing requirements for securities and life and health insurance if they're operating on a commission basis. If they're operating on a fee-only basis and not licensed, then they must be registered as an investment advisor. Candidates must also complete four years of full-time work as a financial planning practitioner. If candidates have completed an approved IARFC examination process, they've met their examination requirements; otherwise, they must pass the RFC Challenge Examination. After an RFC designation, consultants must complete 40 hours of continuing education each year.

The Licenses and Certifications You Need When Trading for Others

If you decide you want to trade for others as well as yourself, you need to become a registered representative. The most comprehensive test you can take is the NASD's Series 7 exam, and you'll need a sponsoring broker. Most times, when you sign up for the required coursework for this examination, either through self-study courses online or through a training school near your home, the school can help you locate a sponsoring broker if you don't already have one.

This license enables you to purchase and/or sell all securities products, including corporate securities, municipal securities, municipal fund securities, options, direct participation programs, investment company products, and variable contracts. Most of the other representative exams are taken whenever you want to sell only a specific type of security rather than the broader options that a Series 7 certification enables you to market.

Professional certifications are not required to sell securities. Most professionals who seek these certifications do so to show their clients that they have attained a certain level of proficiency and met or exceeded the standards within their respective specialties.

As you read through the requirements and courses offered as part of each of the professional designations or NASD Series examinations earlier in this chapter, you may have found subjects that can help you improve the management of your own funds. Many of the schools that train people for the professional designations provide ways for other people like you to take the coursework, even if you don't plan to follow through and get the license or certification.

You can even study for many of these courses at home online. Some of the schools offering online education services in the securities and financial advisor area include

- ✔ American Investment Training (www.aitraining.com), which offers self-study training for all the NASD licenses

- ✔ The American College (www.amercoll.edu), which offers online coursework toward the ChFC, CLU, and CFP designations along with other financial services education

- ✔ College for Financial Planning (www.fp.edu), which offers online coursework for the CFP and CMFC designations along with other financial services education

✔ Empire Stockbroker Training Institute (www.empirestockbroker.com), which offers courses online for all the NASD Series licenses

✔ NASD, which provides detailed outlines of the content that must be covered for all its examinations online at www.nasdr.com/5200_explan.asp

As you probably realize by now, selling securities is a highly regulated field that requires considerable training before you can sell even your first share of stock. Although some people privately trade for others, they risk the possibility of an investigation by the NASD or their state regulators whenever they do so without registering at the state or federal level. Be sure that the trading activities you do for others fit within the law, or you can end up in a legal mess facing significant fines.

Part VI
The Part of Tens

In this part . . .

We join in the *For Dummies* tradition of showing you some special lists of ten (or so) important and key factors that help you with your trading. We review ten common and huge trading mistakes and how to avoid them, and we describe ten basics strategies necessary for your survival and long-term financial well-being as a trader.

Chapter 21

Ten (or More) Huge Trading Mistakes

. . . .

In This Chapter

▶ Trying to trade tops and bottoms (No, this isn't X-rated)

▶ Becoming attached to your trading systems and your stocks

▶ Making decisions on the fly

▶ Losing too much

. . . .

This chapter introduces you to ten (more, actually) huge trading mistakes that befall experienced and novice traders. We offer suggestions for helping you recognize the mistakes and for avoiding and even correcting them.

Fishing for Bottoms

Bottom fishing — trying to catch a stock as it bottoms out — is a great way to get soaked and lose a bucketful of money. In a bear market, stocks get much cheaper than most of us ever expect or want. They won't stop falling until they've run out of gas.

The psychology of a bear market is perverse. As long as traders remain interested in a stock, many are the moments when it seems like the stock may recover. The thing is, stocks rarely turn on a dime and head higher. Only after the momentum crowd loses interest does the stock's downward price slide end. When value investors, who can't resist a bargain, begin nibbling, the stock begins to stabilize; however, it also may spend a very long time bouncing around in a trading range.

Traders have few, if any, reasons for entering the market when a stock is trading in a range. Your best opportunity for profit occurs when the stock breaks out of its trading range. Chapter 9 shows how to identify these trading-range breakout patterns. Instead of risking your trading capital on unreliable bottoming patterns, wait until you're sure.

Timing the Top

Tops and bottoms share something in common. They rarely arrive when they're supposed to. When traders and investors are exuberant, they keep buying even after doing so no longer makes fundamental sense. That's why shorting a stock that's trending higher makes no sense, even if its price is far beyond reasonable.

You don't have to have a lengthy memory or an encyclopedic knowledge of stock market history to remember what happened to Internet stocks in the late 1990s. Those were heady days. Stocks went in only one direction — up. Some of those magically levitating companies had modest revenues, but few had earnings. Nevertheless, traders bid prices into the hundreds of dollars for some of this worthless junk. In retrospect, Internet stocks obviously were a case of mass hysteria, mob mentality, market madness, or all three.

Call it what you will, when the bubble was inflating definitely was not a time to short Internet or technology stocks. Sure, these stocks eventually crashed and burned, but not before depleting the trading accounts of a den full of bearish short sellers. Don't guess. Wait for reliable trading signals, like the ones discussed in Chapters 9 and 10, before entering a position.

You might be asking if there were reliable trading signals before the Internet bubble burst. Not before; traders aren't fortune tellers (see Chapter 8). However, the risks at the time were well-known. And when stocks began heading lower early in 2000, you had all the information you needed to protect your profits and trading capital, and begin selling short. Chapter 13 uses the NASDAQ bubble as an example to show how to evaluate market risk and adjust your trading strategy as the market transitions from a rising to a falling market.

Trading Against the Dominant Trend

Trading against the dominant trend in the market leads to costly mistakes. Unfortunately, misidentifying the trend by focusing on the chart in front of you and forgetting to look at the next higher level chart is an easy thing to do. You may see a promising uptrend occur with a pullback on the intraday charts. But on the daily chart, the trend you saw on the intraday chart actually turns out to be a consolidation rally during a strong downtrend. The promising pullback actually is the beginning of the next leg down on the daily chart. If you buy long in a situation like this one, hoping to capture the next leg up, your position will be swamped (and so will your trading capital) by the flood of sell orders coming from traders who recognize the implications of the longer-term stronger trend.

Regardless of the specific indications of the chart you're looking at, always confirm your analysis by looking at charts that are one time period higher. For example, if you're studying daily charts, confirm your analysis on the weekly charts. If you're studying intraday charts, confirm your analysis on the daily charts. Always know which part of the market cycle you're in and what types of industries excel in that part of the cycle. See Chapters 10 and 13 for additional information.

Don't try to buy long based on a brief intraday move, when the dominant trend on the daily charts is down. Doing so is a great way of giving up your trading capital to someone else.

Winging It

Traders get into big trouble when they wing it. Maybe you heard the guy on business TV say the stock was hot and heading higher. Maybe you saw the news that a new product was bound to be a big hit. Although that may sound like great information, instead it's only a reason to look into the fundamental and technical conditions of a company's stock, but not a reason to buy today.

Devise a strategy. We think that's such great advice, we'll say it again. Devise a strategy. Develop and test a trading system that matches your goals and personality (see Chapter 15). Plan your trades and execute your plan. Wait patiently for your signals to trigger your trades. Pick your entry and exit points before entering your order. Have a plan and stick to it.

Traders also get into trouble when they start second-guessing their trading plans. Sometimes, even in the middle of executing a trade, you need to make a decision but won't be sure which decision is right.

When in doubt, close the position. It's easier to think clearly when your money isn't at risk. You can always buy back the stock if further analysis confirms it's the right thing to do.

Taking Trading Personally

A losing trade is bad for your trading account, but you can't let it get to you. Sure, it makes you feel bad, but a losing trade doesn't impugn your honor or disparage your heritage. A bad trade may reduce your net worth, but it shouldn't damage your self-esteem. Entering a losing trade certainly doesn't mean that you're a nincompoop or blockhead — any more than closing a winning trade signals your brilliance and mastery of all you survey.

The market isn't out to get you; it's out to get your money. Don't take trading personally. A losing trade is just another losing trade. You'll have plenty of them. Get used to it.

Falling In Love

Trading is a business. Your stocks are your inventory. Smart business owners don't fall in love with their inventory. It's there to sell, at a profit if possible, at a loss if necessary. And smart business people don't fall in love with their business models. If it isn't working, they change it; otherwise, they'll be out of business before you can say "liquidation sale."

When you fall in love with your stock, you risk large losses. When you fall in love with your trading plan, you risk many more losses. It's easy to fall in love. After doing hours of research and analysis, you want to be right. You want your trades and your trading plans to generate profits, but hoping doesn't make it so.

Be smart. Don't fall in love. Your trading system doesn't have feelings and your stock won't love you back. Be prepared to jettison positions and trading systems that don't do what they're supposed to do. See Chapter 12 for more about trading as a business and effectively managing your inventory.

Using After-Hours Market Orders

When the market opens and it's off to the races, the market order that you placed last night before going to bed is going to be swept up in a wave of frantic trading. Bad fills are sure to be the result. You're likely to pay considerably more to buy a stock that you want or to sell one for considerably less than you'd planned. You should never place a market order when entering trades after the market is closed (after-hours). Instead, define how much you're willing to buy or sell a stock for by using a stop order, a limit order, or a stop-limit order. Chapter 14 discusses the mechanics of entering these types of orders.

Chasing a Runaway Trend

If you miss the breakout entry point for a stock that you want, waiting is better than entering a position as a trend accelerates. See Chapter 10 for information about identifying and trading a trend. Often, stocks will pull back and test the breakout point. Wait for that point, or wait for the stock to take a short breather after its first leg up. If you're still interested, that's a better entry point than chasing a stock as it accelerates into the trend. Like a fine wine, you sometimes need to let a stock breathe.

On the other hand, if you already have a position in a runaway stock, try planning your exit so that you leave a little money on the table. Capturing every last nickel of the trend is almost impossible, anyway, so don't try. Instead, consider trimming your position as the stock reaches for the stratosphere. If you're using margin, consider taking some profit off the table and reducing your leverage a bit. We discuss this strategy further in Chapter 13, and the mechanics of using margin are covered in Chapter 14. When a runaway stock stops going up and everyone wants out at the same time, the speed at which the price falls is remarkable. Be ready to jettison stocks that rally too fast at the first sign of trouble.

Averaging Down

Averaging down is a below-average idea. You sometimes hear advisors suggesting it as a way of reducing your cost basis, but it's really merely a technique to throw good money after bad. The logic of averaging down is completely contrary to the logic of trading. Traders sell losers. They don't reward them with infusions of trading capital.

However, averaging up makes some sense. Traders call it *pyramiding*. The idea is to add to your winning positions when your trading system triggers new trading signals in the direction of the trend. Pyramiding is a good way of building a large position in a strongly trending stock. Be aware of the risk, though. The larger your position, the more it hurts when the trend ends and the stock's price begins to fall. Be ready to trim your pyramid position at the first sign of trouble.

Ignoring Your Stops

Talking yourself out of honoring your stops is an easy thing to do. You'll be tempted when a trade goes against you. You'll look at your indicators and the support levels on your charts, and you'll be certain that the stock soon will stop falling. When you start thinking you want to give a position a little room to work its way out of losing territory, you're on your way toward a trading debacle. It's wishful thinking, it's hoping against hope, and it's a good way to lose a lot of money. Unless you're omniscient, close the position when the price hits your stop. Take your loss. Chapter 14 discusses stop orders and how to use them.

Diversifying Badly

Exposing all your capital in one trade is a bad idea, and so is trading hundreds of stocks simultaneously. A happy medium can be found somewhere in between.

You can monitor only so many positions and do it well. You need only so many positions to diversify your risk. And although you can have too few or too many stocks in your trading portfolio, no perfect number, one that is right for every trader, exists. That said, you nevertheless have to figure out what the right number is for you. Start with 10 or 15 positions. You may end up deciding that 8 is enough. The Bradford family did. However, unless you have an extremely large portfolio, imagining why you'd need any more than 20 positions is difficult.

The simple wisdom is: Don't put all your eggs in one basket. And don't chop your eggs into little pieces and spread them across many dozens of baskets. You want to diversify, just not too much.

Enduring Large Losses

To trade is to lose. No matter how good your trading system is, no matter how experienced you are, no matter which stocks you pick, you're going to have losing trades.

Your success as a trader depends on how you handle those losing trades. If you dispose of the losers quickly, you can become a very successful trader. But if you hold onto those losing positions, you can lose so much money that it may knock you right out of the trading business.

Using margin (see Chapter 14) exacerbates the problem of losing trades. Margin is a wonderful thing, because with careful application, it can magnify your profits. But on the flip side, with indiscriminate use, it can also magnify your losses. If you want to turn your pool of trading capital into a puddle, leverage a lot of losing trades.

Small losses won't hurt you much, but large losses will. If you use margin and fail to cut your losses, you won't be a trader for long.

Chapter 22

Top Ten Trading Survival Techniques

Trading is not a risk-free activity. Although all traders know that losses are inevitable, they want to minimize those losses and be around to trade another day. In this chapter, we review ten of the top trading survival techniques that can help you enter the world of trading and enable you to continue to trade for a long time to come.

Build Your Trading Tool Chest

Before you buy that first share of stock, that first option or futures contract, or any other security, you need to be certain that you have the right mix of trading software, hardware, and Internet access to be successful. You need the right tools to identify trading candidates; display and interpret charts; research trading opportunities; screen stocks for technical or fundamental constraints; and monitor and analyze your portfolio, open positions, market indexes, sectors, and trading statistics. In summary, the proper tools are critical to finding the right trades and then monitoring those positions after you've found and entered them.

Even after you've found them, if you don't have the right tools, you may not be able to enter and exit positions efficiently, control or track your orders, track your profits and losses, analyze your trading history, or monitor economic reports, earnings, and other business news.

The proper tools help you evaluate your trading system and test your trading ideas. They enable you to keep trading logs to review your trading performance. You also can use tools to stay in touch with other traders and exchange ideas that ultimately may help you improve your trading skills and discover new trading opportunities.

Tools are the core of any good trader's business. Without the right ones, your chances of success drop dramatically. Don't scrimp on the tools you select for your trading activities. (For more information, see Chapter 4.)

Use Both Technical and Fundamental Analyses

You may have heard that all traders use technical analysis and believe that fundamental analysis is a waste of time. Don't believe it. Although technical analysis is critical to finding the right entry and exit points, fundamental analysis improves your ability to make the right stock choices, given market and economic conditions.

You'll find as a trader that knowing the current state of the economy and the state of the market is critical. You obviously want to buy stocks in the bull market and sell them, or short them, in a bear market, but do you know how to recognize when the market is entering a period of transition so you can make your moves when the opportunity for making profitable trades or minimizing potential losses is greatest?

Using a combination of fundamental and technical analyses, your chances of identifying bull and bear markets and finding phases of transition and consolidation improve dramatically. Your best trading opportunities are at the beginning of these phases of change, so be sure that you understand the six phases of the market and know which sectors offer you the best trading opportunities within each of those phases. (For more information, see Parts II and III.)

Choose and Use Your Favorite Tools Wisely

As you begin sorting out your software and hardware and making contact with other traders, you'll probably find out about the hundreds of tools and charts that are out there on the market. You don't need to learn and use them all. Using too many tools can be as dangerous to your trading system and your sanity as using too few. You'll find that you get mixed signals and will probably end up in a state of analysis paralysis trying to figure out which tool is giving you the right signal.

To avoid driving yourself crazy, pick the top two or three trading tools that make sense to you and fit your trading style. Take your time getting to know how they work and how best to interpret the information they generate. Use them to build the types of charts that match your trading style and don't worry about learning all the new gadgets. If your tools are working and you're making a good profit, don't rush to add the newest tool innovation.

Keep your eyes open for new tools that can improve your trading profits, but use caution before making changes to your winning trading system. (For more information, see Chapter 15.)

Count on the Averages to Make Your Moves

You may think that using data from averages to find the right time to enter or exit a position is counterintuitive, but moving averages can be powerful trading indicators. Moving averages actually smooth out the data for you visually and help you identify any trends. Although they cannot predict the future, they nevertheless help you understand the past so you can more effectively extrapolate what may happen to a stock in the future.

Traders use many different types of moving averages in hundreds of different ways. Stock closing prices are the most common data being averaged, but any value on a price chart can be smoothed for interpretation. For example, traders sometimes manipulate the moving averages by using the mid-point between the high and low prices to develop the moving average. Others look for the moving average using the open, high, or low prices. It's all a matter of trading style and how the charts you're developing match your trading system.

Be sure to find out how to use moving averages and what they mean. After you understand them and what goes into them, you can manipulate moving averages to your advantage and to coincide with your trading style. Moving averages are powerful indicators, but they're not the only type of indicator you need to use in choosing your trades; use moving averages in conjunction with other indicators. (For more information, see Chapter 11.)

Develop and Manage Your Trading System

You need to have a road map that helps you find buy and sell signals for your trades. A trading system is such a map, because it's developed using a collection of tools created from technical and fundamental analyses woven together to let you know when it's time to enter or exit positions. You can buy trading systems off the shelf, but these systems are available to thousands of others who ultimately will end up with the same buy and sell signals.

To be able to trade outside the pack, you need to develop your own trading system, using your own favorite tools. Although you can use tools provided in off-the-shelf software packages, you want to develop and adapt a trading system that fits uniquely with your personality and trading objectives.

After initially developing and testing your own trading system, your work is not done. You'll need to constantly monitor your system's successes and failures and look for ways to make improvements. (For more information, see Chapter 15.)

Know Your Costs

Trading isn't cheap. Not only do you have to worry about commissions or transactions fees, you also must watch for any slippage in your trades. Even though you may be using stop or limit orders, you rarely end up executing trades at the exact entry or exit prices you plan. Some slippage, or the difference between the quoted price and the actual price for the security, is bound to occur, so you need to be sure that you carefully monitor your commission costs, transaction fees, and slippage costs.

In addition, don't forget to consider the tax man. If you're trading stocks that you hold for less than a year, any profits you make are taxed as current income rather than at lower capital gains tax rates.

Traders must also avoid being caught by wash sale rules. Most trading losses can be used to offset trading gains and thus reduce your income tax burden, but if you sell a stock for a loss and repurchase the same stock within 30 days, your trading loss for that transaction cannot be deducted. You have to wait until you sell the stock again and use any losses to reduce the cost basis of the trade, which reduces the tax owed when the position is finally closed. Full-time day traders receive special tax treatment, but you must be a bona fide day trader to qualify. (For more information, see Chapters 2 and 14.)

Know When to Hold 'Em and When to Fold 'Em

Knowing when to take your profits and get out and when to accept your losses and close a position before it becomes even more damaging can be among the hardest lessons any trader must learn. All too often you're enticed by the win and want to ride it to the absolute top.

Wise traders plan their exit points at the top and bottom of each position long before they ever enter that position. And, more important, they stick to their plan. Getting caught up in the emotions of a winning trade is easy, but don't forget you're operating a business. Take your profits when you reach your goal and get out, so you don't risk turning a winning position into a loss.

When you make a mistake, own up to it quickly, take your hit, and get out of the position. If the stock recovers, you can always reenter the position at a later time. Don't ride a stock to the bottom just to try to prove you were right. Plan your exit points before you buy and stick to them. (For more information, see Chapter 12.)

Watch for Signals; Don't Anticipate Them

After you make a decision to buy a stock, you may find that you're impatient to actually get into that position. You start watching the charts and waiting for the right signal to buy. Often, you'll see charts move close to your planned signal but not actually reach it.

Be patient. Wait for the signal you've designated in your plan. Don't anticipate any moves, even if the stock price is getting close to that point on your charts. You may miss the perfect entry point, but you'll be less likely to make that fatal mistake of entering a position before the signal is triggered only to see your stock reverse course and thus be forced to take a loss. (For more information, see Chapters 10 and 13.)

Buy on Strength; Sell on Weakness

Buy on strength and sell on weakness is a mantra you've probably heard frequently from investment and trading gurus. The reason for its popularity is a good one. It works! And it needs to become your trading way of life.

When you see a stock showing strength and heading into an uptrend, it's time to buy. When you see a stock falling and showing signs of entering a weakening period, it's time to sell. If a weak stock takes a turn for the better, you can always reenter the position. (For more information, see Chapter 13.)

Keep a Trading Journal and Review It Often

The only way you can ever improve your trading skills is keeping track of what works and what doesn't and trying to gauge why. After each trade, take the time to write down the details of the trade and what went right and/or wrong with that trade. You can only improve what you measure, so measure everything and put it in your trading journal.

Don't forget to review the contents of your journal every week. You may find that reviewing your successes is enjoyable but reviewing your failures is difficult. Failure, however, sometimes is the best teacher. Many people discover more from their failures than from their successes. Try figuring out why your failed trades didn't work and what you could've done to improve your results. Of course, don't ignore your successes. After all, you need to know what works and why and then try to incorporate those winning strategies more consistently into your trading system. (For more information, see Chapter 15.)

Index

• •